Electromagnetic Theory

Electromagnetic Theory

Dr. Prabir K Basu
Ph. D (NPL-New Delhi/BITS, Pilani)
Prof. Echelon Institute of Technology, Faridabad

Hrishikesh Dhasmana
M. Tech., IIT-Mumbai
Asst. Prof. Lingaya's University, Faridabad

Ane Books Pvt. Ltd.

New Delhi ♦ Chennai

Electromagnetic Theory

Prabir K Basu and Hrishikesh Dhasmana

Published by

Ane Books Pvt. Ltd.

4821, Parwana Bhawan, 1st Floor, 24 Ansari Road, Darya Ganj,
New Delhi - 110 002, Tel.: +91(011) 23276843-44, Fax: +91(011) 23276863
e-mail: kapoor@anebooks.com, Website: www.anebooks.com

Branch Office:

- Avantika Niwas, 1st Floor, 19 Doraiswamy Road, T. Nagar,
  Chennai - 600 017, Tel.: +91(044) 28141554, 28141209
  e-mail: anebookschennai@gmail.com, rathinam@anebooks.com

ISBN : 978-93-8015-678-1

Printed at : R.K. Offset Process, New Delhi.

Dedicated to

Our Parents, Better Halfs

Roni, Piu, Saksham and all Our Well-wishers

PREFACE

We are living in the age of communications. Irrespective of its varieties of modes of uses, the fundamental is always linked to the study of electromagnetic waves. Rapid advancement in electrical engineering in the past few decades is due to accurate prediction of complicated electrical network using circuit theory. So circuit theory is essential to understand the performance of any electrical device or component involving various electrical networks. Thus to understand any radio or microwave communication system, circuit theory is needed to design the terminal equipment. But between the output and input terminal, one need to understand the electromagnetic field theory. We thereby feel great pleasure in bringing out our book on Electromagnetic Theory for engineering students. The authors feel the need of writing a book according to the use of engineering students in a simplest possible way. We have tried to deal with the subject contents in a lucid manner so that they are able to understand the realization behind the mathematical concepts which are the backbone of this subject. All the subject fundamentals are discussed in an easy and clear way to make the students strong about the basics of the electromagnetic theory. The philosophy of presentation and material content in the book are based on concept based approach towards the subject.

Besides the theory some mathematical basics has been discussed which will be used later on. Also several interesting numerical problems has been given along with their solution so that the students should have the feeling of the practical usages of the subject. We have tried to put hard efforts in placing contents in this book such that students feel comfortable with the syllabus in an interesting way.

We sincerely express our deep sense of gratitude to the Prof.(Dr.)V.K. Agarwal, Director and the management of Echelon Institute of Technology, Faridabad for their inspirational influence during teaching at EIT. We are grateful to Mr. N. Udayakumar, Chairman, Udhaya Energy Photovoltaics Pvt Ltd, Coimbatore and Prof.(Dr.)Viresh Dutta, Center for Energy Studies, IIT-Delhi, Mr.G.V.K. Sinha, Chairman, Lingaya's University and Prof.(Dr.) D.K.Thakur our colleagues A. K. Shukla, P. Unijal, R. M. Pujahari, Roop Singh, Sunil Bist for their encouragement during preparation of the manuscript. We both are also very much thankful to all our family members for their heartiest cooperation during the preparation of the book. We are also grateful to the publishers, Ane Books Pvt. Ltd., New Delhi, for all cooperation and help related to the timely publication of the book.

It will be kind enough for readers for any suggestions which can easily be accepted for further improvement in next edition.

Dr. P.K. Basu
Hrishikesh Dhasmana

CONTENTS

CHAPTER 1

ELECTROMAGNETIC THEORY FUNDAMENTALS

1.1 Basic Ideas

- The varying electrical and magnetic fields propagating in space in form of waves are called **Electromagnetic waves (e.m.waves).**

The direction of motion of e.m.waves is perpendicular to its both electric and magnetic field components. Examples are light waves, X-ray, etc. Thus the propagation of e.m.waves implies variation in the electrical and magnetic fields.

- As electrical and magnetic fields can exist in vacuum, so e.m.waves can propagate through it.

1.2 A Comparison between the Mechanical Wave and Electromagnetic Waves

S.No.	Mechanical waves	E.m. waves
1	Generated through mechanical oscillations.	Generated through electrical oscillations.
2	Required material medium for propagation.	Do not require any medium for propagation.
3	Velocity of propagation is $v = \frac{I}{\sqrt{T/\rho}}$, where, I, T and ρ are inertia, tension in the medium and density respectively.	Velocity of propagation is $v = \frac{1}{\sqrt{\mu\varepsilon}}$, where, μ and ε are permeability and permittivity of the medium respectively.
4	Potential Energy (P.E.) is stored through 'T' and Kinetic Energy (K.E.) is stored through 'ρ'. Here	Potential Energy (P.E.), *i.e.*, electrical energy is stored through 'ε' and Kinetic Energy (K.E.), *i.e.*,

S.No.	Mechanical waves	E.m. waves
5	'ρ' gives the frictional force comes due to kinetic energy. Particles of the medium execute oscillatory motion and the variable is the displacement of the particles.	magnetic energy is stored through 'μ'. The electric and magnetic fields execute oscillations and the variables are $\vec{E}, \vec{H}$ or $\vec{B}$.

1.3 Some Important Parameters with Symbols and SI Units

S. No.	Physical Quantity	Symbol	Unit
1	Electric field strength	$\vec{E}$	Volt/meter
2	Magnetic field strength	$\vec{H}$	Ampere/meter
3	Electric displacement vector	$\vec{D}$	Coulomb/meter^2
4	Magnetic induction	$\vec{B}$	Tesla or Weber/meter^2
5	Permittivity	ε	Faraday/meter
6	Permittivity of free space	ε_0	Faraday/meter
7	Relative Permittivity	ε_r	No dimension
8	Permeability	μ	Henry/meter
9	Permeability of free space	μ_0	Henry/meter
10	Relative Permeability	μ_r	No dimension
11	Current density	$\vec{J}$	Ampere/meter^2
12	Volume charge density	ρ	Coulomb/meter^3
13	Electrical conductivity	σ	Siemens/meter
14	Displacement current density	$\frac{d\vec{D}}{dt}$	Ampere/meter^2

1.4 Some Useful Relations

(*i*) $\varepsilon_r = \frac{\varepsilon}{\varepsilon_0}$

(*ii*) $\mu_r = \frac{\mu}{\mu_0}$

(*iii*) $\vec{D} = \varepsilon\vec{E}$

(*iv*) $\vec{B} = \mu\vec{H}$

(*v*) $\vec{J} = \sigma\vec{E}$

1.5 Some Sources

(*i*) ρ is the source of $\vec{E}$

(*ii*) $\vec{J}$ and $\frac{\partial \vec{D}}{\partial t}$ are the sources of $\vec{H}$

(*iii*) $\frac{\partial \vec{E}}{\partial t}$ is the sources of $\vec{B}$

(*iv*) $\frac{\partial \vec{B}}{\partial t}$ is the sources of $\vec{E}$

Values: $\varepsilon_0 = 8.8542 \times 10^{-12}$ Faraday/meter, and, $\mu_0 = 4\pi \times 10^{-7}$ Henry/meter

1.6 Basic Concepts of Vectors

1.6.1. Gradient of Scalar Field: The gradient of a scalar field (*e.g.*, grad ϕ, say) at a point is defined as the maximum value of the spatial rate of change of the scalar field at that point.

Mathematically, grad $\phi = \vec{\nabla}\phi = \left(\frac{d\phi}{dr}\right)_{max} .\hat{r} \Rightarrow$ A vector.

- Direction of grad ϕ is normal to the surface level.

(*i*) Understanding: We consider two closely spaced points P and Q (as shown in Fig.1.1) separated by an infinitesimal distance '*dr*'.

Here the coordinates of P and Q are $(x, y, z), (x+dx, y+dy, z+dz)$ respectively.

Now, $\vec{r} = \hat{i}dx + \hat{j}dy + \hat{k}dz$ and $\vec{r} + \vec{dr} = \hat{i}(x+dx) + \hat{j}(y+dy) + \hat{k}(z+dz)$

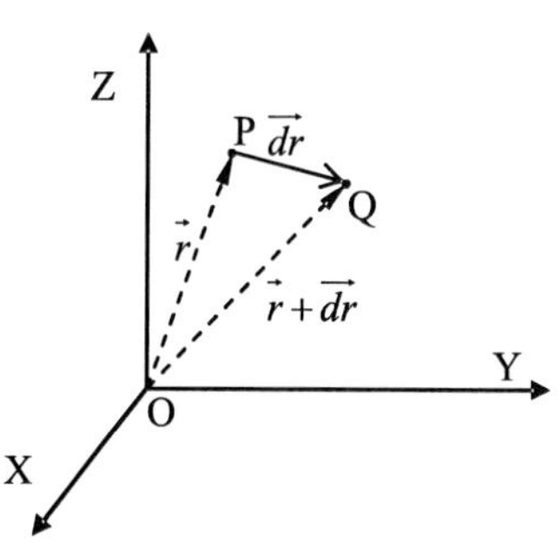

Fig. 1.1 Position of P,Q points in cartesian coordinates.

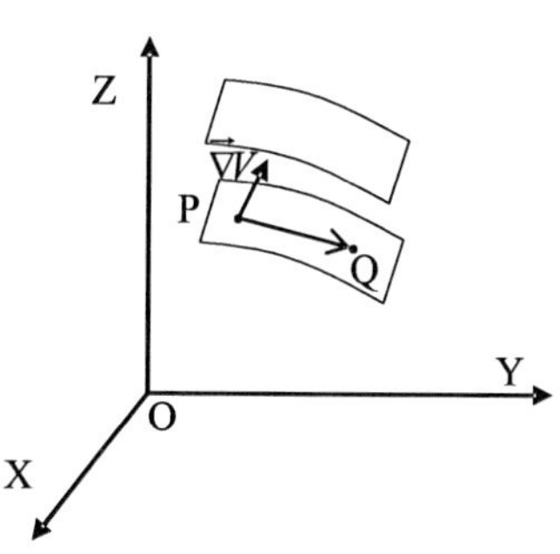

Fig. 1.2 P,Q points are on the surface.

The region contains PQ is also represented by a scalar field 'V' and is shown in Fig.1.2. The change in 'V' from 'P' to 'Q' is given by

$$dV = \frac{\partial V}{\partial x}dx + \frac{\partial V}{\partial y}dy + \frac{\partial V}{\partial z}dz \quad ...(1.1)$$

We can now introduce the 'del' operator '$\vec{\nabla}$' as

$$\vec{\nabla} = \hat{i}\frac{\partial}{\partial x} + \hat{j}\frac{\partial}{\partial y} + \hat{k}\frac{\partial}{\partial z} \quad ...(1.2)$$

So putting eqn. (1.2) into (1.1) we have,

$$dV = \frac{\partial V}{\partial x}dx + \frac{\partial V}{\partial y}dy + \frac{\partial V}{\partial z}dz$$

$$= \left(\hat{i}\frac{\partial V}{\partial x}\right).\hat{i}dx + \left(\hat{j}\frac{\partial V}{\partial y}\right).\hat{j}dy + \left(\hat{k}\frac{\partial V}{\partial z}\right).\hat{k}dz$$

$$= \left(\hat{i}\frac{\partial}{\partial x} + \hat{j}\frac{\partial}{\partial y} + \hat{k}\frac{\partial}{\partial z}\right)V.\left(\hat{i}dx + \hat{j}dy + \hat{k}dz\right) = \vec{\nabla}V.\vec{dr} \quad ...(1.3)$$

This vector field '$\vec{\nabla}V$' is known as GRADIENT of a scalar field or function 'V' or simply called 'GRAD'.

The characteristics of it is given by

(*i*) 'dV' is proportional to $\vec{\nabla}V$, if $|\vec{dr}|$ is constant, *i.e.*, $\vec{\nabla}V$ lies in the direction of maximum increase of 'V'.

(*ii*) If the above points P and Q lies on a equipotential surface, *i.e.*, if we consider 'V' to be a potential function, then, $dV = 0$, hence, from eqn. (1.3), $\vec{\nabla}V.\vec{dr} = 0$, hence, $\vec{\nabla}V$ is perpendicular to $\vec{dr}$. It means that the gradient of a potential function is a vector field and it is everywhere normal to the equipotential surface (as $\vec{dr}$ always lies on the equipotential surface.

As an example if we consider temperature 'T' is the scalar field with its possible variation along one position to the another. Its variation along space coordinate is $\vec{\nabla}T$ and it is a vector quantity.

***(ii)* The Del ($\vec{\nabla}$) Operator:** We already have ideas about operators like '√' for square root, '∫' for integration, or '$\frac{d}{dx}$' for differentiation, etc., the 'del' operator is also one of them. This is a differential vector operator and it is represented by

$$\vec{\nabla} \equiv \left(\vec{\nabla_x}, \vec{\nabla_y}, \vec{\nabla_z}\right) \equiv \left(\frac{\partial}{\partial x}, \frac{\partial}{\partial y}, \frac{\partial}{\partial z}\right)$$

When we operate 'del' upon a scalar quantity, *e.g.*, temperature 'T', $\vec{\nabla}T$ becomes a vector and it represents how fast 'T' is changing with (x, y, z) coordinates.

1.6.2. Flux: When a positive charge is placed at a particular point, electric lines of forces start coming out from it (shown in Fig.1.3). The density of these lines is solely dependent on the magnitude of the charge. These lines of forces flowing out per unit surrounding area per unit time are known as electric flux. Same is true for magnetic flux only with the exception that we can not separate the magnetic opposite poles.

Electric flux is totally dependent on the position of the charge and the area. As shown in the Fig.1.4. the flux coming out of the closed surface 'S' is zero, as there is no difference of numbers of lines of forces between the points A and B.

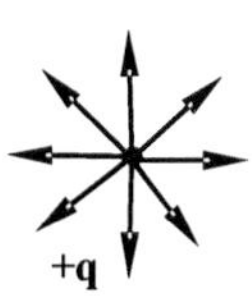

Fig. 1.3 Electric lines of forces from isolated positive charge.

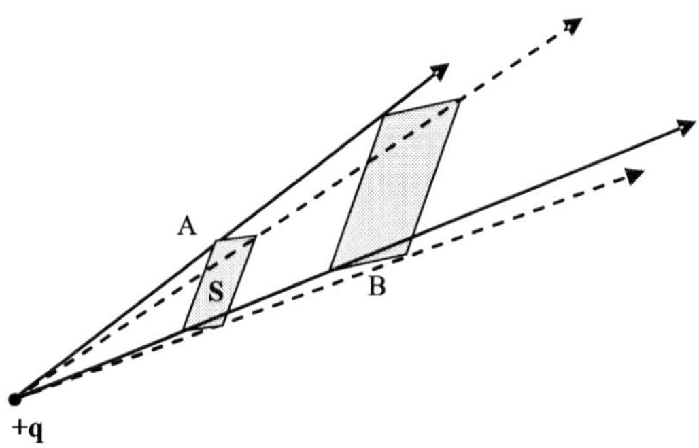

Fig. 1.4 Variation of electric flux from positive charge with distance.

The scalar product of a vector magnetic field $\vec{B}$ at any point and the elementary area $\vec{dS}$ drawn around the point is called Magnetic **Flux** of $\vec{B}$ through the area at that point.

So, Magnetic flux $= d\phi_m = \vec{B}.\vec{dS} \Rightarrow \phi_m = \oint_S \vec{B}.\vec{dS}$ and it is a scalar quantity.

In electrostatics, electric flux is given by

$$\phi_{el} = \oint_S \vec{E}.\vec{dS} \qquad ...(1.4)$$

Physically, for the flow of liquid, if $\vec{v}$ be the velocity of flow of liquid at any point, then, $\left(\vec{v}.\vec{dS}\right)$ gives the volume of liquid flowing through the elementary area in one second and can be known as liquid flux.

1.6.3. Divergence of a Vector Field: We have seen from Fig.1.3 that electric lines of forces are coming out from the positive source charge. If we make an analogy with a point source of light, light rays are coming radially out of it. In this case we normally say that light rays are diverging out from the source. In the same way we can also say for 'electric' case, electric lines of forces are diverging from the positive point source charge. Hence, highly dense divergent lines of forces are an indication of the magnitude of the source charges. Hence, this space variation of the electric field is represented by a new name of 'del, $\vec{\nabla}$' operator as it is now operating on a vector quantity and is known as 'DIVERGENCE' or 'DIV' of the vector.

The total normal flux per unit volume through a closed surface drawn around a point, when the volume enclosed by the surface tends to zero, is called the divergence of the field at that point, *i.e.*, divergence of $\vec{E}$,or,

$$\text{div}\ \vec{E} = \vec{\nabla}.\vec{E} = \underset{V\to 0}{Lt}\left[\frac{1}{V}\oint_S \vec{E}.\vec{dS}\right] \Rightarrow \text{A scalar quantity.} \qquad ...(1.5)$$

Here, V is the volume enclosed by the surface.

A finite positive value of divergence of any vector field indicates the existence of the source and negative value of divergence indicates the existence of the sink. Zero value of divergence shows absolute absence of source or sink.

1.6.4. Curl of a Vector Field: The CURL of a vector field $\vec{A}$ is also a vector unlike 'div' of $\vec{A}$. As shown in Fig.1.5 the point 'X' is on a plate of infinitesimally small area $\vec{S}$ bounded by a closed curve 'C'. The direction of $\vec{S}$, *i.e.*, $\hat{n}$, is obtained from right hand cork screw rule and is shown in Fig.1.5.

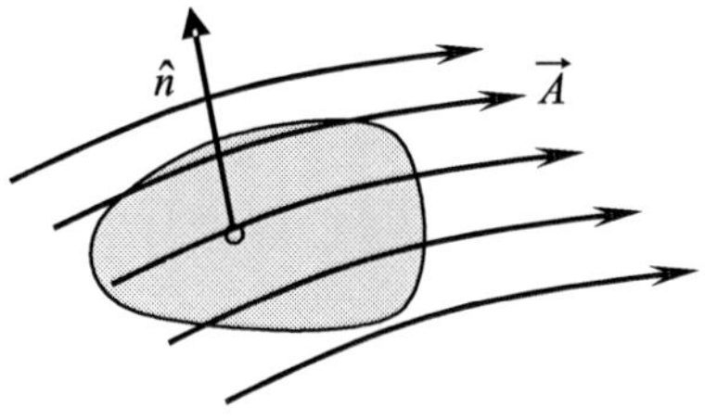

Fig. 1.5 Vector fiels $\vec{A}$ through any abritrary surface

The maximum value of circulation per unit area drawn around a point, when the area enclosed by the closed curve tends to zero, gives the magnitude of the curl of the vector field at that point, *i.e.*,

$$\left[curl\,\vec{A}\right]_{magnitude} = \left|\left[\vec{\nabla}\times\vec{A}\right]\right| = \underset{S\to 0}{Lt}\left[\frac{1}{S}\oint_S \vec{A}.\vec{dl}\right] \qquad ...(1.6)$$

Curl of a vector is also a vector. The direction of curl $\vec{A}$ is same as direction of circulation, *i.e.*, same as direction of area vector S. This is also called as Rotation.

From above discussions on GRADIENT, DIVERGENCE, CURL of the field, we observe that the same 'del, $\vec{\nabla}$' operator operates on the field and yields different results depending on the nature of the fields. These can be summarized as follows.

(*i*) For GRAD of a scalar field 'A', the result is a VECTOR, *i.e.*, '$\vec{\nabla} A$' is a VECTOR.

(*ii*) For DIV of a vector field '$\vec{A}$', the result is a SCALAR, *i.e.*, '$\vec{\nabla}.\vec{A}$' is a SCALAR.

(*iii*) For CURL of a vector field '$\vec{A}$', the result is a VECTOR, *i.e.*, '$\vec{\nabla}\times\vec{A}$' is a VECTOR.

1.6.5. Gauss's Divergence Theorem: It states that the surface integral of a vector field $\vec{A}$ over a closed surface S is equal to the volume integral of the divergence of the vector over the volume enclosed by the Gaussian surface, *i.e.*,

$$\oint_S \vec{A}.\overrightarrow{dS} = \int_V \left(\vec{\nabla}.\vec{A}\right) dV \qquad ...(1.7)$$

This theorem is used to convert the surface integral to volume integral and vice versa. This will be discussed in details in Chapter-II.

1.6.6. Stoke's Theorem: It states that the line integral of a vector field $\vec{A}$ over a curved path C is equal to the surface integral of curl of the vector over the open surface bounded by the curve C, *i.e.*,

$$\oint_C \vec{A}.\overrightarrow{dl} = \oint_S \left(\vec{\nabla}\times\vec{A}\right).\overrightarrow{dS} \qquad ...(1.8)$$

This theorem is used to convert the line integral to surface integral and vice versa.

1.6.7. Some Vector Algebric Relations

(*i*) For rotational or solenoidal vector '$\vec{A}$', CURL $\vec{A}$ exists. Hence $\vec{\nabla}\times\vec{A} = \text{Finite and } \vec{\nabla}.\vec{A} = 0$

(*ii*) For irrotational vector $\vec{A}$, DIV $\vec{A}$ exists. Hence $\vec{\nabla}.\vec{A} =$ Finite and $\vec{\nabla}\times\vec{A} = 0$.

(*iii*) For any vector $\vec{A}$, div (curl $\vec{A}$) = 0 $\Rightarrow \vec{\nabla}.\left(\vec{\nabla}\times\vec{A}\right) = 0$.

(*iv*) For any scalar ϕ, curl (grad ϕ) = 0 $\Rightarrow \vec{\nabla}\times\left(\vec{\nabla}\phi\right) = 0$

(*v*) For any vector $\vec{A}, \vec{\nabla}\times\left(\vec{\nabla}\times\vec{A}\right) = \vec{\nabla}\left(\vec{\nabla}.\vec{A}\right) - \nabla^2\vec{A}$.

1.7 Coordinate Systems

Any point 'P' occupying a particular location in space, can be represented by three space coordinates based on the symmetry of the system. There are three conventional coordinate systems used for identifying the location of 'P' in space. These are CARTESIAN, CYLINDRICAL and SPHERICAL coordinate systems. They are shown in Fig.1.6.

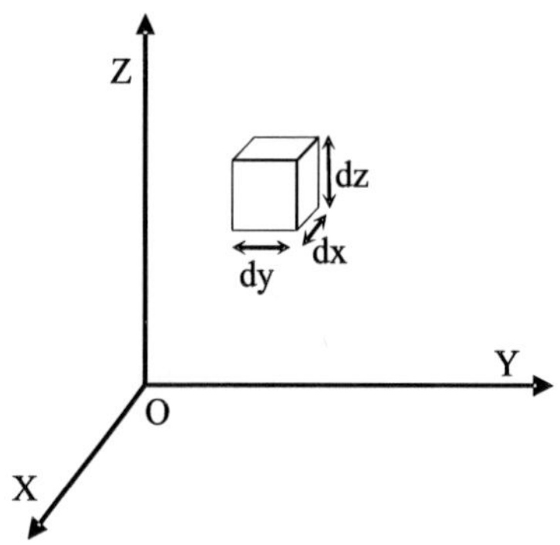

Fig. 1.6 (*a*) Position of point P in cartesian co-ordinate system.

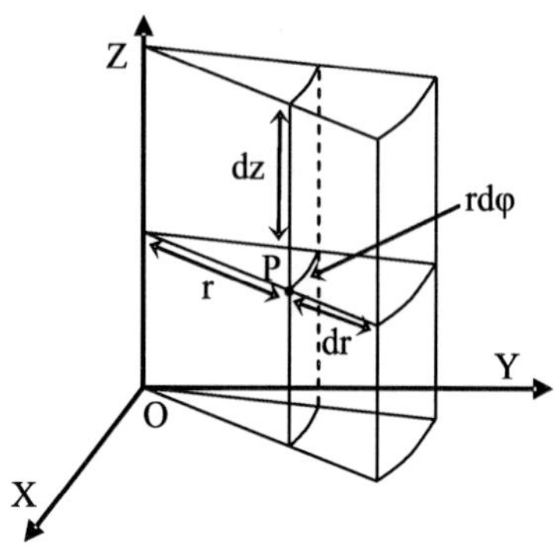

Fig. 1.6 (*b*) Position of point P in cylindrical co-ordinate system.

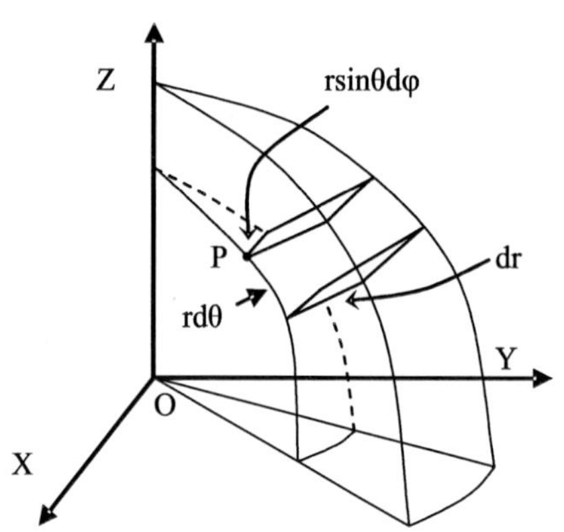

Fig. 1.6 (*c*) Position of point P in spherical co-ordinate system.

An elementary volume 'dV' in the three coordinate systems are shown in Fig.1.6. The volume 'dV' is formed when the point 'P' is moved by an infinitesimal amount along all the three axes in the three different systems.

Now, for Cartesian system: $dV = dxdydz$;

for Cylindrical system: $dV = dr.(rd\phi)dz = rdrd\phi dz$; ...(1.9)

for Spherical system: $dV = dr.(r\sin\theta d\phi).(rd\theta) = r^2 \sin\theta drd\theta d\phi$.

1.8 The '∇^2'

Similar to del, $\vec{\nabla}$' operator, this '∇^2' operator is known as 'del square' operator and based on the nature of the coordinate system its expressions are different.

1.8.1. Cartesian Coordinate System

Here, $\nabla^2 = \vec{\nabla}.\vec{\nabla} = \left[\frac{\partial^2}{\partial x^2} + \frac{\partial^2}{\partial y^2} + \frac{\partial^2}{\partial z^2}\right]$ ...(1.10)

1.8.2. Cylindrical Coordinate System

Here, co-ordinates are (r,ϕ,z) as shown in Fig.1.7.

$x = r\cos\phi, y = r\sin\phi, z = z$

$r = \sqrt{x^2+y^2}; \phi = \tan^{-1}\left(\frac{y}{x}\right); z = z$

$A_r = A_x\cos\phi + A_y\sin\phi; A_\phi = -A_x\cos\phi + A_y\sin\phi; A_z = A_z$

$$A_x = \frac{\overrightarrow{A_r}}{\sqrt{x^2+y^2}}.\hat{i} - \frac{\overrightarrow{A_\phi}}{\sqrt{x^2+y^2}}.\hat{j}$$

$$A_y = \frac{\overrightarrow{A_r}}{\sqrt{x^2+y^2}}.\hat{i} + \frac{\overrightarrow{A_\phi}}{\sqrt{x^2+y^2}}.\hat{j}\ ;\ A_z = A_z$$

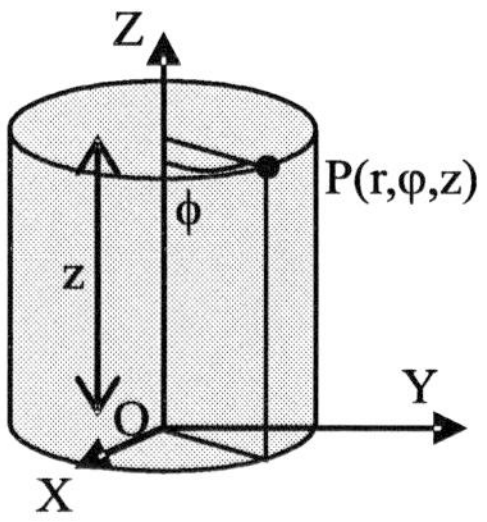

Fig. 1.7 Point P in a cylinder

Hence we have here,

$$\nabla^2 = \frac{1}{\rho}.\frac{\partial}{\partial\rho}\left(\rho\frac{\partial}{\partial\rho}\right) + \frac{1}{\rho^2}.\frac{\partial^2}{\partial\phi^2} + \frac{\partial^2}{\partial z^2} \quad ...(1.11)$$

1.8.3. Spherical Coordinate System

Here, co-ordinates are (r,θ,ϕ) as shown in Fig.1.8.

$x = r\sin\theta\cos\phi, y = r\sin\theta\sin\phi, z = r\cos\theta$

$A_r = A_x\sin\theta\cos\phi + A_y\sin\theta\sin\phi + A_z\cos\theta$

$A_\theta = A_x\cos\theta\cos\phi + A_y\cos\theta\sin\phi - A_z\sin\theta$

$A_\phi = -A_x\sin\phi + A_y\cos\phi$

$r = \sqrt{x^2+y^2+z^2}; \phi = \tan^{-1}\left(\frac{y}{x}\right); \theta = \cos^{-1}\left(\frac{z}{r}\right)$

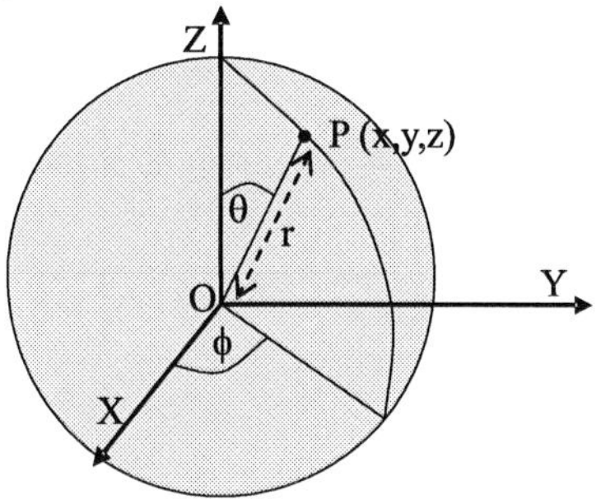

Fig. 1.8 Point P in a sphere.

$$A_x = \frac{\overrightarrow{A_r}}{\sqrt{x^2+y^2+z^2}}.\hat{i} + \frac{\overrightarrow{A_\theta}}{\sqrt{x^2+y^2+z^2}}.\hat{k}.\frac{x}{\sqrt{x^2+y^2}} - \frac{\overrightarrow{A_\phi}}{\sqrt{x^2+y^2}}.\hat{j}$$

$$A_y = \frac{\overrightarrow{A_r}}{\sqrt{x^2+y^2+z^2}}.\hat{i} + \frac{\overrightarrow{A_\theta}}{\sqrt{x^2+y^2+z^2}}.\hat{k}.\frac{y}{\sqrt{x^2+y^2}} + \frac{\overrightarrow{A_\phi}}{\sqrt{x^2+y^2}}.\hat{j}$$

$$A_z = \frac{\overrightarrow{A_r}}{\sqrt{x^2+y^2+z^2}}.\hat{i} + \frac{\overrightarrow{A_\phi}}{\sqrt{x^2+y^2+z^2}}.\hat{j}.\sqrt{x^2+y^2}$$

Hence we have here,

$$\nabla^2 = \frac{1}{r^2}.\frac{\partial}{\partial r}\left(r^2\frac{\partial}{\partial r}\right) + \frac{1}{r^2 \sin\theta}.\frac{\partial}{\partial\theta}\left(\sin\theta\frac{\partial}{\partial\theta}\right) + \frac{1}{r^2\sin^2\theta}.\frac{\partial^2}{\partial\phi^2} \qquad ...(1.12)$$

❑❑❑

CHAPTER 2

STATIC ELECTRIC FIELDS

Electrostatics is developed on a fundamental law, known as 'Coulomb's Law'. This holds for two charged spheres very small radii (small compared to the separation between them) and are immersed in an infinite homogeneous insulating medium.

2.1 Coulomb's Law

For the two spherical charged bodies located far away from conducting surface from other dielectric media, the magnitude of the electrostatic force (F) between them due to their charges is

(*i*) proportional to the product of the interacting charges,
(*ii*) inversely proportional to the distance (r) between the charges.

Mathematically, $$F \propto \frac{q_1 q_2}{r^2} \Rightarrow F = k\frac{q_1 q_2}{r^2} \quad ...(2.1)$$

Here, 'q_1' and 'q_2' are the net charges on charged spheres 1 and 2.
'k' is a constant with value $k = 1$ (CGS system) and $k = 1/4\pi\varepsilon$.
Here ε is the dielectric constant or permittivity of the medium.

For free space or vacuum, $\varepsilon = \varepsilon_0 = 8.854\times10^{-12}$ Farad/meter

Also, $$\varepsilon_0 \approx \frac{1}{36\pi\times10^9}\text{ F/m.}$$

For medium other than free space, $\varepsilon = \varepsilon_0\varepsilon_r$

Here, 'ε_r' is the relative permittivity or dielectric constant of the medium.

Practically, $\varepsilon = \varepsilon_0$.

So, generally we write the Coulomb's law as

$$F = \frac{q_1 q_2}{4\pi\varepsilon_0 r^2}\text{ N} \quad ...(2.2)$$

The direction of the force is along the line joining the two charges.

2.2 Electric Field Strength ($\vec{E}$)

When an electrical charge 'q' is placed, then about the charge there is said to be an electric field of strength '$\vec{E}$'. Its magnitude at any point is force per unit charge at that point. The direction of $\vec{E}$ is the direction of the force on a positive probe charge and is along the radial from the positive charge 'q'.

In the Cartesian coordinate system as shown in Fig.2.1, charge 'q' is located at the point 'Q'. We want to find the electric field at a point 'P' at a distance 'r' from 'Q'.

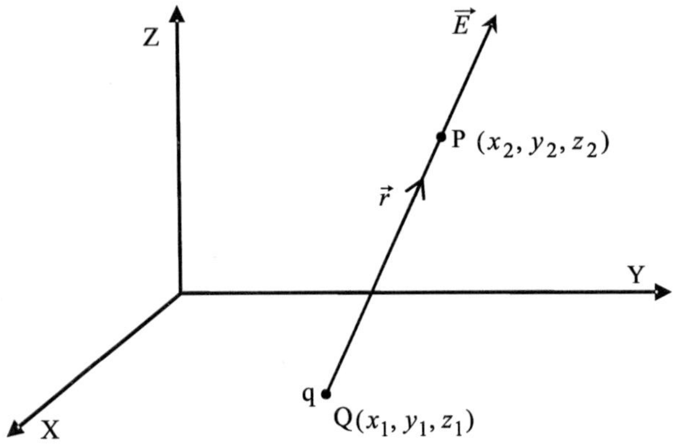

Fig. 2.1 Electric field strengh at a point P in cartesian coordinates.

Here, $\vec{r} = (x_2 - x_1)\hat{i} + (y_2 - y_1)\hat{j} + (z_2 - z_1)\hat{k}$

Using eqn.(2.1), the magnitude of the force on 'Δq' is

$$\Delta F = \frac{q\Delta q}{4\pi\varepsilon_0 r^2} \text{ and, } E = \frac{q}{4\pi\varepsilon_0 r^2}.$$

Vectorically, $$\vec{E} = \frac{q}{4\pi\varepsilon_0 r^2}\hat{r} \quad ...(2.3)$$

2.3 Charge Distributions

Depending on how the charges are uniformly distributed along a particular space, the charge distributions are mainly classified into the following three categories.

2.3.1. Line Charge Distribution: Here charges are distributed over a line 'L' and is shown in Fig.2.2. The differential charge '*dq*' in the elemental line within the line 'L' produces an electric field and its magnitude is given by

$$dE = \frac{dq}{4\pi\varepsilon_0 r^2}$$

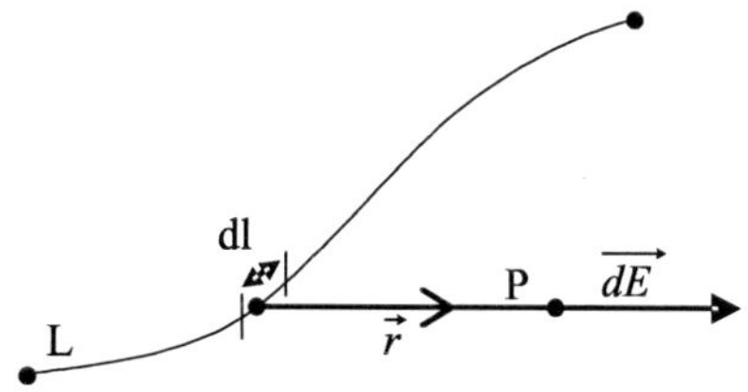

Fig. 2.1 Electric field strength at a point P in cartesian coordinates.

If we consider 'ρ_l' as the line charge density in Coulomb/m, then we have,

$$dq = \rho_l dl$$

So magnitude of the net electric field is given by

$$E = \int_L \frac{dq}{4\pi\varepsilon_0 r^2} = \frac{1}{4\pi\varepsilon_0}\int_L \frac{\rho_l dl}{r^2}$$

NOTE

Current Sheet Density ($\overrightarrow{\rho_{sh}}$)

Sometimes current is confined to the surface of a conductor, such as the inside walls of a waveguide. For such a current sheet it is convenient to define the current density vector $\overrightarrow{\rho_{sh}}$ (in A/m,) which gives the rate of charge transport per unit transverse length. Fig.2.2a shows a total current of I, in the form of a cylindrical sheet of radius r, flowing in the positive Z-direction. Here,

$$\overrightarrow{\rho_{sh}} = \frac{I}{2\pi r}\hat{k}$$

at each point of the sheet. For other sheets, $\overrightarrow{\rho_{sh}}$ might vary from point to point.

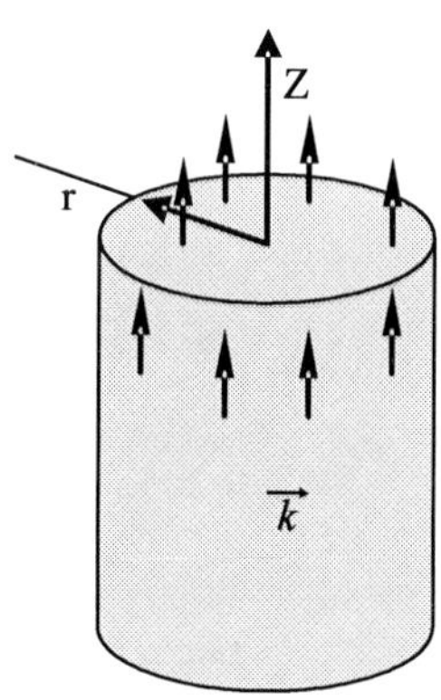

Fig. 2.2 (*a*) Current passing through cylindhical sheet.

In general, the current flowing through a closed path C within current sheet is obtained by integrating the normal component of $\overrightarrow{\rho_{sh}}$ along the contour and is given by

$$I = \int_C \rho_{sh} d\ell$$

2.3.2. Planer or Sheet Charge Distribution: Here charges are distributed over an area 'S' and is shown in Fig.2.3. The differential charge '*dq*' in the elemental area within the area 'S' produces an electric field and its magnitude is given by

$$dE = \frac{dq}{4\pi\varepsilon_0 r^2}$$

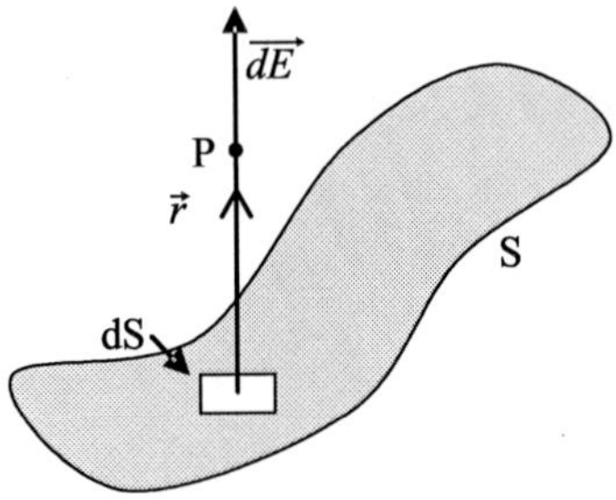

Fig. 2.3 Sheet charge distribution

If we consider 'ρ_s' as the line charge density in Coulumb/m^2, then we have,

$$dq = \rho_s dS$$

So magnitude of the net electric field is given by

$$E = \int_S \frac{dq}{4\pi\varepsilon_0 r^2} = \frac{1}{4\pi\varepsilon_0} \int_S \frac{\rho_s dS}{r^2}$$

2.3.3. Volume Charge Distribution: Here charges are distributed over a volume 'V' and is shown in Fig.2.4. The differential charge '*dq*' in the elemental volume within the volume 'V' produces an electric field and its magnitude is given by

$$dE = \frac{dq}{4\pi\varepsilon_0 r^2}$$

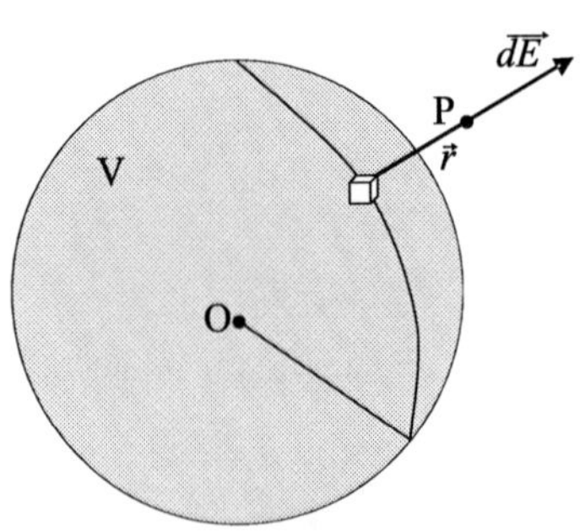

Fig. 2.4 Volume charge distribution.

If we consider 'ρ' as the volume charge density in Coulomb/m^3, then we have,

$$dq = \rho dV$$

So magnitude of the net electric field is given by

$$E = \int_V \frac{dq}{4\pi\varepsilon_0 r^2} = \frac{1}{4\pi\varepsilon_0}\int_V \frac{\rho dV}{r^2}$$

2.4 Electric Displacement 'Ψ' and Displacement Density 'D'

From eqn.(2.3) we see that $\vec{E}$ depends on magnitude and position of charge 'q' and also depends on 'ε' or 'ε_0' of the medium in which the field is measured. Hence, another electrical quantity (excluding q) is also added with 'q' which is independent of the medium and is known as electric displacement or electric flux 'Ψ'.

Example: A sphere with charge 'q' is placed within a larger hollow sphere (without touching). The outer sphere was 'earthed' momentarily and then the inner sphere is removed. The charge on the outer sphere is now measured to be equal (and opposite) to the charge on the inner sphere. This is true for all inner spheres of different sizes and different types of dielectric medium.

Hence, as an explanation we consider that there was an electric displacement through the dielectric media to the outer sphere from the charges on inner to outer sphere. This displacement is only depending on the magnitude of 'q'.

Hence, in SI, $\Psi = q$ Coulomb

Here 'Ψ' is a scalar quantity.

The electric displacement per unit area *i.e.*, electric displacement density, $\vec{D}$, at any point on a spherical surface of radius 'r' centered at the isolated charge 'q' is

$$D = \frac{\Psi}{4\pi r^2} = \frac{q}{4\pi r^2} \text{ Coulomb/mt}^2. \qquad \text{(magnitude only)}$$

'D' at any point depends upon the direction of the area vector, *i.e.*,

$$\vec{D} = \frac{q}{4\pi r^2}\hat{r} \qquad ...(2.4)$$

Hence, comparing eqn.(2.3) and (2.4), $\vec{D} = \varepsilon\vec{E}$ ...(2.5)

This is true for every isotropic media.

'E' is a measurable quantity, but, 'Ψ' or '$\vec{D}$' can not be directly measured, however, their existence was detected even in the 19th century.

2.5 Lines of Force and Lines of Flux

A line of electric force is a curve drawn in such a way that at every point on it shows the direction of electric field. The total numbers of lines per unit area is proportional to $\left|\vec{E}\right|$.

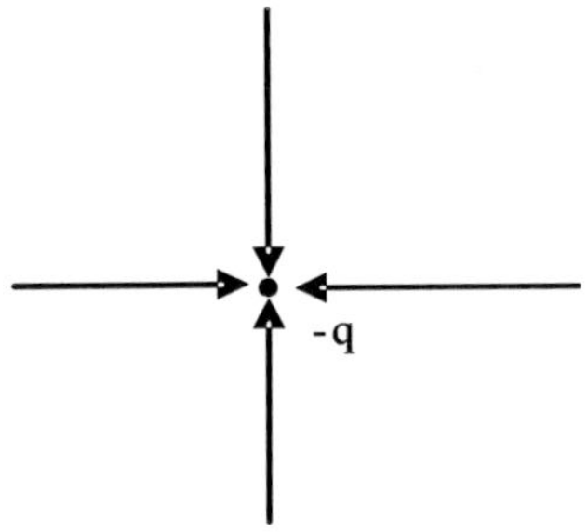

Fig. 2.5 (*a*) A negative charge with electric flux

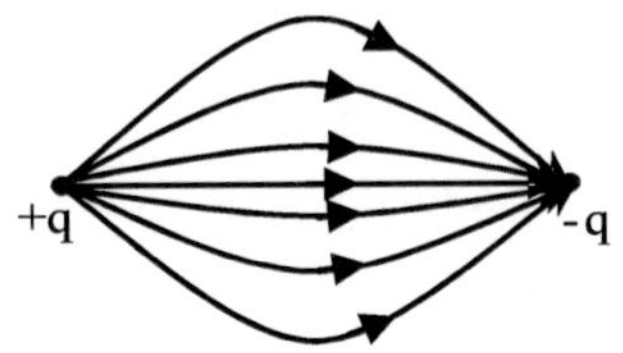

Fig. 2.5 (*b*) Lines of opposite force in opposite charges

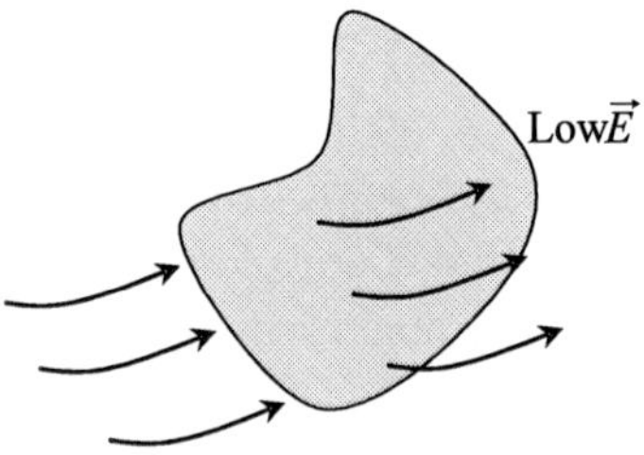

Fig. 2.5 (*c*) Electric flux for low electric field

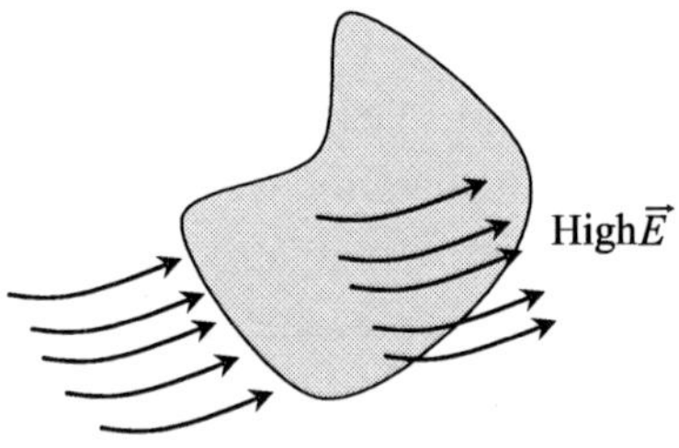

Fig. 2.5 (*d*) Electric flux for high electric field

A line of electric flux is a curve where every point on it has the direction of the electric flux density or displacement density. The total numbers of flux lines per unit area is equal to $\left|\vec{D}\right|$. In homogeneous isotropic media both the lines of force and lines of flux always have the same direction. The lines of forces are shown in Fig.2.5 for different conditions of charges.

2.6 Gauss's Law

Statement: The total displacement or electric flux through any closed surface surrounding charges is equal to the net amount of charge enclosed within the surface, *i.e.*, mathematically,

$$\oint \vec{D}.\vec{dS} = \int_V \rho dV \text{, where, } \rho \text{ is the volume charge density.}$$

Proof: We consider a point charge located in a homogeneous isotropic medium with dielectric constant ' ε '. Here,

$$\vec{E} = \frac{q}{4\pi\varepsilon r^2}\hat{r} \quad ...(2.6)$$

and,

$$\vec{D} = \varepsilon\vec{E} = \frac{q}{4\pi r^2}\hat{r} \quad ...(2.7)$$

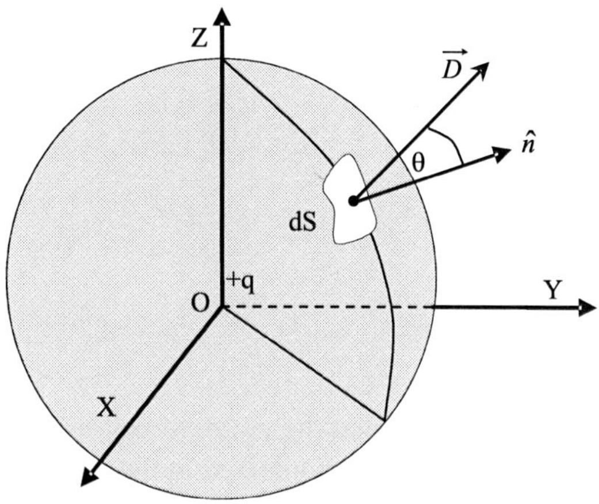

Fig. 2.6 A surface enclosing charge '+q'.

We now consider the displacement through some surface enclosing the charge as in Fig.2.6. The displacement or electric flux through the element of surface '$\overrightarrow{dS}$' is

$$d\Psi = D.dS\cos\theta \quad ... (2.8)$$

where, ' θ ' is the angle between $\vec{D}$ and $\hat{n}$ (direction of $\overrightarrow{dS}$)

[as $d\Psi = \vec{D}.\overrightarrow{dS} = D.dS\cos\theta$].

From the definition of solid angle $d\Omega$ subtended at o by dS is

$$dS\cos\theta = r^2 d\Omega = (2\pi r).(r\sin\theta)d\theta \quad ...(2.9)$$

So, from eqn.(2.9)

$$d\Omega = 2\pi\sin\theta d\theta$$

So,

$$\Omega = \oint d\Omega = \oint 2\pi\sin\theta d\theta = 2\pi\oint\sin\theta d\theta$$

$$= 2\pi\int_0^{\pi}\sin\theta d\theta = 4\pi \quad ...(2.10)$$

Hence,

$$\Psi = \oint d\Psi = \oint D.dS.\cos\theta \quad \text{(using eqn.(2.8))}$$

$$= \oint Dr^2 d\Omega \quad \text{(using eqn.(2.9))}$$

$$= \frac{q}{4\pi} \oint d\Omega \qquad \text{(using eqn.(2.7))} \qquad ...(2.11)$$

From eqn.(2.10) and (2.11),

$$\Psi = \frac{q}{4\pi} \times 4\pi = q \qquad ...(2.12)$$

For a homogeneous medium with charge density ‘ ρ ’, we have,

$$\Psi = q = \int_V \rho dV \qquad ...(2.13)$$

Hence using eqn.(2.8),

$$\Psi = \oint d\Psi = \oint D.dS.\cos\theta = \oint \vec{D}.\vec{dS} \qquad ...(2.14)$$

So from eqns.(2.13) and (2.14),

$$\oint \vec{D}.\vec{dS} = \int_V \rho dV \qquad ...(2.14a)$$

This is Gauss’s law. It indicates that the net outward displacement through a closed surface is equal to the charge contained in the volume by the surface.

2.7 The Potential Function

An electric field is basically a field or region of force. When a body is acted upon by a force and is moved from one position to another, work will be done on or by the body. A charge moving in a static electric field or a mass moving under gravity without friction in both of them, energy is not dissipated. They are the examples of conservative fields. For convenience, a point at infinity is taken as zero point or reference point. The field of force can now be described by the work that must be done in moving the body from the reference point up to any point in the field.

We consider a small body of charge ‘q’ and a second body of charge ‘dq’ is moved from infinity along a radius line to a point ‘P’ at a distance ‘R’ from ‘q’, then, the work done on the system in moving the test charge against the force ‘F’ will be

$$W = -\int_{\infty}^{R} (dF) dr \qquad ...(2.15)$$

Now, from Coulomb’s law, $$dF = \frac{qdq}{4\pi\varepsilon r^2} \qquad ...(2.16)$$

So from eqn.(2.15) and (2.16),

$$W = -\int_{\infty}^{R} \left(\frac{qdq}{4\pi\varepsilon r^2}\right) dr = \frac{qdq}{4\pi\varepsilon R}$$

So the work done on the test charge 'dq' per unit charge is

$$V = \frac{W}{dq} = \frac{q}{4\pi\varepsilon R} \qquad ...(2.17)$$

This 'V' is known as the 'Potential' at the point P due to the charge 'q'. This is scalar and thus it is known as 'Scalar potential'.

For two points separated by an infinitesimal distance 'dr' the work done by the external force in moving a unit positive charge from one point to the other is '*dw*', known as potential difference, '*dV*' and is given by

$$dw = \frac{dW}{q} = dV \qquad = \frac{-\vec{F}.\vec{dr}}{q} = -\vec{E}.\vec{dr} \qquad ...(2.18)$$

But, V is a function of (x,y,z), so we can write the eqn.(2.18) as

$$\frac{\partial V}{\partial x}.dx + \frac{\partial V}{\partial y}.dy + \frac{\partial V}{\partial z}.dz = -\vec{E}.\vec{dr}$$

$$\Rightarrow \left(\hat{i}\frac{\partial V}{\partial x} + \hat{j}\frac{\partial V}{\partial y} + \hat{k}\frac{\partial V}{\partial z}\right)\left(\hat{i}dx + \hat{j}dy + \hat{k}dz\right) = -\vec{E}.\vec{dr}$$

$$\Rightarrow \vec{\nabla}V.\vec{dr} = -\vec{E}.\vec{dr}$$

Hence, $$\vec{E} = -\vec{\nabla}V \qquad ...(2.19)$$

Thus the electric field at any point is just the negative gradient of potential. The direction of the electric field is in the direction, in which the gradient is greatest, *i.e.*, in which direction the potential changes most rapidly.

NOTE

For a problem to find the resultant electric field due to no. of charges, it is simpler to find first the potential field and then determine $\vec{E}$ by using eqn.(2.19). Because $\vec{E}$ is a vector, we require vector addition to calculate the resultant field by resolving each one into three components, then, adding them component wise and then combine them. But potential is a scalar quantity and we can only take the algebric sum of the potentials due to the each charge. So electric field can be determined easily by calculating the potential function.

2.8 Field Due to a Continuous Distribution of Charges

The potential at a point P due to no. of charges is obtained by the simple algebric addition or the superposition of the potentials produced at the point by each of the charges acting alone. We consider charges $q_1, q_2, q_3, ..., q_n$ located at distances $R_1, R_2, R_3, ..., R_n$ respectively from the point 'P'. The potential at 'P' is given by

$$V = \frac{1}{4\pi\varepsilon}\left[\frac{q_1}{R_1} + \frac{q_2}{R_2} + ... + \frac{q_n}{R_n}\right] = \frac{1}{4\pi\varepsilon}\sum_{i=1}^{n}\frac{q_i}{R_i} \quad ...(2.20)$$

If the charge is distributed uniformly in the region, in place of discrete charges, the region can be divided by a no. of elementary volumes '*dV*' and the net charge within the volume '*dV*' can be written as 'ρdV'. Here 'ρ' is the charge density. So eqn.(2.20) can be written as

$$V = \frac{1}{4\pi\varepsilon}\sum_{i=1}^{n}\frac{\rho_i dV_i}{R_i} \quad ...(2.21)$$

Hence, R_1, is the distance of 'P' from ith volume element. When 'dV_i" is infinitesimally small, we can write eqn.(2.21) as

$$V = \frac{1}{4\pi\varepsilon}\int_V \frac{\rho dV}{R} \quad ...(2.22)$$

The integration is preferred where 'ρ' exists. This is not valid when charge distribution extends to infinity.

Also the eqn.(2.22) can be written as

$$V = \int_V \rho G dV \quad ...(2.23)$$

Here, $G = \frac{1}{4\pi\varepsilon R}$ and this is the potential of a unit point charge and is known as the Electrostatic Green's Function for an unbounded homogeneous region.

2.9 Equipotential Surfaces

An equipotential surface is a surface on which the potential is same everywhere. On this surface if a charge moves, it does not do any work as there is zero potential difference and therefore zero electric field everywhere along (tangential to) the surface. It indicates that the electric field must always be perpendicular to an equipotential surface.

Example

2.9.1. Equipotential Surfaces for a Point Charge: We have, $V = \frac{q}{4\pi\varepsilon r}$.

Hence, surface with fixed 'r' have same 'V'. Thus all the equipotential surfaces here are concentric spherical shells.

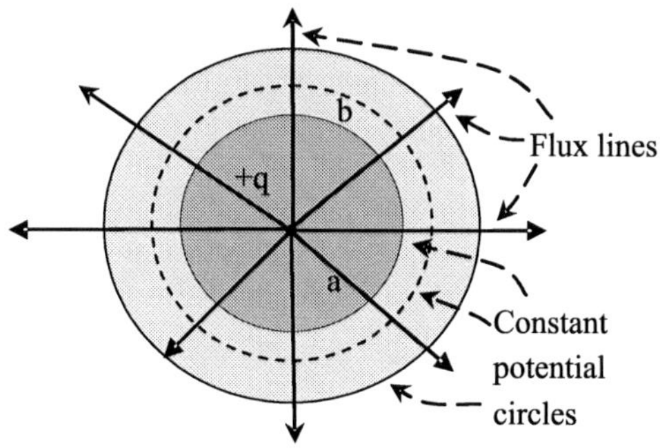

Fig. 2.7 Equipotential surface for a positive point charge

2.9.2. For Parallel Line Charges: The point charge 'P' here is lying in XY plane (shown by the shaded region) as shown in Fig.2.8. 'd' is the distance of separation between the two parallel wires, 'a' and 'b'. The wires of negligible cross-section are parallel to Z-axis. We are determining the potential at 'P' due to the parallel line charges distributed uniformly along them. The Cartesian coordinates of 'P' is $(x, y, 0)$. Here a linear charge density 'ρ_L' Coulomb/m is distributed along wire 'a' and '- ρ_L' Coulomb/m is distributed along wire 'b' as in Fig.2.8.

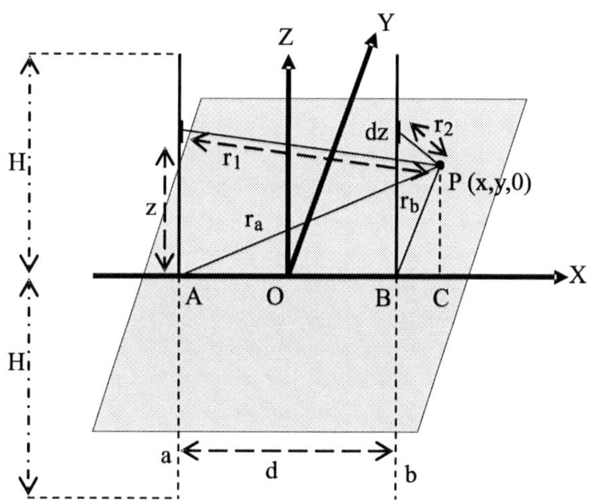

Fig. 2.8 Two parallel line charges separated by a distance

Hence, 'ρdV' is replaced by '$\rho_l dz$' and so potential at point 'P' is given by

$$V = \frac{1}{4\pi\varepsilon}\int_{-H}^{+H}\left[\frac{\rho_l}{r_1} - \frac{\rho_l}{r_2}\right]dz \qquad ...(2.24)$$

$$= \frac{\rho_l}{4\pi\varepsilon}\int_{-H}^{+H}\left[\frac{1}{r_1}-\frac{1}{r_2}\right]dz = \frac{\rho_l}{2\pi\varepsilon}\int_{0}^{+H}\left[\frac{1}{r_1}-\frac{1}{r_2}\right]dz$$

However, $r_1 = \sqrt{\left[r_a^2 + z^2\right]}$ and $r_2 = \sqrt{\left[r_b^2 + z^2\right]}$

Hence from eqn.(2.24),

$$V = \frac{\rho_l}{2\pi\varepsilon}\int_{0}^{+H}\left[\frac{1}{\sqrt{\left[r_a^2+z^2\right]}} - \frac{1}{\sqrt{\left[r_b^2+z^2\right]}}\right]dz$$

$$\Rightarrow V = \frac{\rho_l}{2\pi\varepsilon}\left[\log_e\left(z+\sqrt{r_a^2+z^2}\right) - \log_e\left(z+\sqrt{r_b^2+z^2}\right)\right]_0^H$$

$$\Rightarrow V = \frac{\rho_l}{2\pi\varepsilon}\log_e\left[\frac{z+\sqrt{r_a^2+z^2}}{z+\sqrt{r_b^2+z^2}}\right]_0^H \qquad ...(2.25)$$

As $z \to \infty$, $\left[\frac{z+\sqrt{r_a^2+z^2}}{z+\sqrt{r_b^2+z^2}}\right] \to 1$, hence, if $H >> r_a, r_b$, then, from eqn.(2.25),

$$\Rightarrow V = \frac{\rho_l}{2\pi\varepsilon}\left[\log_e\left[\frac{H+\sqrt{r_a^2+H^2}}{H+\sqrt{r_b^2+H^2}}\right] - \log_e\left[\frac{0+\sqrt{r_a^2+0}}{0+\sqrt{r_b^2+0}}\right]\right] = -\frac{\rho_l}{2\pi\varepsilon}\log_e\left[\frac{r_a}{r_b}\right] \qquad ...(2.26)$$

* If $r_a = r_b \Rightarrow V = 0$.

If we consider the locus of constant potential as constant and thus from eqn.(2.26),

$$V = k_1 = \frac{\rho_l}{2\pi\varepsilon}\log_e\left[\frac{r_b}{r_a}\right] \qquad ...(2.27)$$

$$\Rightarrow \log_e\left[\frac{r_b}{r_a}\right] = \frac{2\pi\varepsilon}{\rho_L}k_1 \Rightarrow \left[\frac{r_b}{r_a}\right] = e^{\frac{2\pi\varepsilon}{\rho_L}k_1} = k$$, we assume,

$$\Rightarrow \left[\frac{r_b}{r_a}\right]^2 = k^2 \qquad ...(2.28)$$

Here, $$k = e^{\frac{2\pi\varepsilon}{\rho_L}k_1} \qquad ...(2.29)$$

From Fig. 2.8, $AP^2 = AC^2 + PC^2 \Rightarrow r_a^2 = \left(x + \frac{d}{2}\right)^2 + y^2$

and $$PB^2 = BC^2 + PC^2 \Rightarrow r_b^{\,2} = \left(x - \frac{d}{2}\right)^2 + y^2 \qquad \text{...(2.30)}$$

From eqns.(2.28) and (2.30),

$$\frac{\left(x - \frac{d}{2}\right)^2 + y^2}{\left(x + \frac{d}{2}\right)^2 + y^2} = k^2 \Rightarrow x^2 - xd + \frac{d^2}{4} + y^2 = k^2\left(x^2 + xd + \frac{d^2}{4} + y^2\right)$$

$$\Rightarrow \left(1-k^2\right)x^2 - xd\left(1+k^2\right) + \frac{d^2}{4}\left(1-k^2\right) + \left(1-k^2\right)y^2 = 0$$

$$\Rightarrow x^2 - xd\frac{\left(1+k^2\right)}{\left(1-k^2\right)} + \frac{d^2}{4} + y^2 = 0$$

$$\Rightarrow x^2 - 2x.\frac{d\left(1+k^2\right)}{2\left(1-k^2\right)} + \left[\frac{d\left(1+k^2\right)}{2\left(1-k^2\right)}\right]^2 + y^2 = \left[\frac{d\left(1+k^2\right)}{2\left(1-k^2\right)}\right]^2 - \frac{d^2}{4}$$

$$\Rightarrow \left[x - \frac{d\left(1+k^2\right)}{2\left(1-k^2\right)}\right]^2 + y^2 = \frac{d^2}{4}\left[\frac{\left(1+2k^2+k^4\right)}{\left(1-2k^2+k^4\right)} - 1\right]$$

$$\Rightarrow \left[x + \frac{d\left(1+k^2\right)}{2\left(k^2-1\right)}\right]^2 + y^2 = \frac{d^2}{4}\left[\frac{\left(1+2k^2+k^4\right)-\left(1-2k^2+k^4\right)}{\left(1-k^2\right)^2}\right]$$

$$\Rightarrow \left[x + \frac{d\left(1+k^2\right)}{2\left(1-k^2\right)}\right]^2 + y^2 = \frac{k^2 d^2}{\left(k^2-1\right)^2} \qquad \text{...(2.31)}$$

Eqn.(2.31) is the equation of a family of circles with radius $\left[\frac{kd}{k^2-1}\right]$ and center at $\left[\frac{d\left(1+k^2\right)}{2\left(1-k^2\right)}, 0\right]$. Due to the invariance in the Z-direction the equipotential surfaces will be cylinders. The cylinders are not concentric as 'k' depends on the potential selected. Fig.2.9. shows the plot of equipotential surfaces about the parallel line charges.

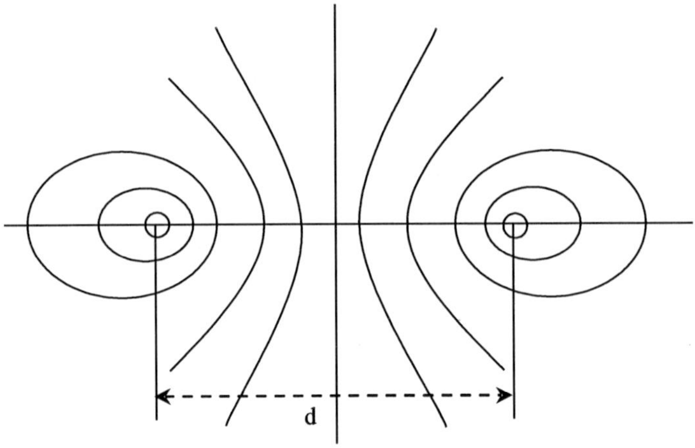

Fig. 2.9 Equipotential surface about the parallel line charges

2.10 Conductors

For a conductor or for a conducting medium, electric field or potential difference is always accompanied by a movement of charges. This is due to free or conduction electrons availability in it. Conduction in metals takes place by the movement of electrons (most loosely bound) in the outermost shells of the atoms inside its crystalline structure. Concentration of atoms in metals is normally $\approx 10^{28}$ atoms/m^3.

NOTE

* Here there can be no static electric field as if any electric field exists; it pushes the charges to redistribute to themselves till 'E' is zero. Hence there is no potential difference to exist between any two points of a conductor. So for static electric fields a conductor surface is always an equipotential surface.
* As there is no net charge anywhere inside a conductor $\rho = 0$ within it. However, there can be a distribution of charge on the surface of the conductor and it results to a normal component of electric field in the dielectric medium outside the conductor. This strength of this normal component of 'E' in terms of surface charge is obtained directly from Gauss's law as discussed next.

2.10.1. Electric Field Due to Surface Charge: We assume here the surface charge density on the surface of the conductor be ρ_s coul/sq. mt. An element of the surface is enclosed in a volume of 'pillbox' shape with its flat surfaces parallel to the conductor surface as in Fig.2.10. 'd' is the depth of the pillbox and is very small as compared with its diameter, then, the electric displacement through its edge surface will be negligible as compared with any displacement through its flat surfaces.

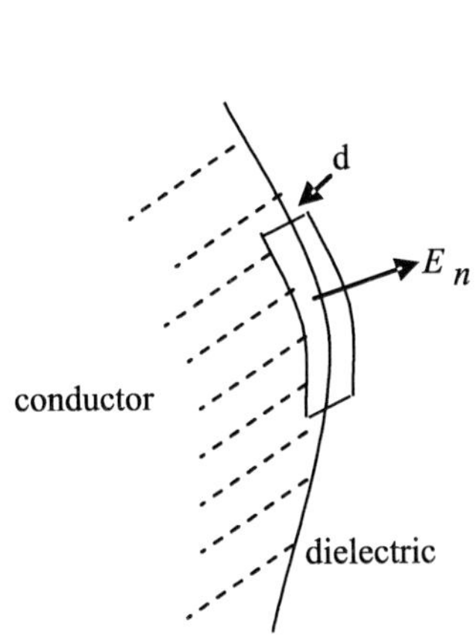

Fig. 2.10 Electric field due to a conductor in a dielectric medium.

There is no displacement through the left hand surface immersed inside the conductor, as no 'E' exists here, so all the electric flux must emerge through the right hand surface. On application of Gauss's law here, $D_n dS = \rho_s dS$, where, 'dS' is the area of one face of the pillbox and 'D_n' is the displacement density normal to the surface.

Hence, $D_n = \rho_s$ and $E_n = \frac{D_n}{\varepsilon} = \frac{\rho_s}{\varepsilon}$.

NOTE

* The electric displacement density at the surface of a conductor is normal to the surface and equal in magnitude to the surface charge density.
* The electric field strength is also normal to the surface and is equal to the surface charge density divided by the dielectric constant.

2.11 Gauss's Divergence theorem

Gauss's law states that the closed surface integral of $\vec{D}$ are equal to the enclosed charges. The DIVERGENCE theorem relates integration throughout a volume to integration over the surface surrounding the volume. Fig.2.11 shows a closed surface S enclosing a volume V containing charges with uniform charge density which produce an electric flux density $\vec{D}$. From the definition of divergence,

$$\vec{\nabla}.\vec{D} = \frac{\partial}{\partial x}D_x + \frac{\partial}{\partial y}D_y + \frac{\partial}{\partial z}D_z,$$

and hence,
$$\int_V \left(\vec{\nabla}.\vec{D}\right)dV = \int_x\int_y\int_z \left[\frac{\partial}{\partial x}D_x + \frac{\partial}{\partial y}D_y + \frac{\partial}{\partial z}D_z\right]dxdydz \qquad ...(2.32)$$

Here, elementary volume is $dV = dxdydz$.

We now consider an elemental rectangular volume (shown in Fig.2.11) having dimensions dy and dz in Y and Z-directions respectively. Let 'D_{x1}' and 'D_{x2}' are the X-components of the electric flux entering left hand side and leaving right hand side of the rectangular volume respectively. The total flux coming out from this volume is the algebric difference of these two.

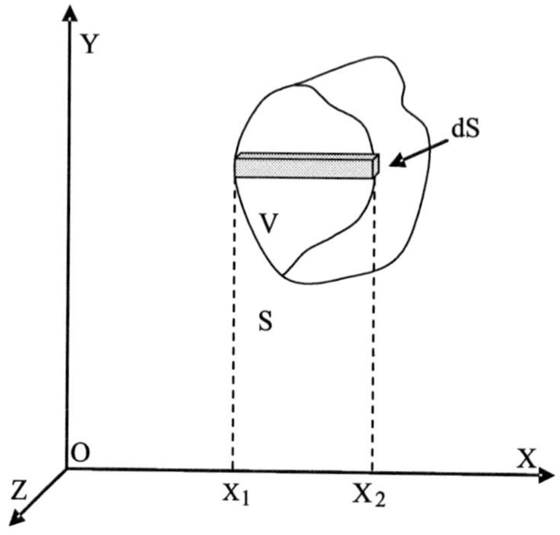

Fig. 2.11 An arbitrary volume bounded by the surface.

Also, $$D_{x2} - D_{x1} = \int_{x_1}^{x_2} \frac{\partial D_x}{\partial x}.dx \qquad ...(2.33)$$

Hence, $$\iiint_{x\,y\,z} \frac{\partial D_x}{\partial x} dxdydz = \iint_{y\,z}\left[\int_x \frac{\partial D_x}{\partial x}\,dx\right]dydz = \iint_{y\,z}[D_{x2} - D_{x1}]dydz \qquad ...(2.34)$$

Now, '$dxdy$' is the X-component of the surface element 'dS' and so eqn.(2.34) is just the integration of the product of 'D_x' times the X-component of 'dS' over the complete surface.

We also have,

$$\vec{D}.\vec{dS} = D_x dS_x + D_y dS_y + D_z dS_z$$

Here, dS_x, dS_y, dS_z are the X, Y and Z-components of $\vec{dS}$ respectively.

For the right face, the flux leaving the surface is '$D_{x2}dydz$', as $\vec{dS}$ is along outward normal, and in the left face, the flux leaving the surface is '$-D_{x1}dydz$', as $\vec{dS}$ is opposite to D_{x1}.

$$\therefore D_x = D_{x_2} - D_{x_1}.$$

So from eqn.(2.34),

$$\iiint_{x\,y\,z} \frac{\partial D_x}{\partial x} dxdydz = \iint_{y\,z} [D_x] dydz = \iint_{y\,z} [D_x] dS_x$$

$$\Rightarrow \iiint_{x\,y\,z} \frac{\partial D_x}{\partial x} dV = \oint_S D_x dS_x \qquad ...(2.35a)$$

Similarly, $$\iiint_{x\,y\,z} \frac{\partial D_y}{\partial y} dV = \oint_S D_y dS_y \qquad ...(2.35b)$$

$$\iiint_{x\,y\,z} \frac{\partial D_z}{\partial z} dV = \oint_S D_z dS_z \qquad ...(2.35c)$$

Using eqn.(2.32) and (2.35), we have,

$$\iiint_{x\,y\,z} \left(\vec{\nabla}.\vec{D}\right) dV = \oint_S \left[D_x dS_x + D_y dS_y + D_z dS_z \right]$$

$$\Rightarrow \iiint_{x\,y\,z} \left(\vec{\nabla}.\vec{D}\right) dV = \oint_S \vec{D}.\vec{dS} \qquad ...(2.36)$$

Hence the divergence theorem is proved. This is true for any vector.

2.12 Integral form of Divergence

The expression on right hand side of eqn.(2.35) indicates that net outward flux (electric) through the closed surface 'S'. The expression on left hand side of eqn.(2.35) represents the average divergence of $\vec{D}$ multiplied by the volume 'V' that is enclosed by 'S'.

NOTE

* Thus the average divergence of a vector is the net outward flux of the vector through a closed surface 'S' divided by the volume enclosed.
* The limit of the average divergence as 'S' is allowed to shrink to zero about a point is the divergence of the vector at that point. Hence,

$$\vec{\nabla}.\vec{D} = \underset{S \to 0}{Lt} \frac{\oint_S \vec{D}.\vec{dS}}{V}$$

$\Rightarrow$ The divergence of $\vec{D}$ is the net outward flux of $\vec{D}$ per unit volume.

2.13 Alternate statement of Gauss's law

From Gauss's law, $$\oint_S \vec{D}.\vec{dS} = \int_V \rho dV \qquad ...(2.37)$$

$$\Rightarrow \int_V \vec{\nabla}.\vec{D}dV = \int_V \rho dV \quad \text{(applying divergence theorem)}$$

As the volume is arbitrary, $\vec{\nabla}.\vec{D} = \rho$ ...(2.38)

This is the alternative statement of Gauss's law.

NOTE

- * It states that at every point in a medium the divergence of electric displacement density is equal to charge density.
- * The net outward flux of electric displacement per unit volume is equal to the charge per unit volume.

2.14 Poission's Equation and Laplace's Equation

Using Gauss's law, we obtain $\vec{D}$ and then $\vec{E}$ is determined. However, as 'ρ' is usually not known, the evaluation of $\vec{E}$ becomes impractical. Also, for evaluating $\vec{E}$ using $\vec{E} = \vec{\nabla}V$, the potential function 'V' should be known throughout the region or field. Laplace's or Poission's equations provide a method to evaluate 'V' by using the relevant prevailing boundary conditions.

For a homogeneous and isotropic medium, ε is constant and we can write from eqn.(2.38),

$$\vec{\nabla}.\vec{D} = \rho \Rightarrow \vec{\nabla}.\varepsilon\vec{E} = \rho \Rightarrow \vec{\nabla}.\vec{E} = \frac{\rho}{\varepsilon} \quad \text{...(2.39)}$$

However, $\vec{E} = -\vec{\nabla}V$ ...(2.40)

Using eqn.(2.40) into eqn.(2.39),

$$\vec{\nabla}.\left(-\vec{\nabla}V\right) = \frac{\rho}{\varepsilon} \quad \text{...(2.41a)}$$

$$\Rightarrow \nabla^2 V = -\frac{\rho}{\varepsilon} \quad \text{...(2.41b)}$$

Eqn.(2.41) is known as Poission's Equation.

For free space, $\rho = 0$, hence eqn.(2.41) becomes

$$\nabla^2 V = 0 \quad \text{...(2.42)}$$

This special case is known as Laplace's equation. This is utmost importance in electromagnetic theory.

For cartesian coordinates, it becomes

$$\nabla^2 V = \frac{\partial^2}{\partial x^2}V + \frac{\partial^2}{\partial y^2}V + \frac{\partial^2}{\partial z^2}V = 0 \quad \text{...(2.43)}$$

This second order partial differential equation relating the rate of change of potential 'V' in three component space must be satisfied for any charge free region.

An alternate of eqn.(2.43) is $\vec{\nabla}.\vec{E} = 0$ ...(2.44)

It means that the numbers of lines of electric field strength emerging from a unit volume is zero, or, lines of electric field strength are continuous.

2.15 Problem of Electrostatics

For a homogeneous, charge free region, the potential 'V' should satisfy eqn.(2.42) with the boundary conditions of the particular problem. For charges 'V' can be found directly as

$$V = \frac{1}{4\pi\varepsilon}\int_V \frac{\rho dV}{R} \quad \text{(from eqn.(2.22))}$$

Also, $\rho_s = D_n = \varepsilon E_n$.

However, for any general problem, neither potential nor the charge distribution from ρ_s is known. They have to be determined.

2.16 Solution for Some Simple Cases

2.16.1. In Rectangular Coordinates: Two Parallel Planes: We consider two parallel planes of infinite extent in X and Y-directions and are separated by a distance 'd' along the Z-direction, have a potential difference applied between them as shown in Fig.2.12.

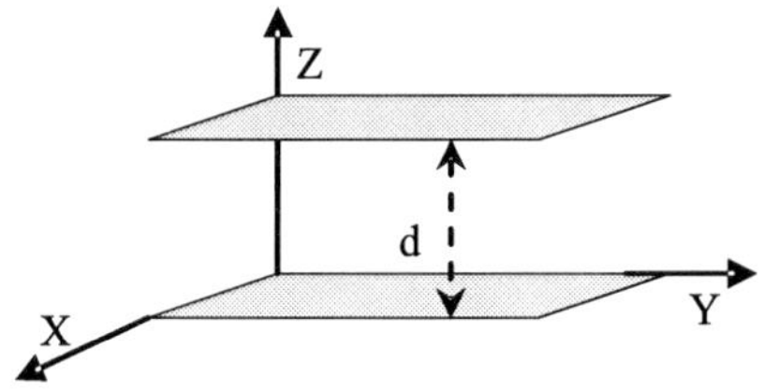

Fig. 2.12 Two parallel plane in Z-direction.

We have to find the potential distribution and electric field strength in the region between them.

We have the Laplace's equation as $\nabla^2 V = 0$

In Cartesian coordinate system from eqn.2.43, we have then,

$$\nabla^2 V = \frac{\partial^2}{\partial x^2}V + \frac{\partial^2}{\partial y^2}V + \frac{\partial^2}{\partial z^2}V = 0 \quad ...(2.45)$$

Here, there is no variation of 'V' along X and Y-directions. It varies only in Z-direction.

Hence from eqn.(2.45), $\frac{\partial^2}{\partial z^2}V = 0$ ...(2.46)

The solution of eqn.(2.46) is $V = k_1 z + k_2$ ...(2.47)

Here k_1 and k_2 are arbitrary constants.
The boundary conditions are,

$$V = V_0 \text{ at } z = 0 \qquad ...(2.48a)$$

$$V = V_1 \text{ at } z = d \qquad ...(2.48b)$$

Using eqn.(2.48a) into (2.47), $k_2 = V_0$,

hence, eqn.(2.47) now becomes, $V = k_1 z + V_0$ ...(2.49)

Using eqn.(2.48b) into (2.49), $V_1 = k_1 z + V_0 \Rightarrow k_1 = \dfrac{V_1 - V_0}{d}$ ...(2.50)

Hence from eqns.(2.49) and (2.50) we have,

$$V = \left(\frac{V_1 - V_0}{d}\right) z + V_0 \qquad ...(2.51)$$

The electric field strength becomes,

$$\vec{E} = -\vec{\nabla} V = -\frac{\partial V}{\partial z}\hat{k} = -\left(\frac{V_1 - V_0}{d}\right)\hat{k} \qquad ...(2.52)$$

So '$\vec{E}$' is constant between the plates having value $-\left(\dfrac{V_1 - V_0}{d}\right)$ and it is directed along the Z-axis and toward the plate of lower potential.

2.16.2. In Cylindrical Coordinates: Concentric Cylinders: In cylindrical coordinates, using eqn.1.11, the Laplace's equation becomes

$$\nabla^2 V = \frac{1}{r}.\frac{\partial}{\partial r}\left(r\frac{\partial V}{\partial r}\right) + \frac{1}{r^2}.\frac{\partial^2 V}{\partial \phi^2} + \frac{\partial^2 V}{\partial z^2} = 0 \qquad ...(2.53)$$

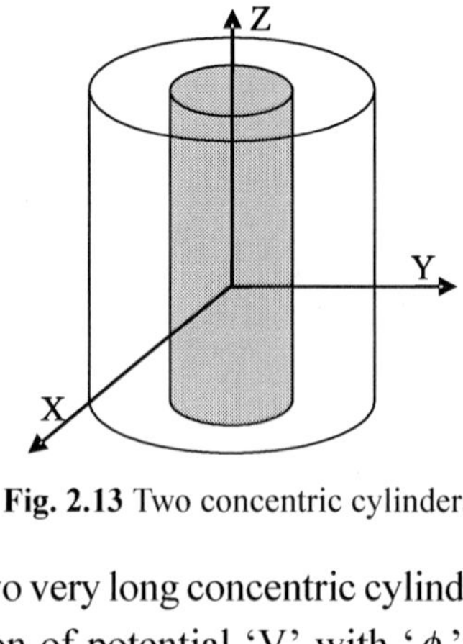

Fig. 2.13 Two concentric cylinders.

For the space between two very long concentric cylinders (as shown in Fig.2.13), there will be no variation of potential 'V' with 'ϕ' or 'z', but only with 'r'. Hence, eqn.(2.53) becomes

$$\frac{1}{r}.\frac{\partial}{\partial r}\left(r\frac{\partial V}{\partial r}\right)=0 \qquad ...(2.54)$$

$$\Rightarrow \frac{\partial}{\partial r}\left(r\frac{\partial V}{\partial r}\right)=0 \Rightarrow \left(r\frac{\partial V}{\partial r}\right)=k_1=\text{constant}$$

$$\Rightarrow k_1\frac{dr}{r}=dV \Rightarrow V=k_1\log r+k_2 \qquad ...(2.55)$$

Here k_1 and k_2 are arbitrary constants.

Hence, $\vec{E}=-\vec{\nabla}V=-\frac{\partial V}{\partial r}\hat{r}=\frac{k_1}{r}\hat{r}$

2.16.3. In Spherical Coordinates: Concentric Spheres: In spherical coordinates, using eqn.1.12, the Laplace's equation becomes

$$\nabla^2 V=\frac{1}{r^2}.\frac{\partial}{\partial r}\left(r^2\frac{\partial V}{\partial r}\right)+\frac{1}{r^2\sin\theta}.\frac{\partial}{\partial\theta}\left(\sin\theta\frac{\partial V}{\partial\theta}\right)+\frac{1}{r^2\sin^2\theta}.\frac{\partial^2 V}{\partial\phi^2}=0 \qquad ...(2.56)$$

For a constant 'θ,ϕ', we have

$$\frac{\partial}{\partial r}\left(r^2\frac{\partial V}{\partial r}\right)=0 \Rightarrow \left(r^2\frac{\partial V}{\partial r}\right)=k_1=\text{constant}$$

$$\Rightarrow dV=k_1\frac{dr}{r^2} \Rightarrow V=-\frac{k_1}{r}+k_2 \qquad ...(2.57)$$

Here k_1 and k_2 are arbitrary constants. Hence,

$$\vec{E}=-\vec{\nabla}V=-\frac{\partial V}{\partial r}\hat{r}=\frac{k_1}{r^2}\hat{r}$$

2.17 Electrical Image Method

For a positive point charge near the surface of a curved conductor 'C' (as shown in Fig.2.14), the lines of forces coming out from the point charge is stopped at the surface of 'C'. However, if we close all the lines of forces as in Fig.2.14, we found that the whole region can be divided into the two regions,

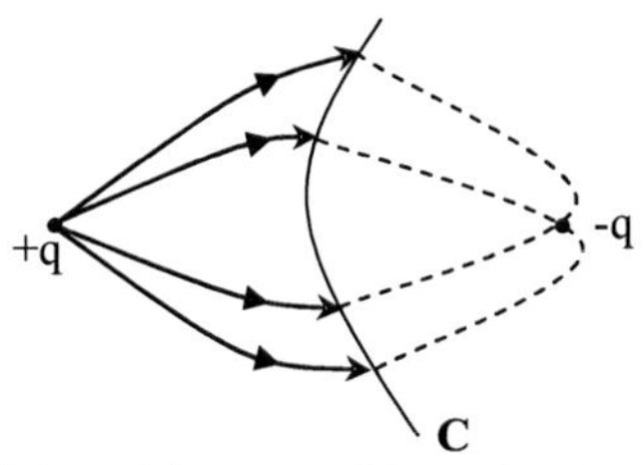

Fig. 2.14 Lines of forces originated from a positive point charge near a curved conductor.

one inside the conductor and another at the outside. It seems all the lines of force emanating from the point charge reaches another equal but opposite charge (like mirror image of the actual point charge) inside the conductor. This is the basic idea behind the solution of electrostatic problems by the electrical image method.

The image method involves conversion of an electrostatic field into another equivalent field which is easier to calculate. In this method it is possible to replace the conducting surface by one or more point charges in such a way that the conductor surfaces are replaced by equipotential surface. In this technique mirror image of the conductor in the ground plane is taken and the image carries a negative of the charge distribution on actual conductor. Then the ground plane is removed and by symmetry there is equipotential surface where the ground plane was earlier. This can be understood by considering following example. Let us consider a line charge ' ρ_l ' Coulomb/m parallel to and at a distance' h ' from a perfectly conducting plane of infinite extent. We have to determine the resulting potential 'V' and ' $\vec{E}$ '.

The boundary conditions here are that the conducting plane must be an equipotential surface. Also, potential at infinity is considered to be zero, so the potential of the conducting plane must be zero since it extends to infinity. The electric lines of flux start on the positive charge must terminate on negative charges on the plate and at infinity. These negative charges on the conducting surface are require to distribute themselves so that there is no tangential component of electric field along the surface of the conductor, *i.e.*, so the conducting plane is an equipotential surfaces as in Fig.2.15. Fig.2.15(*a*) indicates the line charge near a conducting surface and Fig.2.15(*b*) indicates that the

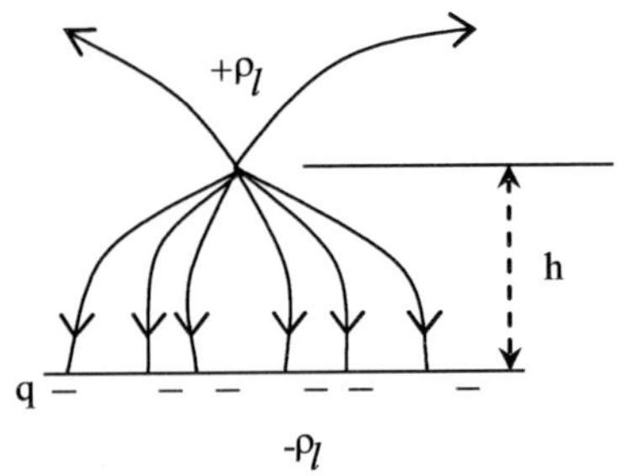

Fig. 2.15 (*a*) Line charge near a conducting. surface

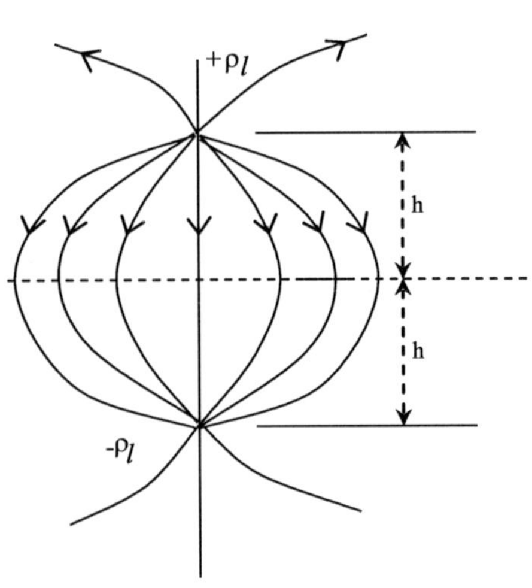

Fig. 2.15 (*b*) Image charge near a conducting. suface

charges on the conducting surface have been replaced by an appropriately located image charges. The electric field due to a line charge at a distance ‘h’ from an infinite conducting plane is exactly the same as the field (on one side of a zero potential plane) produced by that line charge and an equal and opposite line charge located parallel at a distance ‘h’ away. This second line charge (totally hypothetical) is called the electrical image of the other. Thus we can compute the fields in Fig.2.15(b) by computing the field due to ‘+q’ and ‘–q’ at a suitable point. In the ground plane, the electric field is zero and the field outside the conductor will remain same.

Similarly we can apply this method to calculate the field produce by a point charge ‘+q’ near a right angle corner between two conducting plane boundaries at zero potential. So this method helps to calculate the electric field produce by charges concentrated or distributed on spheres, lines, cylinder or planes without knowing the surface charge density distribution.

2.18 Example

Point Charge above a Grounded Conducting Plane: Here, a point charge ‘+q’ is located above a distance of ‘h’ from the grounded conducting surface as shown in Fig.2.16(a).

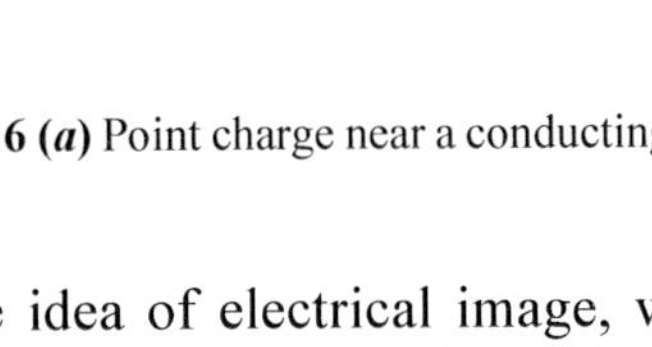

Fig. 2.16 (*a*) Point charge near a conducting plane.

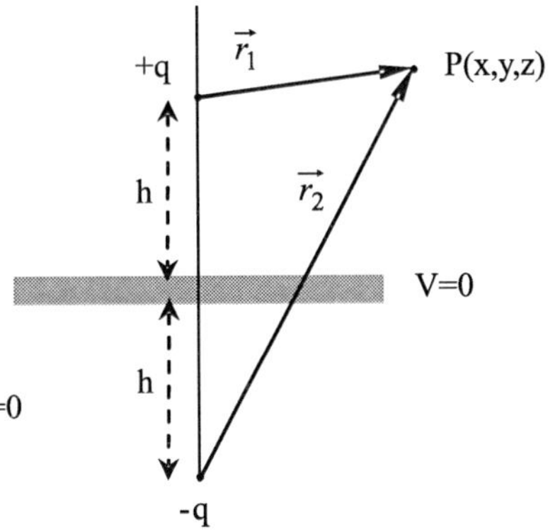

Fig. 2.16 (*b*) Image charge of a point charge near a conducting plane.

Using the idea of electrical image, we consider the presence of a second hypothetical image charge of magnitude ‘-q’ located at a distance of ‘h’ just inside the conductor as shown in Fig.2.16 (b). This situation is equivalent to the problem of two equal and opposite charges located at height ‘h’ from conducting plane. Then negative charge would not have effect on the field of opposite side of the conductor. Then every point of the plane will be at equal distance from charges ‘+q’ an ‘–q’ and hence the plane will be at zero potential.

Net electric field at the point P is

$$\vec{E} = \overrightarrow{E_{+q}} + \overrightarrow{E_{-q}} = \frac{q}{4\pi\varepsilon} \cdot \frac{\vec{r_1}}{r_1^3} + \frac{-q}{4\pi\varepsilon} \cdot \frac{\vec{r_2}}{r_2^3}$$

Here, $\vec{r_1} = x\hat{i} + y\hat{j} + (z-h)\hat{k}$

$\vec{r_2} = x\hat{i} + y\hat{j} + (z+h)\hat{k}$

So, $$\vec{E} = \frac{q}{4\pi\varepsilon} \cdot \left[\frac{x\hat{i} + y\hat{j} + (z-h)\hat{k}}{\left[x^2 + y^2 + (z-h)^2\right]^{3/2}} - \frac{x\hat{i} + y\hat{j} + (z+h)\hat{k}}{\left[x^2 + y^2 + (z+h)^2\right]^{3/2}} \right] \qquad ...(2.58)$$

At the conducting surface $z = 0$.
The potential at the point 'P' is

$$V = V_{+q} - V_{-q} = \frac{q}{4\pi\varepsilon} \left[\frac{1}{r_1} - \frac{1}{r_2} \right]$$

$$= \frac{q}{4\pi\varepsilon} \left[\frac{1}{\left[x^2 + y^2 + (z-h)^2\right]^{1/2}} - \frac{1}{\left[x^2 + y^2 + (z+h)^2\right]^{1/2}} \right]$$

At equipotential surface $V = 0$ and then $z = 0$. So the surface charge density of the induced charge is

$$D_n = \frac{\Psi}{A} = \rho_s = \varepsilon\, E\big|_{z=0} \qquad ...(2.59)$$

Using eqns.(2.58) and (2.59) at $z = 0$, we have,

$$D_n = \varepsilon\, E\big|_{z=0} = \varepsilon \times \frac{q}{4\pi\varepsilon} \cdot \left[\frac{x\hat{i} + y\hat{j} + (-h)\hat{k}}{\left[x^2 + y^2 + (-h)^2\right]^{3/2}} - \frac{x\hat{i} + y\hat{j} + (h)\hat{k}}{\left[x^2 + y^2 + (h)^2\right]^{3/2}} \right]$$

$$= -\frac{qh\hat{k}}{2\pi\left[x^2 + y^2 + (h)^2\right]^{3/2}}$$

So, $$\rho_s = D_n = -\frac{qh\hat{k}}{2\pi\left[x^2 + y^2 + (h)^2\right]^{3/2}}$$

The total charge induced on the conducting plane is

$$Q = \int \rho_s dS = \int \left[-\frac{qh}{2\pi\left[x^2 + y^2 + (h)^2\right]^{3/2}} \right] dxdy$$

Now here for a cylindrical symmetry,

$$x^2 + y^2 = r^2 \text{ and } dS = dxdy = rdrd\phi \,.$$

So,
$$Q = -\frac{qh}{2\pi}\iint\left[\frac{1}{\left[x^2 + y^2 + (h)^2\right]^{3/2}}\right]dxdy$$

$$= -\frac{qh}{2\pi}\iint\left[\frac{rdrd\phi}{\left[r^2 + (h)^2\right]^{3/2}}\right]$$

$$= -\frac{qh}{2\pi}\int_0^{2\pi} d\phi \int_0^{\infty}\frac{rdr}{\left[r^2 + (h)^2\right]^{3/2}} \qquad \left(\text{given, } r^2 + h^2 = t^2 \Rightarrow rdr = tdt, \int \frac{dt}{t^2} = -\frac{1}{t}\right)$$

$$= -\frac{qh}{2\pi}\times 2\pi \times \left[-\frac{dt}{t^1}\right]_{r=0}^{r=\infty}$$

$$= qh\left[\frac{1}{\sqrt{r^2 + h^2}}\right]_0^{\infty} = q\left[\frac{1}{\sqrt{\frac{r^2}{h^2} + 1}}\right]_0^{\infty}$$

$$= q\left[0 - 1\right] = -q$$

This shows that a total charge '-q' is induced on the conducting plane.

2.19 Capacitance

The capacitance is a property of a electrical device or component to hold or store electrical energy. Any two conducting surfaces having equal but opposite charges separated by any insulating or dielectric medium or even free space, have a capacitance. It depends on the geometry of the system and the dielectric involved. The capacitance between two conductors is defined as $C = \frac{Q}{V}$. Here 'V' is voltage or potential difference between the conductors due to equal and opposite charges 'Q' on them.

2.19.1. Parallel Plate Capacitor: We have a parallel capacitor of plate area 'A' each and separation 'd' and is shown in Fig.2.17a. Here, 'd' is much smaller with the length or width of the plates. For a charge 'Q' on plates, the surface charge density is $\rho_S = \frac{Q}{A}$ and electric field 'E' between plates is $E = \frac{\rho_S}{\varepsilon}$.

Here, ε is dielectric constant of the medium between the plates. The distribution of electric field lines is shown in Fig.2.17(a) and Fig.2.17(b).

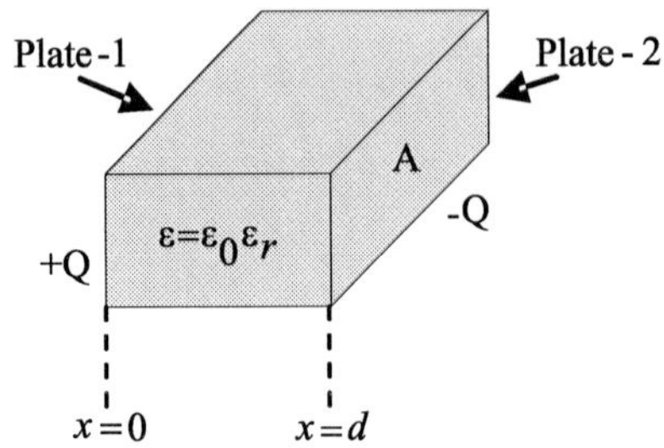

Fig. 2.17 (*a*) A parallel plate capacitor.

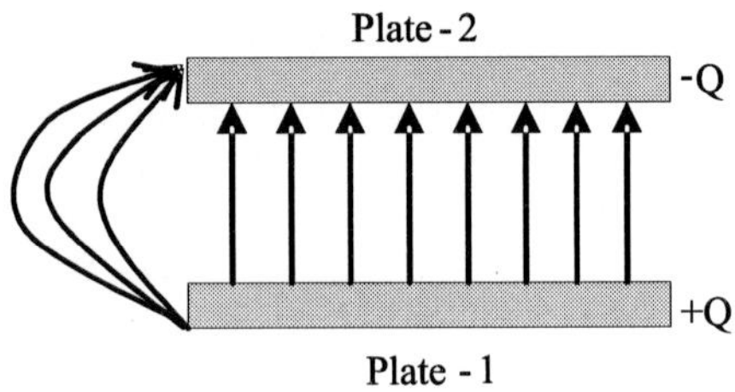

Fig. 2.17 (*b*) A parallel plate capacitor with field lines.

The voltage between the plates then,

$$V = \int_{l=0}^{l=d} \vec{E}.\vec{dl} = Ed$$

Hence,
$$C = \frac{Q}{V} = \frac{Q}{Ed} = \frac{Q}{\frac{\rho_S}{\varepsilon}.d} = \frac{Q\varepsilon}{\frac{Q}{A}.d} = \frac{\varepsilon A}{d}$$

$$\Rightarrow C = \frac{\varepsilon A}{d} \text{ Farad}$$

2.19.2. Concentric Conductors: Here we consider two infinitely long concentric conducting cylinders of radius 'a' and 'b' for inner cylinder radius and for outer

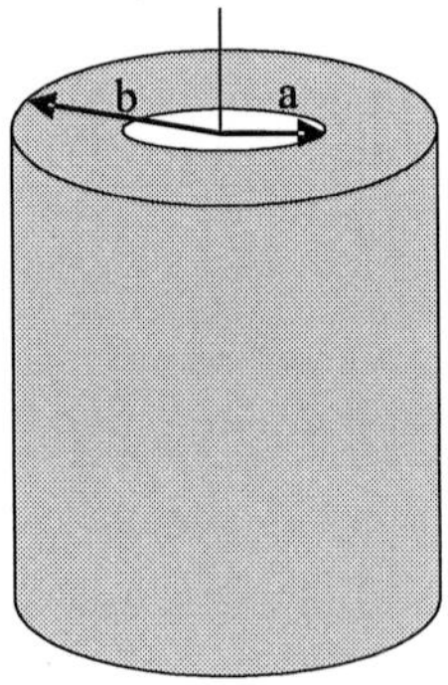

Fig. 2.18 (*a*) A cylindrical capacitor

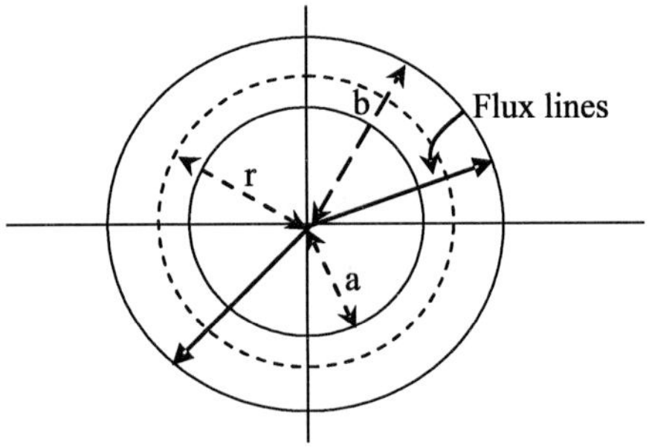

Fig. 2.18 (*b*) Electric field lines in a cylindrical capacitor

cylinder radius respectively as shown in Fig.2.18(a). We assume a charge distribution 'ρ_l' Coulomb/m on the inner conductor and an equal and opposite charge on the outer conductor. Due to the symmetry the flux will be radial and the displacement through any cylindrical shell will be 'ρ_l' Coulomb/length and is shown in Fig.2.18(b). Hence, the magnitude of the displacement density is

$$D = \frac{\rho_l}{2\pi r} \quad [D \times 2\pi r L = \rho_l \times L = q] \qquad ...(2.60)$$

and,

$$E = \frac{\rho_l}{2\pi\varepsilon r} \qquad ...(2.61)$$

The voltage then,

$$V = \int_a^b E dr = \int_a^b \frac{\rho_l}{2\pi\varepsilon r} dr = \frac{\rho_L}{2\pi\varepsilon} \int_a^b \frac{dr}{r}$$

$$\Rightarrow V = \frac{\rho_L}{2\pi\varepsilon} \ln\left(\frac{b}{a}\right) \qquad ...(2.62)$$

Hence, capacitance per meter will be

$$C = \frac{\rho_l}{V} = \frac{2\pi\varepsilon}{\ln\left(\frac{b}{a}\right)} \text{ F/m} \qquad ...(2.63)$$

2.20 Electrostatic Energy Stored in a Capacitor

A capacitor stores energy which can be converted into heat by discharging the capacitor through a resistance. The potential is defined as the work done per unit charge, the work done in moving a small charge 'dq' against a potential 'V' is 'Vdq'. Also, $V = \frac{q}{C}$.

Hence, the work done in increasing the charge on a capacitor by an amount 'dq' is '$\frac{q}{C} dq$'.

The total work done in charging a capacitor to 'Q' Coulomb is given by

$$W = \int_0^Q \frac{q}{C} dq = \frac{1}{2} \frac{Q^2}{C}.$$

So the energy stored by a charged capacitor is

$$W = \frac{1}{2} \frac{Q^2}{C} = \frac{1}{2} CV^2 \qquad ...(2.64)$$

2.21 Energy Associated to An Electrostatic Field

Electrostatic energy may also be considered as the energy necessary to establish a given charge distribution in space.

We here first determine the amount of work necessary to assemble them. For simplicity we consider three charges q_1, q_2, q_3 placed in an empty space. So no work is required to transfer 'q_1' from infinity to point 'P_1' as the space initially is charge free. This is represented in Fig.2.19.

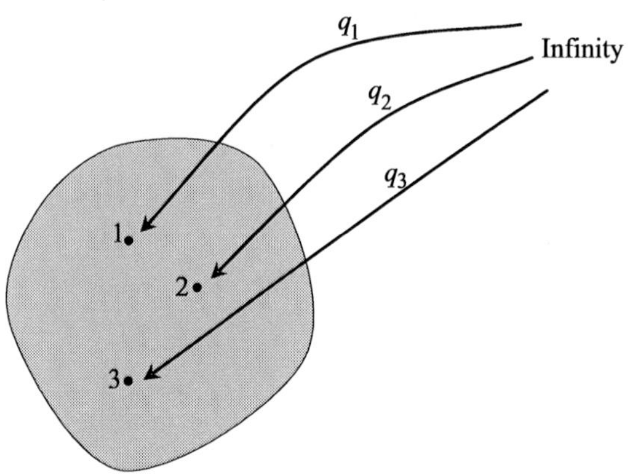

Fig. 2.19 A space where 3 charges are drawn from infinity.

Hence, work done in bringing 'q_2' is q_2V_{21} (due to 'q_1'),

work done in bringing 'q_3' is $q_3(V_{31}+V_{32})$ (due to 'q_1 & q_2')

So, the total work done is

$$W = 0 + q_2V_{21} + q_3(V_{31}+V_{32}) \quad ...(2.65)$$

If the charges are placed in a reverse order, the, the total work done is

$$W = 0 + q_2V_{23} + q_1(V_{12}+V_{13}) \quad ...(2.66)$$

Hence total work done in both the cases is equal.

So, adding eqn.(2.65) and (2.66), we have,

$$2W = q_1(V_{12}+V_{13}) + q_2(V_{21}+V_{23}) + q_3(V_{31}+V_{32}) = q_1V_1 + q_2V_2 + q_3V_3 \quad ...(2.67)$$

Here, $V_1 = V_{12} + V_{13}$

This is the potential due to the effect of other two charges and similarly for others we have, $V_2 = V_{21} + V_{23}$ and $V_3 = V_{32} + V_{31}$.

Eqn.(2.67) can now be expressed as

$$W = \frac{1}{2}[q_1V_1 + q_2V_2 + q_3V_3] = \frac{1}{2}\sum_{i=1}^{3} q_iV_i$$

Hence for an isolated system of 'n' charges, we have,

$$W = \frac{1}{2}\sum_{i=1}^{n} q_i V_i$$

For continuous volume charge distribution, we have for a volume 'v', total charge can be represented by $q = \int_v \rho_v dv$

Hence, eqn.(2.67) for continuous volume charge distribution can be modified as

$$W = \frac{1}{2}\int_v \rho_v V dv = \frac{1}{2}\int_v \left(\vec{\nabla}.\vec{D}\right) V dv \qquad ...(2.68)$$

We know, $\vec{\nabla}.\left(V\vec{D}\right) = \vec{D}.\left(\vec{\nabla}V\right) + V\left(\vec{\nabla}.\vec{D}\right)$

$$\Rightarrow V\left(\vec{\nabla}.\vec{D}\right) = \vec{\nabla}.\left(V\vec{D}\right) - \vec{D}.\left(\vec{\nabla}V\right)$$

Using this into eqn.(2.68) we have,

$$W = \frac{1}{2}\int_\vartheta \left[\vec{\nabla}.\left(V\vec{D}\right) - \vec{D}.\left(\vec{\nabla}V\right)\right] d\vartheta = \frac{1}{2}\int_\vartheta \left[\vec{\nabla}.\left(V\vec{D}\right)\right] d\vartheta - \frac{1}{2}\int_\vartheta \left[\vec{D}.\left(\vec{\nabla}V\right)\right] d\vartheta$$

$$= \frac{1}{2}\int_\vartheta \left[\vec{\nabla}.V\vec{D}\right] d\vartheta - \frac{1}{2}\int_\vartheta \left[\vec{D}.\left(-\vec{E}\right)\right] d\vartheta$$

$$= \frac{1}{2}\int_S \left[V\vec{D}\right] dS + \frac{1}{2}\int_\vartheta \left[\vec{D}.\vec{E}\right] d\vartheta$$

As $V \propto \frac{1}{r}\left[\because V = \frac{1}{4\pi\varepsilon}.\frac{q}{r}\right]$ and, $D \propto \frac{1}{dS} \Rightarrow D \propto \frac{1}{r^2}$;

so 'VD' varies as '$\frac{1}{r^3}$'.

Hence on combining

$$\left(V\vec{D}\right).\vec{dS} \propto \frac{1}{r^3} \times r^2 = \frac{1}{r}.$$

On integration over the whole surface for $r \to \infty$, value of the integral becomes zero. So we only have now,

$$W = \frac{1}{2}\int_\vartheta \left[\vec{D}.\vec{E}\right] d\vartheta = \frac{1}{2}\int_\vartheta \varepsilon E^2 d\vartheta$$

Here the electrostatic energy density (energy per unit volume) is given by

$$w = \frac{1}{2}\varepsilon E^2$$

Alternate Approach

We consider that all of space is initially field-free and that 'N' point charges are brought in form infinity and located at specific points. The energy expended is locating the ith charge at the point $\vec{r_i}$ (a vector indicating the point x_i, y_i, z_i, where the potential is V_i) is given by

$$W_i = q_i V_i = \frac{q_i}{4\pi\varepsilon}\sum_{j=1}^{i-1}\frac{q_j}{R_{ij}} \qquad ...(2.69)$$

Here, $R_{ij} = \left|\vec{r_i} - \vec{r_j}\right|$.

As no energy is used up in locating the first charge and thus total energy is

$$W = \sum_{i=2}^{N} W_i = \frac{1}{4\pi\varepsilon}\sum_{i=2}^{N}\sum_{j=1}^{i-1}\frac{q_j}{R_{ij}} \qquad ...(2.70)$$

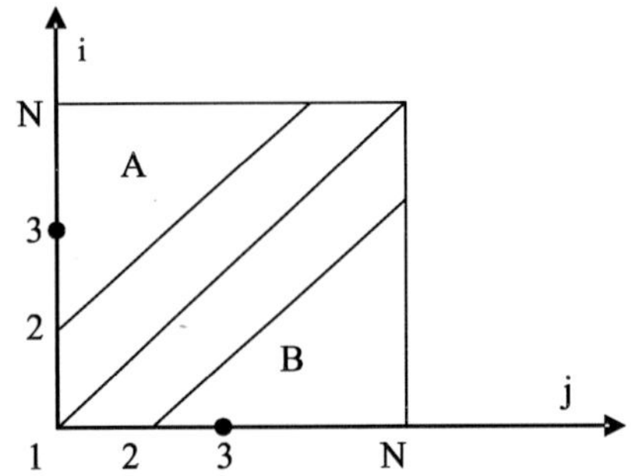

Fig. 2.20 A plane consisting of N point charges.

In eqn.(2.70) we have ignored the energy necessary to form each point charge. The numbers over which the summation is carried out may be depicted as points in the i-j plane as shown in Fig.2.20. Since the quantity is symmetric in 'i' and 'j', the same energy 'W' would be obtained by a summation over triangle 'B'. Hence, summation over both triangles must give '2W' and can be written as

$$W = \frac{1}{2}\times\frac{1}{4\pi\varepsilon}\sum_{i=1}^{N}\sum_{j=1}^{i-1}\frac{q_j\, q_i}{R_{ij}}, i \neq j \qquad ...(2.71)$$

A continuous charge distribution can be used in place of q_i and q_j as

$$q_i = \rho\left(\vec{r}\right)d\vartheta \quad q_j = \rho\left(\vec{r}\,'\right)d\vartheta'$$

Also we can remove the condition $i \neq j$ as no point charges are present in continuous distribution, hence the energy necessary to form a continuous charge distribution is

$$W = \frac{1}{8\pi\varepsilon}\int_{\vartheta}\int_{\vartheta'}\frac{\rho(\vec{r})\rho(\vec{r}')d\vartheta d\vartheta'}{R} \qquad ...(2.72)$$

Here, $R = |\vec{r} - \vec{r}'|$

From earlier section we know the potential function as,

$$V(\vec{r}) = \frac{1}{4\pi\varepsilon}\int_{\vartheta'}\frac{\rho(\vec{r}')d\vartheta'}{R} \qquad ...(2.73)$$

Hence from eqn.(2.72) and (2.73),

$$W = \frac{1}{2}\int_{V}\rho(\vec{r})V(\vec{r})d\vartheta \qquad ...(2.74)$$

From vector algebra we know,

$$\vec{\nabla}.(V\vec{D}) = V(\vec{\nabla}.\vec{D}) + \vec{D}.(\vec{\nabla}V)$$

$$\Rightarrow V(\vec{\nabla}.\vec{D}) = \vec{\nabla}.(V\vec{D}) - \vec{D}.(\vec{\nabla}V) \qquad ...(2.75)$$

On applying it in eqn.(2.74) we get

$$W = \frac{1}{2}\int_{\vartheta}\rho V d\vartheta = \frac{1}{2}\int_{\vartheta}\left[V(\vec{\nabla}.\vec{D})\right]d\vartheta = \frac{1}{2}\int_{\vartheta}\left[\vec{\nabla}.(V\vec{D}) - \vec{D}.(\vec{\nabla}V)\right]d\vartheta$$

$$\Rightarrow W = \frac{1}{2}\int_{\vartheta}\left[\vec{\nabla}.(V\vec{D}) - \vec{D}.(\vec{\nabla}V)\right]d\vartheta$$

$$= \frac{1}{2}\int_{S}\left[V\vec{D}\right]dS + \frac{1}{2}\int_{\vartheta}\left[\vec{D}.\vec{E}\right]d\vartheta \quad \text{(as in earlier section)} \qquad ...(2.75a)$$

If $S \to \infty$ the integrand in the surface integral must drop off as fast as $(1/r^3)$ as thus the surface integral vanishes. Hence eqn.(2.75a) becomes,

$$W = \frac{1}{2}\int_{\vartheta}\left[\vec{D}.\vec{E}\right]d\vartheta = \frac{1}{2}\int_{\vartheta}DEd\vartheta = \frac{1}{2}\int_{\vartheta}\varepsilon E^2 d\vartheta \qquad ...(2.76)$$

Eqn.(2.76) is often interpreted as everywhere in space that there exists an energy density as

$$w = \frac{1}{2}\varepsilon E^2 \qquad ...(2.77)$$

Some Cases

2.21.1. Charge on a Conducting Surface: If charge is assembled on the surface of a conductor the surface must be an equipotential, then, as we know,

$$W = \frac{1}{2}\int_v \rho_v V dv = \frac{1}{2}V\int_v \rho_v dv$$

so for the surface,

$$W = \frac{1}{2}V\int_S \rho_S dS = \frac{1}{2}QV \quad ...(2.78)$$

Here 'V' is the potential of the surface and 'Q' is the total charge on it.

2.21.2. Force on a Charged Conductor: We consider an elemental area 'ΔS' on a charged conductor and is depressed a distance 'Δl', the increase in stored energy is

$$\Delta W = w\Delta S\Delta l \quad ...(2.79)$$

Such a depression must be carried out against a force 'F' and thus,

$$\Delta W = F\Delta l = (f\Delta S)\Delta l \quad ...(2.80)$$

Here 'f' is the force per unit area, *i.e.*, pressure.
Using eqn.(2.79) and (2.80),

$$\Delta W = w\Delta S\Delta l = (f\Delta S)\Delta l$$

$$\Rightarrow f = w \quad ...(2.81)$$

If the surface charge density is ρ_S, then,

$$f = \frac{1}{2}\varepsilon E^2 = \frac{1}{2\varepsilon}D^2 = \frac{1}{2\varepsilon}\rho_S{}^2 \quad ...(2.82)$$

2.22 Boundary Conditions Between the Two Dielectrics

We consider a interface between two dielectrics in an electric field. Let the dielectric constants of the mediums ε_1 and ε_2 respectively and we also assume that there are no free charges available on the boundary surface. We now apply

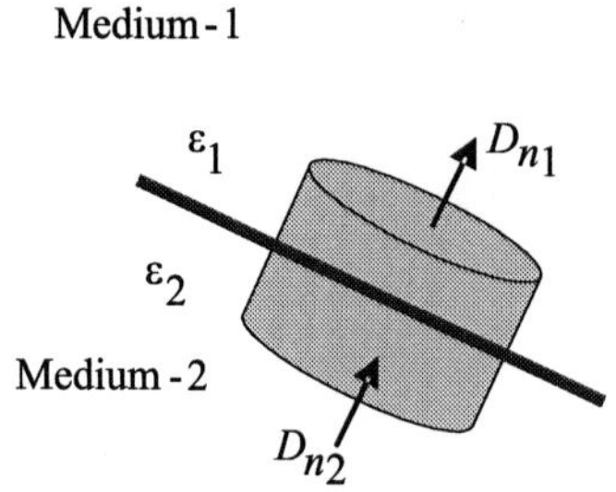

Fig. 2.21 (*a*) A shallow cylindrical box enclosing a boundary.

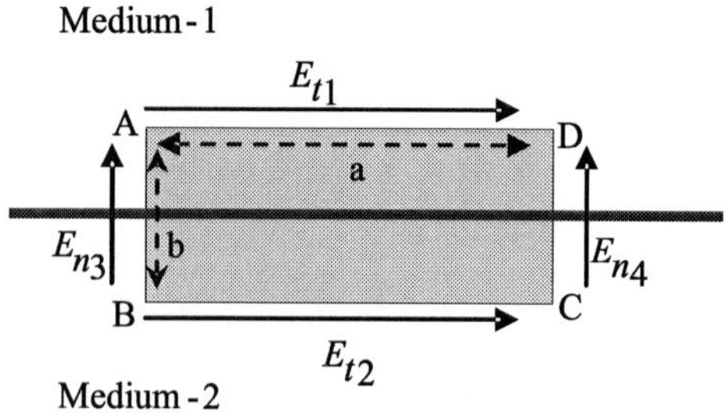

Fig. 2.21 (*b*) A shallow rectangular box enclosing a boundary.

Gauss's law to the shallow cylindrical box that encloses a portion of the boundary as in Fig.2.21(a). Since there are no charges present within the volume, the net outward displacement through the surface of the box is zero,

$$i.e., \ \vec{\nabla}.\vec{D} = 0 \Rightarrow \vec{D} = \text{constant}.$$

When the depth of the box is allowed to approach zero, always keeping the boundary surface between its two flat faces, the displacement through the curved edge surface becomes negligible. Then Gauss's law requires that the displacement through the upper face be equal to the displacement through the lower face. Because the area of the faces are equal, the normal components of the displacement densities must be equal, *i.e.*, $D_{n_1} = D_{n_2}$. So there is the same numbers of lines of displacement flux entering one face as are leaving the outer face. The lines of electric displacement are continuous across a boundary surface, whereas, the normal component of $\vec{D}$ is the same on bothsides of a boundary.

Fig.2.21(b) shows a face 'ABCD' of a rectangular box of length 'a' and depth 'b'. There are electric field strengths $\vec{E_1}$ and $\vec{E_2}$ respectively in medium-1 and 2 respectively. In the electrostatic field, the voltage around any closed path must be zero, *i.e.*,

$$V_{closedpath} = \oint \vec{E}.\vec{dl} = 0$$

Applying this for ABCD, where AD is just inside medium-1 and BC just inside medium-2, we have,

$$\oint \vec{E}.\vec{dl} = -bE_{n_3} + aE_{t_2} + bE_{n_4} - aE_{t_1} \qquad ...(2.83)$$

Here, E_{t_1}, E_{t_2} are the average tangential components of $\vec{E}$ along AD and BC; E_{n_3}, E_{n_4} are the average normal components of $\vec{E}$ along BA and CD respectively. As the sides AD and BC are brought closer, the lengths AB and CD approach to zero, *i.e.*, $b \to 0$, we have from eqn.(2.83)

$$aE_{t_2} - aE_{t_1} = 0 \Rightarrow E_{t_1} = E_{t_2} \qquad ...(2.84)$$

Hence, the tangential component of $\vec{E}$ is continuous at the boundary. So the two boundary conditions are:

(*i*) Normal $\vec{D}$ is continuous at the boundary, and,

(*ii*) Tangential $\vec{E}$ is continuous at the boundary.

They are used to solve problems involving dielectrics.

2.23 The Electrostatic Uniqueness Theorem

Statement: Any solution to Laplace's or Poission's equation which also satisfies the boundary conditions must be the only solution that exists. It gives the uniqueness of the solution.

Till now we have only specified about the boundary conditions without assuring about the possibility of uniqueness in solution. We are now looking for it. We consider a problem in which a given charge density 'ρ' is contained in a volume 'V' surrounded by a surface 'S'. Let V_1 and V_2 are two potentials satisfying Poisson's equations as

$$\nabla^2 V_1 = -\frac{\rho}{\varepsilon} \quad \text{and} \quad \nabla^2 V_2 = -\frac{\rho}{\varepsilon} \qquad ...(2.85)$$

Eqn.(2.85) suggest the formation of a difference potential as and it satisfies the Laplace's equation as (from eqn.(2.85)),

$$\nabla^2 V_1 = \nabla^2 V_2 \Rightarrow \nabla^2 (V_1 - V_2) = 0 \Rightarrow \nabla^2 (V_0) = 0 \qquad ...(2.86)$$

We know the identity from vector algebra,

$$\vec{\nabla}.\left(V_0 \vec{\nabla} V_0\right) = V_0 \nabla^2 V_0 + \left(\vec{\nabla} V_0 . \vec{\nabla} V_0\right) \qquad ...(2.87)$$

Using eqn.(2.86) into (2.87) and for the whole volume,

$$\int_v \vec{\nabla}.\left(V_0 \vec{\nabla} V_0\right) dv = 0 + \int_v \left(\vec{\nabla} V_0\right)^2 dv$$

$$\Rightarrow \oint_S \left[V_0 \vec{\nabla} V\right] \overrightarrow{dS} = \int_v \left(\vec{\nabla} V_0\right)^2 dv \quad \text{(using divergence theorem)} \qquad ...(2.88)$$

The component of the gradient normal to S can be written as '$\frac{\partial}{\partial n}$' and hence from eqn.(2.88),

$$\Rightarrow \oint_S \left[V_0 \frac{\partial V_0}{\partial n}\right] dS = \int_v \left(\vec{\nabla} V_0\right)^2 dv \qquad ...(2.89)$$

Uniqueness of the electric field means

$$\overrightarrow{E_1} = -\vec{\nabla} V_1 = \overrightarrow{E_2} = -\vec{\nabla} V_2 \Rightarrow -\vec{\nabla}(V_1 - V_2) = 0 \Rightarrow \vec{\nabla}(V_0) = 0 \text{ everywhere in volume.}$$

Eqn.(2.89) shows that this is possible only when $V_0 = 0$ or $\frac{\partial V_0}{\partial n} = 0$ at all points on 'S'.

(*i*) $V_0 = 0 \Rightarrow V_1 = V_2 = V_s$, say on 'S'. This specification of potential function on 'S' is called '**Dirichlet** boundary condition'.

(ii) $\frac{\partial V_0}{\partial n} = 0 \Rightarrow -\frac{\partial V_1}{\partial n} = -\frac{\partial V_2}{\partial n} = E_S$ on 'S'. This specification of the normal derivative of the potential on 'S' is called the '**Neumann** boundary condition'.

If both the Dirichlet and Neumann conditions are given over part of 'S', then the problem is said to be over specified or improperly posed.

We have seen that from the uniqueness of $\vec{E}$,

$$\vec{\nabla} V_1 = \vec{\nabla} V_2 \Rightarrow V_1 = V_2 + \text{constant} \quad ...(2.90)$$

This eqn.(2.90) indicates that throughout the volume the constant maintains the non-uniqueness of the potential. However, if the potential is specified at any point on 'S', then, $V_1 = V_2$ at that point and the constant is zero. It indicates that the Dirichlet boundary condition specified on any portion on 'S' guarantees the uniqueness of the potential.

2.24 Dirac-delta Representation for a Point Charge

When a point charge 'q' Coulomb is located within the volume 'V' and we use continuous distribution of charges within the volume with a charge density 'ρ' Coulomb/m^3,

then, $\int_V \rho dV = q$.

If 'q' lies outside 'V' then, $\int_V \rho dV = q$.

Both the above conditions are satisfied if 'ρ' is expresses in a new form as

$$\rho(\vec{r}) = q\delta(\vec{r} - \vec{r}_0) \quad ...(2.91)$$

Here, 'δ' is known as Dirac delta function and as 'ρ' is a function of '$\vec{r}$', hence, 'δ' is a function of $(\vec{r} - \vec{r}_0)$.

In one dimension the Dirac delta function at the point $x = x_0$ is designated by $\delta(x - x_0)$ and at $x_0 = 0$, it is designated by $\delta(x - x_0)$. It has the property as

$$\int_a^b \delta(x - x_0)dx = 1 \text{; if } x_0 \text{ lies within the range } (a,b)$$

$$= 0 \text{; if } x_0 \text{ is not lying within the range in } (a,b) \quad ...(2.92)$$

Thus $\delta(x - x_0)$ behaves as a very sharply peak function of unit area and can be represented as a vanisingly thin width, but infinitely large peak Gaussian function

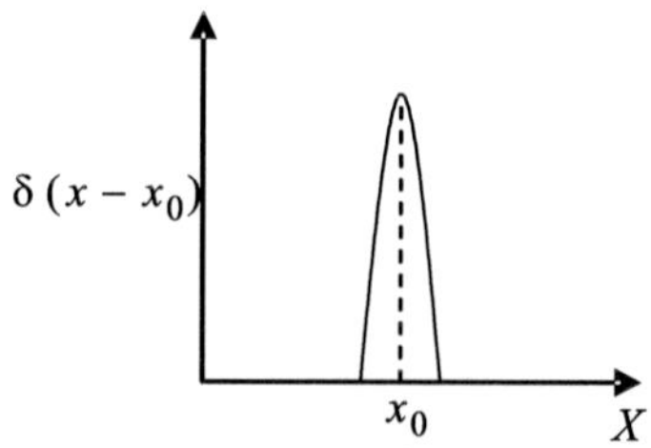

Fig. 2.22 (*a*) Distribution of dirac delta function along X-direction with finite peak.

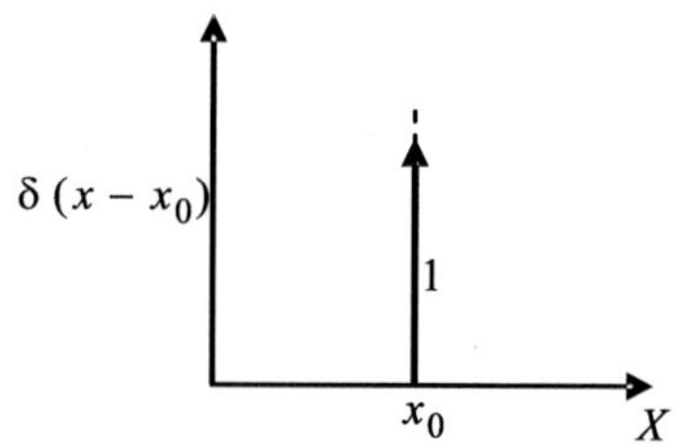

Fig. 2.22 (*b*) Dirac delta function along X-direction.

of unit area as shown in Fig.2.22(a) and 2.22(b). Fig.2.22(b) represents the delta function as straight line existing only at $x = x_0$.

Another fundamental property of δ - function can be stated as

$$\int_a^b f(x)\delta(x - x_0)dx = f(x_0) \text{ if } x_0 \text{ lies within the range } (a,b)$$

$$= 0\,; \text{ if } x_0 \text{ is not lying within the range in } (a,b) \qquad ...(2.93)$$

Under integral operation the 'δ' has the property of selecting the value of the function f (x) at the point 'x_0'. Hence, in terms of one-dimensional deltas, eqn.(2.91) is given by

$$\rho(\vec{r}) = q\delta(\vec{x} - \vec{x_0})\delta(\vec{y} - \vec{y_0})\delta(\vec{z} - \vec{z_0}) \qquad ...(2.94)$$

For a point charge 'q' at the origin, *i.e.*, $(0,0,0)$, eqn.(2.94) becomes,

$$\rho(\vec{r}) = q\delta(\vec{x})\delta(\vec{y})\delta(\vec{z}) \qquad ...(2.95)$$

For line distributions of charge, the charge density is given by

$$\rho(\vec{r}) = q_L\delta(\vec{x})\delta(\vec{y}) \qquad ...(2.96)$$

Here, 'ρ_L' is the line charge in Coulomb/m.

For sheet distributions of charge, the charge density is given by

$$\rho(\vec{r}) = q_S\delta(\vec{z}) \qquad ...(2.97)$$

The Poisson's equation is now

$$\nabla^2 V = -\frac{q}{\varepsilon} = -\frac{\rho}{\varepsilon}\delta \qquad ...(2.98)$$

Also if the point charge is located at '$\vec{r_0}$', the Green's function must satisfy Poisson's equation in the form of

$$\nabla^2 G(\vec{r},\vec{r_0}) = -\frac{\rho}{\varepsilon}\delta(\vec{r} - \vec{r_0}) \qquad ...(2.99)$$

2.25 Dirac Delta (δ) Representation for an Infinitesimal Dipole

The infinitesimally small charge dipole is shown in Fig.2.23. It has charges '+q' and '-q' with a distance of separation 'l' between them. We have to determine the effect of this dipole at a point 'P' with a distance of 'r' away from the center of the dipole. Here, $l << r$.

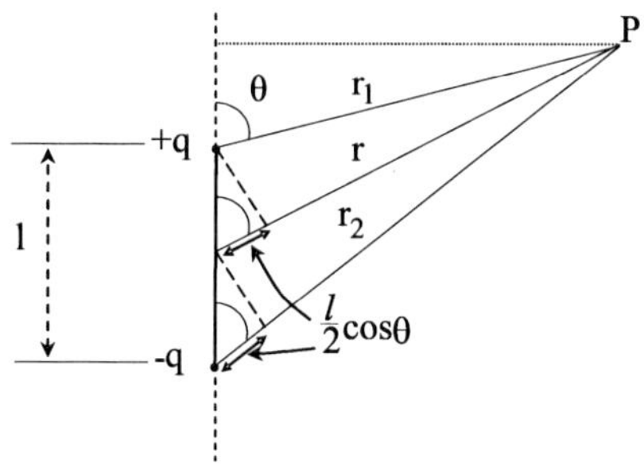

Fig. 2.23 Infinitesimal electric dipole.

Here, $r_1 \approx r - \frac{l}{2}\cos\theta$ and $r_2 \approx r + \frac{l}{2}\cos\theta$ as $l << r$.

So,

$$4\pi\varepsilon V = \frac{q}{r_1} - \frac{q}{r_1} = \frac{q}{r - \frac{l}{2}\cos\theta} - \frac{q}{r + \frac{l}{2}\cos\theta}$$

$$= \frac{q \times 2 \times \frac{l}{2}\cos\theta}{r^2 - \frac{l^2}{4}\cos^2\theta}$$

$$\approx \frac{ql\cos\theta}{r^2} \qquad (\text{as } l^2 << r^2)$$

Now the volume density of charge '$\rho(\vec{r})$' may be represented by

$$\rho(\vec{r}) = q\delta(\vec{x})\delta(\vec{y})\left[\delta(\vec{z} - \frac{l}{2}) - \delta(\vec{z} + \frac{l}{2})\right]$$

This may be written for an infinitesimal dipole with finite spacing and spacing approaches zero as

$$\rho(\vec{r}) = \underset{l \to 0}{Lt}\left\{q\delta(\vec{x})\delta(\vec{y})\left[\delta(\vec{z} - \frac{l}{2}) - \delta(\vec{z} + \frac{l}{2})\right]\right\}$$

$$= \underset{l \to 0}{Lt}\left\{-ql\delta(\vec{x})\delta(\vec{y})\frac{\left[\delta(\vec{z}+\frac{l}{2})-\delta(\vec{z}-\frac{l}{2})\right]}{l}\right\} \quad ...(2.99)$$

The quantity in square brackets is the derivative of the Dirac delta and if the dipole moment 'p' is defined as

$$p = \underset{l \to 0}{Lt}(ql) \quad ...(2.100)$$

then the charge density of an infinitesimal dipole becomes from eqn.(2.99) and (2.100) as

$$\rho(\vec{r}) = \underset{l \to 0}{Lt}(ql)\left\{-\delta(\vec{x})\delta(\vec{y})\delta'(\vec{y})\right\} = -p\delta(\vec{x})\delta(\vec{y})\delta'(\vec{z}) \quad ...(2.101)$$

Normally 'p' is expressed as a vector '$\vec{p}$'. Its direction is along the line drawn from the negative charge to the positive charge.

Thus for the charge distribution we have $\vec{p} = p\hat{z}$.

❑❑❑

CHAPTER 3

STEADY MAGNETIC FIELDS

3.1 The Steady Magnetic Field

Electric charges at rest produce an electric field (electrostatic field) and when they are in motion form electric current and thus produces magnetic field. A static magnetic field is originated from a constant current or from a permanent magnet. However, we are interested about the magnetic field produced by the current in electromagnetic theory.

The force on an electric charge depends on its position and its velocity. The electric force on the charge is dependent of the motion of the charge, however, the other component, magnetic force, is dependent on how fast the charge is moving. The total electromagnetic force on a charge can thus be written as

$$\vec{F} = q\left(\vec{E} + \vec{v} \times \vec{B}\right)$$

This force is also known as the Lorentz force.

3.2 Magnetic Induction and Faraday's Law

In 1820 for the first time it was discovered that there is a close relationship between electricity and magnetism. Earlier to that, both electricity and magnetism are treated as separate subjects. The first discovery showed that a current carrying wire produces a magnetic field, with this as a background people immediately started believing that magnets might also produce electric field. Finally in 1840, Faraday discovered that electric effects exist only there is something 'changing'. It might be a pair of wires with a 'changing' current, or, the magnet is moved near an electric circuit. It shows the induction effect. This can be explained by the Lorentz magnetic force (although this theory comes into existence at a later time), *i.e.*, $\left(\vec{v} \times \vec{B}\right)$ force. We consider an wire AB passing through the vicinity of a magnet as shown in Fig.3.1. with its ends connected to a galvanometer 'G'. When the wire is just shaked at the proximity of the magnet, the galvanometer needle moves.

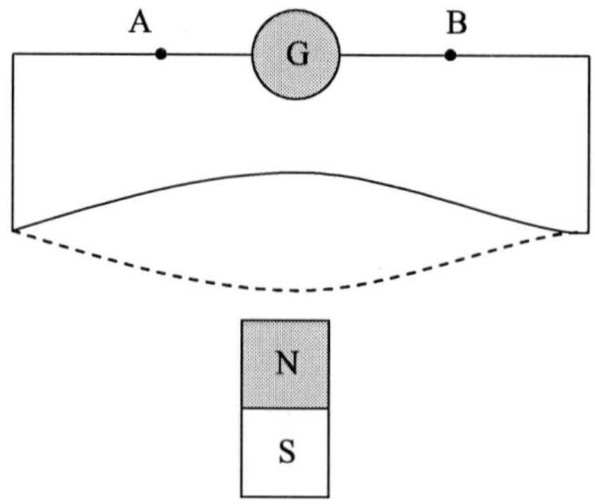

Fig. 3.1 A magnet near a wire.

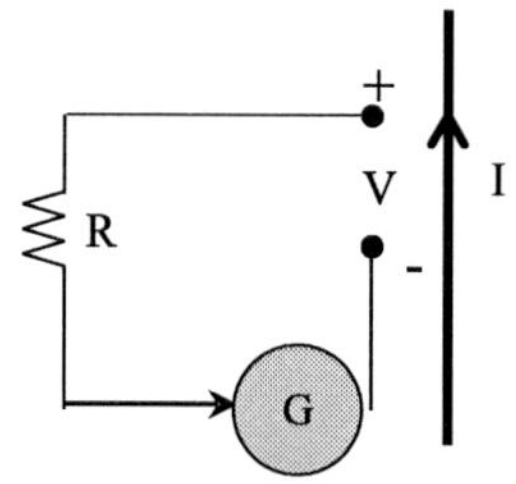

Fig. 3.2 A currect carriying wire near a loop.

Fig. 3.2 shows a ballistic galvanometer and it is connected to a loop placed near a long straight wire, carrying a current 'I'. Magnetic compass needle indicates that there is a magnetic field in the region about the wire. At the position of the loop system, the direction of the field is out of the plane of the paper for an outward flow of the current. If now 'I' is reduced to zero, the galvanometer is deflected, the amount of the deflection being independent of the rate at which the current is reduced to zero, so long as the time required is short compared with the period of the galvanometer.

The current 'I_g' through the 'G' flows as a result of 'V' induced in the loop and is $I_g = \frac{V}{R}$. Here 'R' is the total resistance (normally very large) in the galvanometer circuit. This deflection in 'G' is a measure of charge 'Q' or the time integral of the current through it, so that

$$Q = \int_0^t I_g \, dt = \frac{1}{R}\int_0^t V dt$$

This 'Q' is an experimentally determinable quantity.

Magnetic flux 'ϕ' through the loop is defined as the time integral of voltage induced in the loop throughout the interval during which the magnetic field is being established; or, having been established, the time integral of voltage throughout the interval in which the field is reduced to zero. Both these quantities are equal but with opposite sign and is given by

$$\phi = \pm\int_0^t V dt \qquad ...(3.1)$$

Here, the time interval '0' to 't' is that required to establish the field or reduce it to zero. On differentiation of eqn.(3.1), we have,

$$V = -\frac{d\phi}{dt} \qquad ...(3.2)$$

This is the Faraday's induction law. The negative sign indicates that with increase in flux, the induced voltage is negative. From eqn.(3.1), the unit of flux is 'Volt-sec' and this is named as 'Weber'.

3.3 Some Parameters

3.3.1. Magnetic Flux Density, $\vec{B}$: The magnetic flux per unit area through a loop of small area is called the magnetic flux density $\vec{B}$ at the location of the loop. As flux through the loop depends upon the orientation of the loop and also on its area, $\vec{B}$ is vector. The direction is taken as the normal to the plane of the loop when oriented to enclose maximum flux. Its unit is 'Tesla' or 'Weber per sq. mt.'.

Hence, $$\phi = \oint_S \vec{B}.\vec{dS}$$.

3.3.2. Magnetic Field Strength $\vec{H}$ and Ampere's Circuital Law: Using the Fig.3.3 it is possible to determine $\vec{B}$ at all points in a region about a long current carrying wire. For a homogeneous medium, amount of magnetization, $\vec{B}$, due to a current carrying wire is proportional to the permeability (μ) of the medium ($B \propto \mu$), proportional to current 'I' flowing ($B \propto I$)and inversely proportional

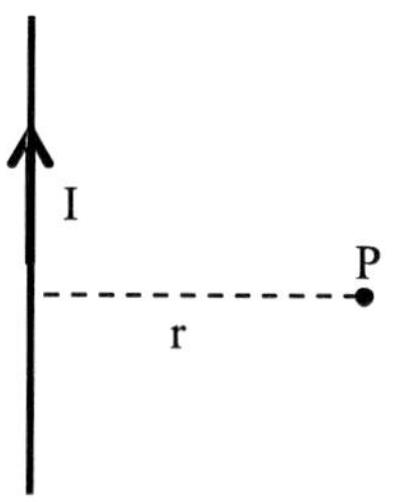

Fig. 3.3 A point P near a current carrying wire.

to the distance (r) from the current carrying wire ($B \propto 1/r$), *i.e.*, $B \propto \dfrac{\mu I}{r}$ ...(3.3)

Here, $\mu = \mu_0 \mu_r$.

μ_0 is the permeability of vacuum or free space and $\mu_0 = 4\pi \times 10^{-7}$ Henry/mt in SI, μ_r is the relative permeability (relative to vacuum).

Hence using eqn.(3.3) with a proportionality constant $\left(\dfrac{1}{2\pi}\right)$, we have,

$$B = \frac{\mu I}{2\pi r}$$

But $B = \mu H$,

hence, $$B = \frac{\mu I}{2\pi r} = \mu H \qquad ...(3.4)$$

and, $$H = \frac{I}{2\pi r} \text{ Amp/m} \qquad ...(3.4a)$$

Hence magnetic field strength ' $\vec{H}$ ' is defined by the current which produces it and the geometry of the system, with its direction same as $\vec{B}$, *i.e.*,

$$\vec{B} = \mu \vec{H} \qquad ...(3.4b)$$

In earlier example, $|\vec{H}|$ is independent of ' μ ' depending only on 'I' and 'r', while $|\vec{B}|$ is dependent on ' μ '. So 'H' may be considered as magnetic stress that drives a resultant flux density throughout the medium. Hence we can say that 'H' is analogous to 'E' and 'B' is analogous to 'D'.

Now the line integral, $F_M = \int_a^b \vec{H}.\vec{dl}$ is defined as the **magnetomotive force** between the points 'a' to 'b'.

For a circular path of radius 'r' we have, $L = 2\pi r$, hence,

$$F_M = \oint \vec{H}.\vec{dl} = HL = H.2\pi r = I \text{ (using eqn.(3.4a))} \qquad ...(3.5)$$

This is the Ampere's work law or Circuital law.

Statement: The line integral of the tangential component of magnetic field strength around a closed path is equal to the current enclosed by the path, *i.e.*,

$$\oint \vec{H}.\vec{dl} = I_{enclosed}$$

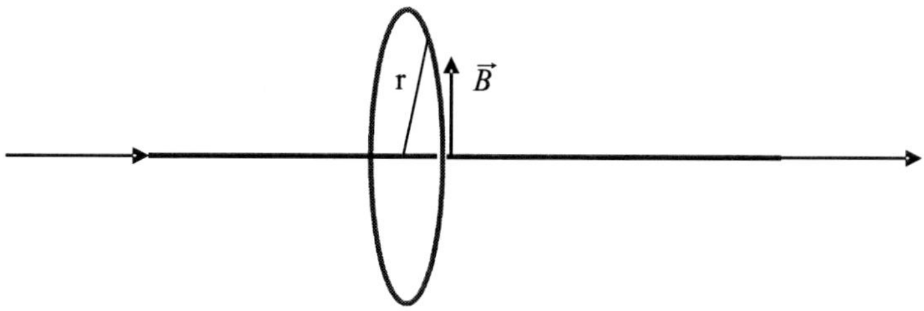

Fig. 3.4 A current carrying loop.

The law is similar to Gauss's law for $\vec{D}$ for a distribution of charges. However, following two conditions must be satisfied before the application of Ampere's law.

(*i*) At each point of the closed path, $\vec{H}$, is either tangential or normal to the path.

(*ii*) '$\vec{H}$' has the same value at all points of the path, where is tangential. This is shown in Fig.3.4.

3.4 Ampere's Work Law in the Differential Form

Ampere's work law states that the magnetomotive (MMF) force around a closed path is equal to the current enclosed by the path as

$$\oint \vec{H}.\vec{dl} = I \quad ...(3.5)$$

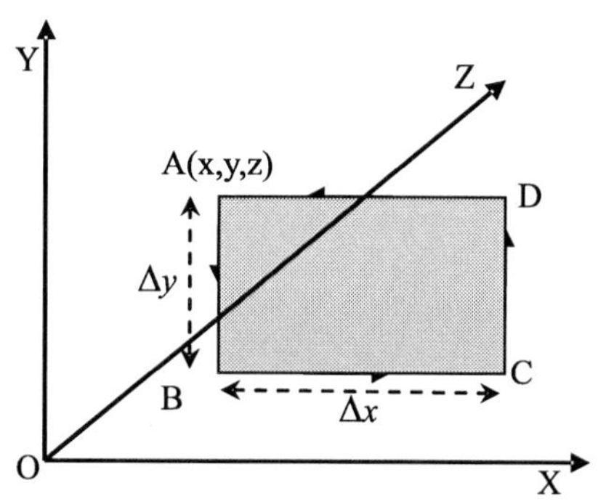

Fig. 3.5 A current carrying rectangular loop ABCD.

We consider a conducting region with current density $\vec{J}$ as shown in Fig.3.5. Let ABCD be an element of area parallel to the XY-plane and the coordinate of the point $A(x, y, z)$ and the value of 'H' at A is (H_x, H_y, H_z). The MMF around the closed path ABCDA can be obtained by summing the MMFs along the four sides of the rectangle.

MMF from A to B $= H_y(-\Delta y)$ (as ' Δy ' is decreasing)

MMF from B to C $= \left[H_x + \dfrac{\partial H_x}{\partial y}(-\Delta y) \right] \Delta x$

MMF from C to D $= \left[H_y + \dfrac{\partial H_y}{\partial x}(\Delta x) \right] \Delta y$

MMF from D to A $= H_x(-\Delta x)$ (as ' Δx ' is decreasing)

Adding both sides of the above we get, MMF around the closed path ABCDA

$$= H_y(-\Delta y) + \left[H_x + \frac{\partial H_x}{\partial y}(-\Delta y) \right] \Delta x + \left[H_y + \frac{\partial H_y}{\partial x}(\Delta x) \right] \Delta y + H_x(-\Delta x)$$

$$= \left[\frac{\partial H_y}{\partial x} - \frac{\partial H_x}{\partial y} \right] (\Delta x \Delta y)$$

The current flowing through this rectangle is

$$dI = J_Z \Delta x \Delta y$$

Hence using the Ampere's law by eqn.(3.5) we have,

$$\left[\frac{\partial H_y}{\partial x} - \frac{\partial H_x}{\partial y} \right] \Delta x \Delta y = J_Z \Delta x \Delta y$$

$$\Rightarrow J_Z = \left[\frac{\partial H_y}{\partial x} - \frac{\partial H_x}{\partial y} \right] \quad \text{...(3.6a)}$$

If we consider this elemental area to be taken parallel to the YZ plane and then parallel to the ZX plane, we have,

$$J_x = \left[\frac{\partial H_z}{\partial y} - \frac{\partial H_y}{\partial z} \right] \quad \text{...(3.6b)}$$

$$J_y = \left[\frac{\partial H_x}{\partial z} - \frac{\partial H_z}{\partial x} \right] \quad \text{...(3.6c)}$$

Arranging (3.6a), (3.6b) and (3.6c) as

$$\hat{i}J_x + \hat{j}J_y + \hat{k}J_z = \hat{i}\left[\frac{\partial H_z}{\partial y} - \frac{\partial H_y}{\partial z} \right] + \hat{j}\left[\frac{\partial H_x}{\partial z} - \frac{\partial H_z}{\partial x} \right] + \hat{k}\left[\frac{\partial H_y}{\partial x} - \frac{\partial H_x}{\partial y} \right]$$

$$\Rightarrow \vec{J} = \vec{\nabla} \times \vec{H} \quad \text{...(3.6)}$$

This is an alternative statement in the differential form of Ampere's law.

The differential form given in eqn.(3.6) requires a homogeneous medium, because the space derivative has no meaning at a discontinuity of the medium.

However, when the path under consideration crosses a discontinuity, the integral form given in eqn.(3.5) is more suitable.

NOTE

Interpretation of $\vec{\nabla}\times\vec{H}$

From eqn.(3.6) taking its integral over an area we get,

$$\oint_S \left(\vec{\nabla}\times\vec{H}\right).\overrightarrow{dS} = \oint_S \vec{J}.\overrightarrow{dS} \qquad ...(3.7)$$

$$\Rightarrow \oint_S \left(\vec{\nabla}\times\vec{H}\right).\overrightarrow{dS} = I$$

However, $I = \oint_l \vec{H}.\vec{dl}$, hence we have,

$$\oint_S \left(\vec{\nabla}\times\vec{H}\right).\overrightarrow{dS} = \oint_l \vec{H}.\vec{dl} \qquad ...(3.8)$$

Eqn.(3.8) relates the surface integral of $\left(\vec{\nabla}\times\vec{H}\right)$ over a surface to the line integral of $\vec{H}$ or MMF around the closed path bounding the surface.

If the surface is reduced to an element of area 'dS', the result is

$$\left(\vec{\nabla}\times\vec{H}\right).\hat{n} = \frac{\oint_l \vec{H}.\vec{dl}}{dS}.$$

Hence, $\left(\vec{\nabla}\times\vec{H}\right)$ equals the 'MMF' per unit area. Its direction is such that the direction of '$\hat{n}$' of the area '$\overrightarrow{dS}$' results in a maximum MMF around its edge and the space variation of '$\vec{H}$' depends on '$\frac{1}{dS}$', *i.e.*, for spherical symmetry,

$$dH \propto \frac{1}{dS} \propto \frac{1}{r^2}.$$

3.5 Ampere's Law for a Current Element or Biot-Savart's Law

We now consider the total magnetic field strength at any point as the sum of the contributions from elemental lengths 'dl' of the circuit, each carrying a current 'I'. This quantity '*Idl*' is called a current element. It is a vector quantity having the direction of the current or the direction of the element 'dl' in which the current flows. So this may be written as $\vec{I}dl$ or $I\vec{dl}$. Here, as shown in Fig.3.6 AB is a current element '$I\vec{dl}$'. Current elements do not have separate existence.

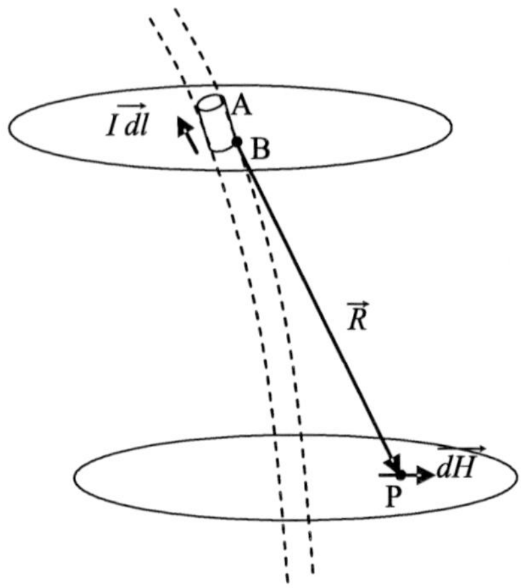

Fig. 3.6 Magnetic field at a point P due to current carriying element.

All these elements are summed up to make the complete current carrying wire. The elemental magnetic field, '$\vec{dH}$' is to be determined at a point 'P' at a distance, '$\vec{R}$', away from AB.

A differential magnetic field strength '$\vec{dH}$', infers from the experiment results from the current element '$I\vec{dl}$'as in the followings.

(*i*) '$\vec{dH}$' is proportional to '$I\vec{dl}$', *i.e.*, $\vec{dH} \propto I\vec{dl}$;

(*ii*) Proportional to the 'sin' of the angle 'ψ', *i.e.*, $\vec{dH} \propto \sin\Psi$; '$\psi$' is the angle between the direction of '$I\vec{dl}$' and the direction of $\vec{R}$,and,

(*iii*) Inversely proportional to square of the distance, 'R', between the current element and the point of observation 'P' as shown in Fig. *i.e.*, $\vec{dH} \propto \frac{1}{R^2}$.

On combining and considering the constant of proportionality as '$1/4\pi$, we have for the magnitude of '*dH*' as

$$dH = \frac{(Idl)\,Sin\psi}{4\pi R^2} \qquad ...(3.9)$$

Hence, this complete statement can be written vectorically as

$$\vec{dH} = \frac{\left(I\vec{dl}\right)\times\hat{R}}{4\pi R^2} \qquad ...(3.10)$$

Here, $\hat{R}$ is a unit vector in the direction of $\vec{R}$.

Hence, the total magnetic field strength $\vec{H}$ at a point 'P' is given by

$$\vec{H} = \oint_C \frac{\left(I\vec{dl}\right)\times\hat{R}}{4\pi R^2} \qquad ...(3.11)$$

The direction of $\vec{H}$ is perpendicular to the plane containing ‘ $I\vec{dl}$ ’ and $\vec{R}$, in the direction in which a right hand screw would progress in turning from ‘ Idl ’ to $\vec{R}$. Eqn.(3.10) is known as Ampere’s law for a current element or also known as Biot-Savart law as deduced firstly by them.

3.6 Magnetic Field Due to Volume Distribution of Current and the Dirac Delta

We have seen that currents are not necessarily confined to filamentary paths, so the eqn.(3.11) should be generalized by including a current density ‘ $\vec{J}$ ’ flowing within a volume ‘V’ as shown in Fig. 3.7. Hence the net current ‘I’ can be represented by

$$I = \oint_S \vec{J}(\vec{r}).\vec{dS}$$

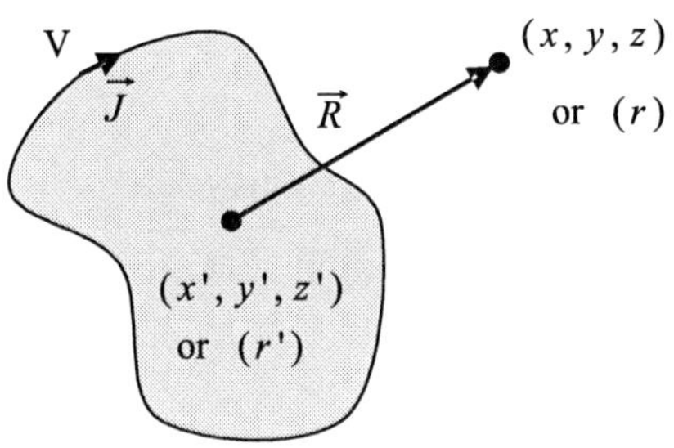

Fig. 3.7 An arbitrary current carrying volume bounded by the surface.

Using it into eqn.3.11 of Biot-savart’s law, we have,

$$\vec{H}(\vec{r}) = \oint_C \frac{\left(I\vec{dl}\right)\times\hat{R}}{4\pi R^2} = \frac{1}{4\pi}\oint_C\oint_S \frac{\left(\left(\vec{J}(\vec{r}).\vec{dS}\right)\vec{dl}\right)\times\hat{R}}{4\pi R^2}$$

$$= \frac{1}{4\pi}\int_V \frac{\vec{J}\left(\vec{r'}\right)\times\hat{R}}{R^2}dV \qquad ...(3.12)$$

Here the prime is used to denote the coordinates of the source region.

The current density may be used to represent filamentary currents by making use of the properties of the Dirac delta. If the current is confined to a straight filament along the Z-axis and if the total current is ‘I’ Amp., then,

$$\vec{J} = \hat{k}I\delta(x)\delta(y).$$

Similarly, if the current ‘I’ is confined to a filamentary loop of radius ‘a’, then the current density is given by

$$\vec{J} = \hat{\phi}I\delta(x-a)\delta(z)$$

The above representations satisfy the relation between current and current density as

$$I = \int_S \vec{J}.\overrightarrow{dS} \quad ...(3.13)$$

Here 'S' is an open surface. If 'S' is a closed one, then conservation of charge requires that the net steady current passing through the surface 'S' is zero, *i.e.*,

$$\int_S \vec{J}.\overrightarrow{dS} = 0 \Rightarrow \int_V \left(\vec{\nabla}.\vec{J}\right) dV = 0 \quad \text{(applying divergence theorem)}$$

Here volume 'V' is enclosed by the surface 'S' and as it is arbitrary, we have,

$$\left(\vec{\nabla}.\vec{J}\right) = 0 \quad ...(3.14)$$

This is the equation of continuity for steady currents.

3.7 Ampere's Force Law

We now consider two loops C_1 and C_2 carrying currents I_1 and I_2 as shown in Fig.3.8. 'dl_1' and 'dl_2' are directed distance between them is $\overrightarrow{R_{12}}$, where, $\overrightarrow{R_{12}} = R\hat{R}_{12}$, $\hat{R}_{12}$ is the unit vector drawing from point '1' to point '2'.

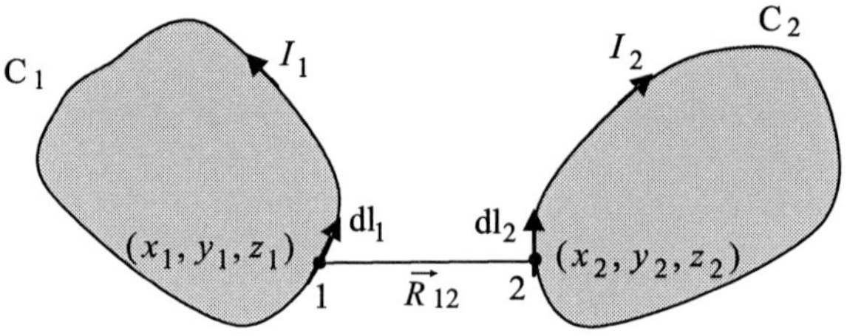

$\vec{R}_{12} = R\hat{R}_{12}$

Fig. 3.8 Two current carrying loops in proximity.

So Ampere's force law now may be expressed as

$$\overrightarrow{F_{21}} = \frac{\mu I_1 I_2}{4\pi} \oint_{C_1} \oint_{C_2} \frac{\overrightarrow{dl_2} \times \left(\overrightarrow{dl_1} \times \hat{R}_{12}\right)}{R^2} \quad ...(3.15)$$

Here, $\overrightarrow{F_{21}}$ is the force on C_2.

Now we can consider this force as acting at a distance on C_2 through the intermediary of a magnetic field produced by the current flowing in C_1, *i.e.*, we can write eqn.(3.15) as

$$\overrightarrow{F_{21}} = \mu I_2 \oint_{C_1} \overrightarrow{dl_2} \times \overrightarrow{H_{21}} \quad ...(3.16)$$

Here,
$$\overrightarrow{H_{21}} = \frac{I_1}{4\pi} \oint_{C_1} \frac{\left(\overrightarrow{dl_1} \times \hat{R}_{12}\right)}{R^2} \quad ...(3.17)$$

$\overrightarrow{H_{12}}$ is the magnetic field strength due to the current 'I_1' in C_1.

Hence we can rewrite eqn.(3.16) as

$$\overrightarrow{F_{21}} = I_2 \oint_{C_2} \overrightarrow{dl_2} \times \overrightarrow{B_{21}} \quad ...(3.18)$$

and thus,
$$\overrightarrow{B_{21}} = \frac{\mu I_1}{4\pi} \oint_{C_2} \frac{\left(\overrightarrow{dl_1} \times \hat{R}_{12}\right)}{R^2} \quad ...(3.19)$$

3.8 Magnetic Vector Potential

Same concept of electric potential in electrostatics has been incorporated in magnetostatics also in the concept of magnetic potential for magnetic field. Corresponding to the individual charges in electric field case, the sources of the magnetic field would be the current elements '$\overrightarrow{Idl}$' of the circuits that produce the field. So the magnetic potential would therefore depend upon these current elements. In electrostatics we have $\vec{E} = -\vec{\nabla}V$

Like electric potential 'V', the space derivative of magnetic potential give $\vec{B}$ or $\vec{H}$. As the magnetic field that is to be derived from the potential, it is proportional to '$\overrightarrow{Idl}$', the potential itself must be proportional to '$\overrightarrow{Idl}$'. Because the magnetic field strength due to a current element varies inversely as the square of the distance 'R' from the element (Ampere's law) $\left[H \propto \frac{1}{R^2}\right]$, the magnetic potential due to the current elements must vary inversely as the first power of the distance (because magnetic field is the space derivative of potential).

The magnetic potential is a vector quantity and is represented by '$\vec{A}$'. $\vec{A}$ refers to the vector potential developed due to the currents (other than 'I' flowing in the wire) responsible of producing $\vec{B}$. The definition of $\vec{A}$ is consistent with the requirement of

$$\vec{\nabla}.\vec{B} = 0 \cdot$$

The unit of $\vec{A}$ is Weber/m or T/m.

The electric charges are scalar and hence electric potential is a scalar quantity. However, current elements are vector, so the potential in this case must be a vector. There are two vector space derivatives of a vector, divergence and curl. However, divergence of a vector yields a scalar, therefore, for the suitable magnetic vector potential $\vec{A}$, we have,

$$\vec{H} = \vec{\nabla} \times \vec{A} \text{ or } \vec{B} = \vec{\nabla} \times \vec{A} \cdot$$

Both the above relations are true, but normally we use,

$$\vec{B} = \vec{\nabla} \times \vec{A} \qquad ...(3.20)$$

For magnetically isotropic and homogeneous medium, μ is constant. So both the above relations are equivalent.

We have from the definition of $\vec{A}$,

$$\overrightarrow{dA} = R\overrightarrow{dB}$$

$$= \mu R\overrightarrow{dH} = \mu R \frac{I\overrightarrow{dl} \times \hat{R}}{4\pi R^2} \quad \text{(from Biot-Savart's law in eqn.(3.11))}$$

$$= \mu \frac{I\overrightarrow{dl}}{4\pi R} \qquad ...(3.21)$$

Hence, the relation between $\vec{A}$ and current element source as

$$\overrightarrow{dA} = k \frac{I\overrightarrow{dl}}{R} \qquad ...(3.22)$$

Here, 'k' is a constant and is given by

$$k = \frac{\mu}{4\pi}.$$

Hence, the magnetic vector potential due to a current flow in a complete circuit is obtained by the integration of vector potentials caused by all the current elements that comprise the circuit as

$$\vec{A} = \oint_C \frac{\mu I \overrightarrow{dl}}{4\pi R} \qquad ...(3.23)$$

The general form of this expression is obtained by replacing 'I' by '$\vec{J}$' and then integrating over the volume 'V' in which the current density exists. Thus we have,

$$\vec{A} = \int_V \frac{\mu \vec{J}}{4\pi R} dV$$

3.9 The Vector Potential (Alternate Approach)

We know from eqn.(3.12),

$$\vec{H}(\vec{r}) = \frac{1}{4\pi} \int_V \frac{\vec{J}(\vec{r}\,') \times \hat{R}}{R^2} dV' \qquad ...(3.24)$$

Now we can write,

$$\frac{\vec{J}\left(\vec{r}'\right)\times\hat{R}}{R^2} = -\vec{J}\left(\vec{r}'\right)\times\vec{\nabla}\left(\frac{1}{R}\right)$$

$$= \vec{\nabla}\left(\frac{1}{R}\right)\times\vec{J}\left(\vec{r}'\right) \qquad \text{(as '}\vec{J}\left(\vec{r}'\right)\text{' is independent of '}R\text{')}$$

$$= \vec{\nabla}\times\left[\frac{\vec{J}\left(\vec{r}'\right)}{R}\right] \qquad ...(3.25)$$

Using eqns.(3.24) and (3.25),

$$\vec{B}\left(\vec{r}\right) = \mu\vec{H}\left(\vec{r}\right) = \frac{\mu}{4\pi}\int_V \vec{\nabla}\times\left[\frac{\vec{J}\left(\vec{r}'\right)}{R}\right]dV'$$

$$= \vec{\nabla}\times\frac{\mu}{4\pi}\int_V\left[\frac{\vec{J}\left(\vec{r}'\right)}{R}\right]dV' \qquad ...(3.26)$$

Eqn.(3.26) represents the magnetic vector potential $\vec{A}$ and we know from eqn.(3.20),

$$\vec{A}(\vec{r}) = \frac{\mu}{4\pi}\int_V\left[\frac{\vec{J}\left(\vec{r}'\right)}{R}\right]dV' \qquad ...(3.27)$$

Thus from eqns.(3.26) and (3.27),

$$\vec{B} = \vec{\nabla}\times\vec{A} \qquad ...(3.28)$$

Example

Magnetic field about a long straight wire using $\vec{A}$

Here, $$\vec{A} = \int_V \frac{\mu\vec{J}}{4\pi R}dV'$$

Fig.3.9 shows a current carrying wire where current is along Z-direction only, so, we have only one component of $\vec{A}$, *i.e.*, A_Z.

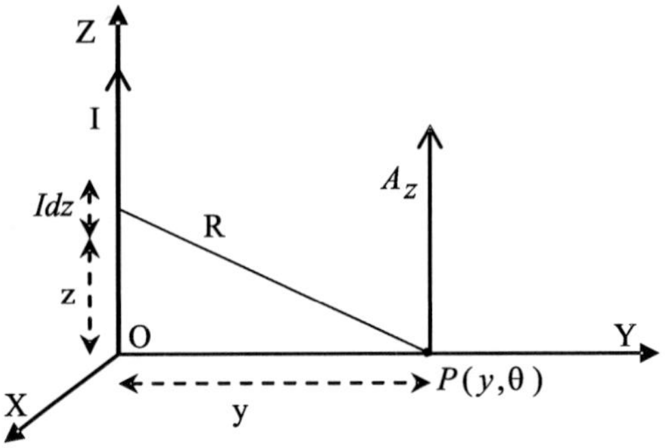

Fig. 3.9 Magnetic vector potential at a point P due to a current element.

So in a homogeneous medium,

$$A_z = \frac{\mu}{4\pi}\int_{-L}^{L}\frac{Idz}{R} \text{ (as '}\vec{J}dV'\text{' is replaced by '}Idz\text{')}$$

$$= \frac{\mu}{4\pi}\int_{-L}^{L}\frac{Idz}{\sqrt{y^2+z^2}} = \frac{\mu I}{2\pi}\int_{0}^{L}\frac{dz}{\sqrt{y^2+z^2}}$$

$$= \frac{\mu I}{2\pi}\left[\ln\left\{z+\sqrt{y^2+z^2}\right\}\right]_0^L$$

$$= \frac{\mu I}{2\pi}\left[\ln\left\{L+\sqrt{y^2+L^2}\right\}-\ln(y)\right]$$

For, $L >> y$, we have,

$$y^2 + L^2 \approx L^2,$$

hence, $$A_Z = \frac{\mu I}{2\pi}\left[\ln\{2L\}-\ln(y)\right] \quad ...(3.29)$$

Now for a point in YZ-plane from the vector potential,

$$H_x = \frac{1}{\mu}\left[\left(\vec{\nabla}\times\vec{A}\right)_x\right] = \frac{1}{\mu}\left(\frac{\partial A_Z}{\partial y}\right)$$

$$\left[\text{As 'X' component of } \begin{bmatrix}\hat{i} & \hat{j} & \hat{k}\\ \frac{\partial}{\partial x} & \frac{\partial}{\partial y} & \frac{\partial}{\partial z}\\ A_x & A_y & A_z\end{bmatrix} \textit{ is } \begin{bmatrix}\hat{i} & \hat{j} & \hat{k}\\ \frac{\partial}{\partial x} & \frac{\partial}{\partial y} & \frac{\partial}{\partial z}\\ 0 & 0 & A_z\end{bmatrix} = \hat{i}\left[\frac{\partial A_z}{\partial y}-\frac{\partial A_y}{\partial x}\right] = \hat{i}\left[\frac{\partial A_z}{\partial y}\right]\right]$$

$$\Rightarrow \quad H_x = \frac{1}{\mu}\frac{\partial}{\partial y}\left[\frac{\mu I}{2\pi}\left[\ln\{2L\}-\ln(y)\right]\right] \quad \text{(using eqn. (3.29))}$$

$$\Rightarrow \quad H_x = \frac{1}{\mu}\left[\frac{\mu I}{2\pi}\left[0-\left(\frac{1}{y}\right)\right]\right] = -\frac{I}{2\pi y} \quad ...(3.30)$$

So the lines of magnetic field strength will be circles about the wire.

3.10 The Far Magnetic field of a Current Distribution

The magnetic vector potential integral of eqn.(3.27) is valid for any observation point. If the observation point is far away from the source potential responsible for current distribution, approximation is possible for eqn.(3.27) under this practical condition. The distribution is shown in Fig.3.10.

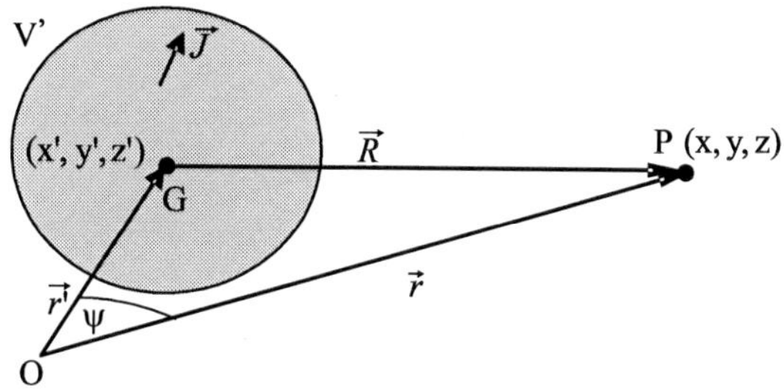

Fig. 3.10 Point P far away from source G..

Here the source potential is at a point 'G' with coordinates (x', y', z') and point of observation is at 'P' with coordinates (x, y, z) with a distance of 'R' between them. Points 'G,P' are at a distances of '$|\vec{r'}|$' and '$|\vec{r}|$' from the origin 'O' respectively. 'ψ' is the angle between $\vec{r}$ and $\vec{r'}$.

We have, $$R^{-1} = \frac{1}{R} = \frac{1}{\sqrt{(x-x')^2+(y-y')^2+(z-z')^2}}$$

$$= \left[r^2 - 2rr'\cos\psi + r'^2\right]^{-\frac{1}{2}}$$

$$\Rightarrow R^{-1} = \frac{1}{\sqrt{r^2 - 2rr'\cos\psi + r'^2}}$$

$$= \frac{1}{r}\cdot\frac{1}{\sqrt{1-2\left(\frac{r'}{r}\right)\cos\psi + \left(\frac{r'}{r}\right)^2}}$$

$$= \frac{1}{r}\cdot\left[1-2\left(\frac{r'}{r}\right)\cos\psi + \left(\frac{r'}{r}\right)^2\right]^{-\frac{1}{2}} \quad \text{(here r>>r')}$$

$$=\frac{1}{r}\cdot\left[1-\left(-\frac{1}{2}\right)2\left(\frac{r'}{r}\right)\cos\psi+\frac{1}{2}\left(3\cos^2\psi-1\right)\left(\frac{r'}{r}\right)^2+\ldots\ldots\right]$$

(Expanding the infinite series using binomial theorem)

$$=\frac{1}{r}\sum_{n=0}^{\infty}P_n(\cos\psi)\left(\frac{r'}{r}\right)^n$$

Here, P_n is called a Legendre function and

$$P_0=1, P_1=\cos\psi, P_2=\frac{1}{2}\left[3\cos^2\psi-1\right]\cos\psi \text{, and so on.}$$

We can write,

$$r'\cos\psi=\vec{r}'.\hat{n}=\frac{\vec{r}'.\vec{r}}{r}\quad\left[\hat{n}=\frac{\vec{r}}{|\vec{r}|}=\frac{\vec{r}}{r}\text{ is the unit vector along }'\vec{r}'\right]$$

Hence,
$$R^{-1}=\frac{1}{r}\cdot\left[1+\left(\frac{r'}{r}\right)\cos\psi+\frac{1}{2}\left(3\cos^2\psi-1\right)\left(\frac{r'}{r}\right)^2+\ldots\ldots\right]$$

$$=\frac{1}{r}\cdot\left[1+\left(\frac{\vec{r}'.\hat{n}}{r}\right)+\frac{1}{2}\left(3\left(\frac{\vec{r}'.\hat{n}}{r}\right)^2-\left(\frac{r'}{r}\right)^2\right)+\ldots\ldots\right]\quad\ldots(3.31)$$

From eqn.(3.27) we have,

$$\vec{A}(\vec{r}')=\frac{\mu}{4\pi}\int_V\frac{\vec{J}dV'}{R}$$

Hence substituting the value of '$\frac{1}{R}$' from eqn.(3.31), we get

$$\vec{A}(\vec{r}')=\frac{\mu}{4\pi}\int_V\frac{\vec{J}\left(\vec{r}'\right)dV'}{R}$$

$$=\frac{\mu}{4\pi}\int_V\left(\vec{J}\left(\vec{r}'\right)dV'\right)\cdot\frac{1}{r}\cdot\left[1+\left(\frac{\vec{r}'.\hat{n}}{r}\right)+\frac{1}{2}\left(3\left(\frac{\vec{r}'.\hat{n}}{r}\right)^2-\left(\frac{r'}{r}\right)^2\right)+\ldots\ldots\right]$$

$$=\frac{\mu}{4\pi r}\int_V\vec{J}(\vec{r}')dV'+\frac{\mu}{4\pi r^2}\int_V\vec{J}(\vec{r}')(\vec{r}'.\hat{n})dV'+\frac{\mu}{8\pi r^3}\int_V\vec{J}(\vec{r}')\left[3(\vec{r}'.\hat{n})^2-r'^2\right]dV'+..\quad\ldots(3.32)$$

Since current must flow in closed loops, 1st term of eqn.(3.32) must be zero. The first non-zero term predominates for arbitrary large values of 'r'.

3.11 Equation of Continuity (Conservation of nos. of Charges)

Here we are determining the current 'I' crossing through any surface 'S' and '$\vec{J}$' is known. When there is no steady state, the change of increase of charge equals to the net flow of charge into the volume. So, mathematically,

$$-\frac{\partial q}{\partial t} = \text{time rate at which charge leaves the volume.}$$

$$\Rightarrow -\frac{\partial q}{\partial t} = \oint_S \vec{J}.\overrightarrow{dS} \Rightarrow -\frac{\partial}{\partial t}\oint_V \rho dV = \oint_S \vec{J}.\overrightarrow{dS}$$

$$\Rightarrow -\oint_V \frac{\partial}{\partial t}\rho dV = \oint_V (\vec{\nabla}.\vec{J})dV$$

$$\Rightarrow \oint_V \left[\vec{\nabla}.\vec{J} + \frac{\partial \rho}{\partial t}\right]dV = 0$$

Since the equation is true for all values, integrand must vanish.

So, $$\vec{\nabla}.\vec{J} + \frac{\partial \rho}{\partial t} = 0 \qquad ...(3.33)$$

This is the equation of continuity for current and 'ρ' is the net charge density.

At steady state, 'ρ' is constant and so from eqn.(3.33), $\vec{\nabla}.\vec{J} = 0$. This is equivalent to Kirchoff's law for current flow. In the conduction process, valence electrons move freely under the external electric field. Here, for the electrons in motion, static condition does not exist.

❑❑❑

CHAPTER 4

TIME VARYING FIELDS AND MAXWELL'S EQUATIONS

4.1 Inconsistency of Ampere's Law

Upto now for static electric field, charges are at rest and the static magnetic field is due to the steady current. We have attained the following equations.

From Gauss's law of electrostatics,

$$\vec{\nabla}.\vec{D} = \rho \Rightarrow \oint \vec{D}.\vec{dS} = \int_V \rho dV$$

$$\Rightarrow \oint \vec{D}.\vec{dS} = \int_V \rho dV \text{ (using Gauss's divergence theorem)} \quad ...(4.1)$$

For '$\vec{E}$' is an irrotational vector, we have

$$\vec{\nabla} \times \vec{E} = 0$$

$$\Rightarrow \oint \vec{E}.\vec{dl} = 0 \text{ (using Stoke's theorem)} \quad ...(4.2)$$

From Ampere's law,

$$\vec{\nabla} \times \vec{H} = \vec{J}$$

$$\Rightarrow \oint \vec{H}.\vec{dl} = \int \vec{J}.\vec{dS} \text{ (using Stoke's theorem)} \quad ...(4.3)$$

For '$\vec{B}$' is an rotational vector, we have

$$\vec{\nabla}.\vec{B} = 0$$

$$\Rightarrow \oint \vec{B}.\vec{dS} = 0 \text{ (using Gauss's divergence theorem)} \quad ...(4.4)$$

The continuity equation for steady current is

$$\vec{\nabla}.\vec{J} = 0$$

$$\Rightarrow \int \vec{J}.\vec{dS} = 0 \text{ (using Gauss's divergence theorem)} \quad ...(4.5)$$

The modified equation of continuity for time varying field is

$$\vec{\nabla}.\vec{J} = -\frac{\partial \rho}{\partial t} \qquad ...(4.6)$$

Taking the divergence of eqn.(4.3) (Ampere's law), we only get,

$$\vec{\nabla}.\vec{J} = 0$$

This is the equation of continuity for steady current as given in eqn.(4.5).

Thus it can not arrive the equation of continuity for time varying field as given in eqn.(4.6). So it is not consistent with the time varying field. This is one of the factors which lead J.C.Maxwell to seek modification to Ampere's law.

A suggestion to the correct modification is found by substituting Gauss's law (eqn.(2)) into the equation of continuity (eqn.(4.6)), *i.e.*,

$$\vec{\nabla}.\vec{J} = -\frac{\partial \rho}{\partial t} = -\frac{\partial\left(\vec{\nabla}.\vec{D}\right)}{\partial t} \Rightarrow \vec{\nabla}.\left[\frac{\partial \vec{D}}{\partial t} + \vec{J}\right] = 0 \qquad ...(4.7)$$

In integral form (by integrating over a volume and then applying the divergence theorem) we have from eqn.(4.7) as

$$\int_V \vec{\nabla}.\left[\frac{\partial \vec{D}}{\partial t} + \vec{J}\right] dV = 0 \Rightarrow \oint_S \left[\frac{\partial \vec{D}}{\partial t} + \vec{J}\right].\overrightarrow{dS} = 0 \qquad ...(4.8)$$

This equation suggests that $\left[\frac{\partial \vec{D}}{\partial t} + \vec{J}\right]$ may be taken as the total current density for time varying fields. $\left[\frac{\partial \vec{D}}{\partial t}\right]$ is known as 'displacement current density'.

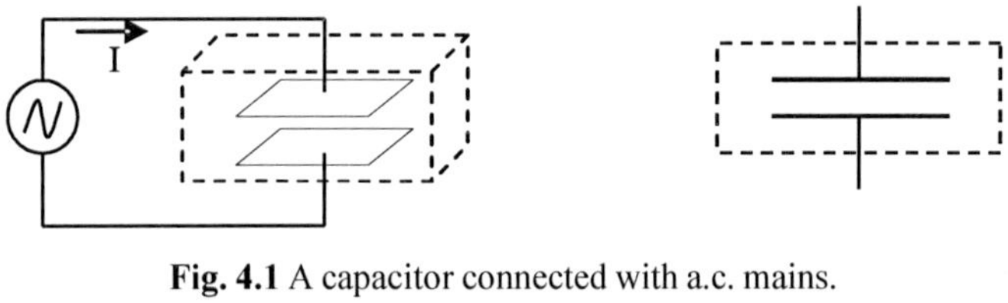

Fig. 4.1 A capacitor connected with a.c. mains.

Fig.4.1 above shows a surface enclosing one plate of a two plate capacitor. On applying eqn.(4.8) we found that during charging or discharging, the conduction current in the wire attached to the plate is equal to the displacement current passing between the plates.

Maxwell has given an answer to that. According to him the total current density should replace '$\vec{J}$' in Ampere's law and the result would be

$$\vec{\nabla} \times \vec{H} = \vec{J} + \frac{\partial \vec{D}}{\partial t} \qquad ...(4.9)$$

Taking the divergence we have,

$$\vec{\nabla}.\left(\vec{\nabla}\times\vec{H}\right)=\vec{\nabla}.\left(\vec{J}+\frac{\partial\vec{D}}{\partial t}\right)$$

$$\Rightarrow 0=\frac{\partial}{\partial t}\left(\vec{\nabla}.\vec{D}\right)+\left(\vec{\nabla}.\vec{J}\right)$$

$$\Rightarrow\left(\vec{\nabla}.\vec{J}\right)=-\frac{\partial}{\partial t}\left(\vec{\nabla}.\vec{D}\right)=-\frac{\partial\rho}{\partial t}$$

$$\Rightarrow\left(\vec{\nabla}.\vec{J}\right)=-\frac{\partial\rho}{\partial t}$$

This gives the equation of continuity for a time varying field. Therefore, when it was obtained by Maxwell, eqn.(4.9) was a postulate whose validity had to be established by the experiment.

Maxwell's assumption that a changing displacement density (*i.e.*, a changing electric field '$\frac{\partial\vec{D}}{\partial t}$') equivalent to an current density '$\vec{J}$' and that can produce a magnetic field. Combining this with Faraday's law we get that changing magnetic field will produce an electric field and it leads to the 'wave equations'. This result enabled Maxwell to predict electromagnetic wave propagation some 30 years before Hertz's experimental verification.

Now on integration of eqn.(4.9) over a surface we have,

$$\oint_S\left(\vec{\nabla}\times\vec{H}\right).\overrightarrow{dS}=\oint_S\left(\vec{J}+\frac{\partial\vec{D}}{\partial t}\right).\overrightarrow{dS}$$

$$\Rightarrow\oint_l\left(\vec{H}\right).\overrightarrow{dl}=\oint_S\left(\vec{J}+\frac{\partial\vec{D}}{\partial t}\right).\overrightarrow{dS}\quad\text{(applying Stoke's Theorem)}\qquad ...(4.10)$$

Eqn.(10) states that MMF around a closed path is equal to the total current enclosed by the path. Thus eqn.(4.9) and (4.10) replace the static form of Ampere's law.

The wave theory received additional support from the electromagnetic theory of James Clark Maxwell (1864), who showed that electric and magnetic fields were propagated together and that their speed was identical with the speed of light. It thus became clear that visible light is a form of electromagnetic radiation, constituting only a small part of the electromagnetic spectrum. Maxwell's theory was confirmed experimentally with the discovery of radio waves by Heinrich Hertz in 1886.

4.2 Maxwell's Equations

There are four fundamental equations by Maxwell on which the subject of electromagnetism developed.

First Equation: $\boxed{div\vec{D} = \vec{\nabla}.\vec{D} = \rho}$

This is the Differential form of Gauss's law in Electrostatics.

Second Equation: $\boxed{div\vec{B} = \vec{\nabla}.\vec{B} = 0}$

This is the Differential form of Gauss's law in Magnetostatics.

Third Equation: $\boxed{curl\vec{E} = \vec{\nabla}\times\vec{E} = -\frac{\partial\vec{B}}{\partial t}}$

This is the Differential form of Faraday's law of Electromagnetic induction.

Fourth Equation: $\boxed{curl\vec{H} = \vec{\nabla}\times\vec{H} = \vec{J} + \frac{\partial\vec{D}}{\partial t}}$

This is the Maxwell's modification of Ampere's law.

All these Maxwell's Equations are the mathematical expressions of a certain experimental results. He expressed them in differential forms. During his time 'del ($\vec{\nabla}$)' notation was not developed, but it is him, who has developed the importance on combinations of derivatives. These combinations were later known as GRAD, DIV, CURL.

4.3 Maxwell's Equations in Static Field

We consider now both '$\vec{E}$' and '$\vec{H}$' are constant with time. Hence,

$$\frac{\partial\vec{E}}{\partial t} = 0 = \frac{\partial\vec{D}}{\partial t}, \text{ and, } \frac{\partial\vec{H}}{\partial t} = 0 = \frac{\partial\vec{B}}{\partial t}$$

Applying these into Maxwell's equations we obtain,

$$div\vec{D} = \vec{\nabla}.\vec{D} = \rho$$

$$div\vec{B} = \vec{\nabla}.\vec{B} = 0$$

$$curl\vec{E} = \vec{\nabla}\times\vec{E} = 0$$

$$curl\vec{H} = \vec{\nabla}\times\vec{H} = \vec{J}$$

Hence we see for Electrostatics the equations are:

$$div\vec{D} = \vec{\nabla}.\vec{D} = \rho$$

$$curl\vec{E} = \vec{\nabla}\times\vec{E} = 0$$

For Magnetostatics the equations are:

$$div\vec{B} = \vec{\nabla}.\vec{B} = 0$$

$$curl\vec{H} = \vec{\nabla}\times\vec{H} = \vec{J}$$

These equations clearly indicate separate equations for electricity amd magnetism and these does not indicate any inter-relationship between the '$\vec{E}$' and '$\vec{H}$'.

4.4 Derivation: (Maxwell's Equations in Differential Form)

4.4.1. First Equation: $\vec{\nabla}.\vec{D} = \rho$

We consider a surface S bounding a volume V in a dielectric medium. In the dielectric, total charge consists of free charges plus polarization charges. Let 'ρ' and 'ρ_ρ' are the free charge density and polarization charge density at a point in a small volume element 'dV' respectively, then, from Gauss's law of Electrostatics,

$$\oint_S \vec{E}.\vec{dS} = \frac{1}{\varepsilon}\int_V \left(\rho + \rho_p\right)dV \qquad ...(4.11)$$

But, $\rho_p = -\vec{\nabla}.\vec{P}$

Hence, using eqn.(4.11), $\varepsilon\oint_S \vec{E}.\vec{dS} = \int_V \left(\rho - \vec{\nabla}.\vec{P}\right)dV \qquad ...(4.12)$

Using Gauss's divergence theorem (to change surface integral to a volume integral), we have,

$$\varepsilon\oint_S \vec{E}.\vec{dS} = \int_V \left(\rho - \vec{\nabla}.\vec{P}\right)dV$$

$$\Rightarrow \varepsilon\int_V (\vec{\nabla}.\vec{E})dV = \int_V \rho dV - \int_V \left(\vec{\nabla}.\vec{P}\right)dV \Rightarrow \int_V \vec{\nabla}.\left(\varepsilon\vec{E} + \vec{P}\right)dV = \int_V \rho dV$$

$$\Rightarrow \int_V \left[\vec{\nabla}.\vec{D} - \rho\right]dV = 0 \quad \text{[as we know, } \vec{D} = \vec{P} + \varepsilon\vec{E}\,] \qquad ...(4.13)$$

Since this eqn.(4.13) is true for all volumes, then, the integrand must vanish, *i.e.*,

$$\vec{\nabla}.\vec{D} - \rho = 0 \Rightarrow \vec{\nabla}.\vec{D} = \rho\,.$$

This is Maxwell's first equation.

4.4.2. Second Equation: $div\vec{B} = \vec{\nabla}.\vec{B} = 0$

The isolated magnetic poles and magnetic currents due to them has no physical significance. So magnetic lines of force are either curved or go to infinity. Consequently, the number of magnetic lines of force entering any closed surface is same as leaving it. It means that the flux of magnetic induction $\vec{B}$ across any closed surface is always zero, *i.e.*,

$$\oint_S \vec{B}.\overrightarrow{dS} = 0$$

On applying Gauss's divergence theorem here we get, $\int_V \vec{\nabla}.\vec{B}dV = 0$.

As the surface bounding the volume is arbitrary, this holds true for all volume and integrand must vanish.

Hence, $div\vec{B} = \vec{\nabla}.\vec{B} = 0$. This is Maxwell's second equation.

4.4.3. Third Equation: $curl\vec{E} = \vec{\nabla}\times\vec{E} = -\frac{\partial \vec{B}}{\partial t}$

From Faraday's law of electromagnetic induction, we know that electro motive force (emf) induced in a closed loop is equal to the rate of change of magnetic flux, *i.e.*,

$$e = -\frac{d\phi}{dt} \quad ...(4.14)$$

However, the magnetic flux, ϕ, from its definition is given by

$$\phi = \oint_S \vec{B}.\overrightarrow{dS}.$$

Here, S is any surface having loop as boundary.
So, using eqn.(4.14),

$$e = -\frac{d\phi}{dt} = -\oint_S \frac{\partial}{\partial t}\left(\vec{B}.\overrightarrow{dS}\right) = -\oint_S \frac{\partial \vec{B}}{\partial t}.\overrightarrow{dS} \quad ...(4.15)$$

Now, the emf 'e' can be computed by calculating the work done in carrying a unit charge round a closed loop C. Thus if electric field intensity, E, at a small element 'dl' of loop is present, then, we have,

$$e = \int_C \vec{E}.\overrightarrow{dl} \Rightarrow -\oint_S \frac{\partial \vec{B}}{\partial t}.\overrightarrow{dS} = \int_C \vec{E}.\overrightarrow{dl} \quad \text{[using eqn.(4.15)]} \quad ...(4.16)$$

Using Stokes's theorem for the conversion of line integral to surface integral, we have from eqn.(4.16),

$$\oint_S \left(\vec{\nabla}\times\vec{E}\right).\overrightarrow{dS} = -\oint_S \frac{\partial \vec{B}}{\partial t}.\overrightarrow{dS}$$

$$\Rightarrow \oint_S \left[\left(\vec{\nabla}\times\vec{E}\right) + \frac{\partial \vec{B}}{\partial t}\right].\overrightarrow{dS} = 0 \quad ...(4.17)$$

As surface is arbitrary, equation (4.17) holds only when integrand vanishes, so,

$$\left(\vec{\nabla}\times\vec{E}\right) + \frac{\partial \vec{B}}{\partial t} = 0$$

$$\Rightarrow \left(\vec{\nabla}\times\vec{E}\right) = -\frac{\partial \vec{B}}{\partial t} \qquad ...(4.17a)$$

This is Maxwell's third equation.

One interesting point to note that as $\left(\vec{\nabla}\times\vec{E}\right) = -\frac{\partial \vec{B}}{\partial t}$, the dimensional equation becomes

$$\frac{E}{L} = \frac{B}{T} \Rightarrow E = \frac{LB}{T} = \frac{L}{T}B = cB$$

Here, 'L, T, c' denote length dimension, time dimension and velocity of the e.m. wave respectively. It means that the magnitude of '$\vec{E}$' is 'c' times higher than that of '$\vec{B}$'. Hence electrical effect in e.m. wave is totally dominant over the magnetic effect.

4.4.4. Fourth Equation: $curl\vec{H} = \vec{\nabla}\times\vec{H} = \vec{J} + \frac{\partial \vec{D}}{\partial t}$

Ampere's Circuital law states that the line integral of the magnetic induction around any closed path is numerically equal to permeability multiplied by the current enclosed in the path as shown in Fig.4.1. So, we have,

$$\oint_C \vec{B}.\vec{dl} = \mu I \Rightarrow \oint_C \vec{H}.\vec{dl} = I \qquad ...(4.18)$$

However, the current is

$$I = \oint_S \vec{J}.\vec{dS}.$$

So, using eqn.(4.18) here,

$$\oint_C \vec{H}.\vec{dl} = I = \oint_S \vec{J}.\vec{dS}$$

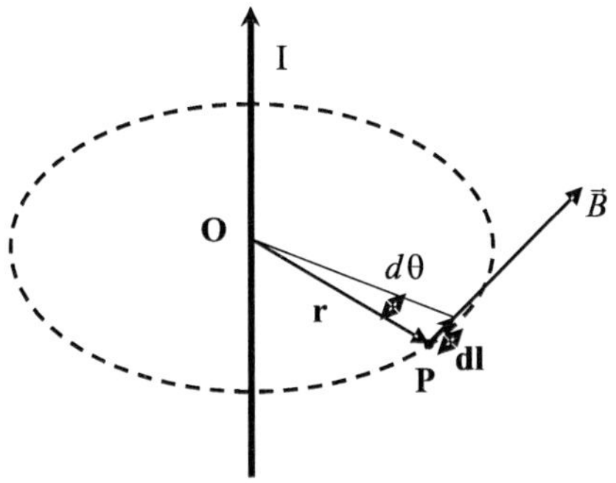

Fig. 4.2 A current carrying wire with producing a magnetic field.

Using Stokes's theorem,

$$\oint_S \left(\vec{\nabla}\times\vec{H}\right).\vec{dS} = \oint_S \vec{J}.\vec{dS}$$

$$\Rightarrow \oint_S \left[\left(\vec{\nabla}\times\vec{H}\right)-\vec{J}\right].\vec{dS} = 0$$

As the surface is arbitrary, integrand must vanish, so,

$$\left[\left(\vec{\nabla}\times\vec{H}\right)-\vec{J}\right]=0 \Rightarrow \vec{\nabla}\times\vec{H} = \vec{J} \qquad ...(4.19)$$

Now, we know that for any vector $\vec{A}$, div (curl $\vec{A}$) = 0

$$\Rightarrow \vec{\nabla}.\left(\vec{\nabla}\times\vec{A}\right)=0$$

So here from eqn.(4.19), div (curl $\vec{H}$) = 0

$$\text{div}\,(\vec{J}) = 0 \qquad ...(4.20)$$

However, from continuity equation for the conservation of charge,

$$\vec{\nabla}.\vec{J} + \frac{\partial \rho}{\partial t} = 0$$

$$\Rightarrow \vec{\nabla}.\vec{J} = -\frac{\partial \rho}{\partial t} \qquad ...(4.21)$$

So from eqns.(4.20) and (4.21), we see that div ($\vec{J}$) = 0 only when 'ρ' is constant with time.

Thus we found that Ampere's law is valid only for steady state condition. For time varying field this equation must be modified. Maxwell investigated this to make it consistent with the equation of continuity for all practical time varying field. He assumed that the definition of current density is insufficient and a part $\vec{J_d}$ must be added to it. So the total current density becomes $\left[\vec{J}+\vec{J_d}\right]$.

As, from eqn.(4.19), $\vec{\nabla}\times\vec{H} = \vec{J}$,

we have now, $\vec{\nabla}\times\vec{H} = \vec{J} + \vec{J_d}$

$$\Rightarrow div(\vec{\nabla}\times\vec{H}) = div(\vec{J}+\vec{J_d})$$

$$\Rightarrow 0 = div(\vec{J}+\vec{J_d})$$

$$\Rightarrow div(\vec{J_d}) = -div\vec{J} = \frac{\partial \rho}{\partial t} \qquad \text{(using equation of continuity)}$$

$$\Rightarrow div(\vec{J_d}) = \frac{\partial}{\partial t}\left[\vec{\nabla}.\vec{D}\right] \qquad \text{(using Maxwell's first equation)}$$

$$\Rightarrow div(\vec{J_d}) = \vec{\nabla}.\left[\frac{\partial}{\partial t}\vec{D}\right]$$

$$\Rightarrow \overrightarrow{J_d} = \left[\frac{\partial}{\partial t}\vec{D}\right] \qquad ...(4.22)$$

Hence, total current density becomes '$\vec{J} + \frac{\partial \vec{D}}{\partial t}$'. So, we have,

$$\vec{\nabla} \times \vec{H} = \vec{J} + \overrightarrow{J_d} = \vec{J} + \frac{\partial \vec{D}}{\partial t}$$

$$\Rightarrow \vec{\nabla} \times \vec{H} = \vec{J} + \frac{\partial \vec{D}}{\partial t}$$

This is the Maxwell's fourth equation, as well as, the modified form of Ampere's law.

4.4.5. Characteristics of Displacement current ($\overrightarrow{J_d}$)

1. This is a current only in sense that it produces a magnetic field. It is not linked with motion of charges. It is having a finite value even in a perfect vacuum.
2. $\overrightarrow{J_d} = \left[\frac{\partial}{\partial t}\vec{D}\right]$
3. $\overrightarrow{J_d}$ makes the total current continuous across the discontinuity in a conduction current. Example: A battery charging a capacitor produces a closed current loop with $\overrightarrow{J_{total}} = \vec{J} + \overrightarrow{J_d}$.
4. For a good conductor less than optical frequency (10^{15} hz), $\vec{J} >> \overrightarrow{J_d}$.

4.5 Physical Significance of Maxwell's Equations

(Maxwell's Equations in Integral Form)

4.5.1. First Equation

Here, $\vec{\nabla}.\vec{D} = \rho \Rightarrow \int_V \vec{\nabla}.\vec{D}.dV = \int_V \rho dV$

$$\Rightarrow \oint_S \vec{D}.\overrightarrow{dS} = \int_V \rho dV = q \qquad \text{(using Gauss's divergence theorem).}$$

$\Rightarrow$ Net outward flux of displacement vector through the surface enclosing a volume, is equal to the net charge contained within the volume. This is Gauss's law of Electrostatics.

4.5.2. Second Equation

Here, $\vec{\nabla}.\vec{B}=0 \Rightarrow \oint_S \vec{B}.\overrightarrow{dS}=0$ (using Gauss's divergence theorem).

$\Rightarrow$ Net outward flux of magnetic induction vector through the surface enclosing a volume, is zero. This is Gauss's law of Magnetostatics.

4.5.3. Third Equation

Here, $$\vec{\nabla}\times\vec{E}=-\frac{\partial\vec{B}}{\partial t}$$

$$\Rightarrow \oint_S \left(\vec{\nabla}\times\vec{E}\right).\overrightarrow{dS}=\oint_S -\frac{\partial\vec{B}}{\partial t}.\overrightarrow{dS}=-\frac{\partial}{\partial t}\oint_S \vec{B}.\overrightarrow{dS}$$

$$\Rightarrow \int_C \vec{E}.\vec{dl}=-\frac{\partial}{\partial t}\oint_S \vec{B}.\overrightarrow{dS}$$ (Using Stoke's theorem)

$$\Rightarrow e=-\frac{\partial}{\partial t}\phi$$

$\Rightarrow$ The emf 'e' around a closed path is equal to negative rate of change of magnetic flux linked with the path. This is Faraday's law of electromagnetic induction.

4.5.4. Fourth Equation

Here, $$\vec{\nabla}\times\vec{H}=\vec{J}+\frac{\partial\vec{D}}{\partial t}$$

$$\Rightarrow \oint_S \left(\vec{\nabla}\times\vec{H}\right).\overrightarrow{dS}=\oint_S \left[\vec{J}+\frac{\partial\vec{D}}{\partial t}\right].\overrightarrow{dS}$$

$$\Rightarrow \int_C \vec{H}.\vec{dl}=\oint_S \left[\vec{J}+\frac{\partial\vec{D}}{\partial t}\right].\overrightarrow{dS}$$ (Using Stoke's theorem)

$\Rightarrow$ The magneto motive force (MMF), $MMF=\int_C \vec{H}.\vec{dl}$, around a closed path is equal to the conduction current plus displacement current through any surface bounded by the path. This is the modified form of Ampere's circuital law for time varying field.

4.6 Plane Wave Equation in a Homogeneous Medium

A **homogeneous medium** is one for which the quantities 'ε,μ,σ' are constant throughout the medium. The medium is **isotropic** if 'ε' is a scalar constant so that ' $\vec{D},\vec{E}$ ' have same values everywhere in all direction. A **source free region** is that where there are impressed voltages or currents (no generators).

We now consider a uniform linear medium having permittivity ' ε ', conductivity 'σ', but does not have any free charge or any current other than that determined by Ohm's law.

So, in this medium, we have,

$$\vec{D}=\varepsilon\vec{E},\quad \vec{B}=\mu\vec{H},\quad \vec{J}=\sigma\vec{E}\text{, and, }\rho=0 \qquad ...(4.23)$$

Thus using eqn.(4.23) all the Maxwell's equations become,

$$\vec{\nabla}.\vec{D}=\rho\Rightarrow\varepsilon\vec{\nabla}.\vec{E}=0\Rightarrow\vec{\nabla}.\vec{E}=0 \qquad ...(4.24)$$

$$\vec{\nabla}.\vec{B}=0\Rightarrow\mu\vec{\nabla}.\vec{H}=0\Rightarrow\vec{\nabla}.\vec{H}=0 \qquad ...(4.25)$$

$$\vec{\nabla}\times\vec{E}=-\frac{\partial\vec{B}}{\partial t}$$

$$\Rightarrow\vec{\nabla}\times\vec{E}=-\mu\frac{\partial\vec{H}}{\partial t} \qquad ...(4.26)$$

$$\vec{\nabla}\times\vec{H}=\vec{J}+\frac{\partial\vec{D}}{\partial t}$$

$$\Rightarrow\vec{\nabla}\times\vec{H}=\sigma\vec{E}+\varepsilon\frac{\partial\vec{E}}{\partial t} \qquad ...(4.27)$$

Taking the curl of equation (4) we have,

$$\vec{\nabla}\times\left[\vec{\nabla}\times\vec{E}\right]=\vec{\nabla}\times\left[-\frac{\partial\vec{B}}{\partial t}\right]\quad\Rightarrow\vec{\nabla}\times\left[\vec{\nabla}\times\vec{E}\right]=\mu\vec{\nabla}\times\left[-\frac{\partial\vec{H}}{\partial t}\right]$$

$$\Rightarrow\vec{\nabla}.\left(\vec{\nabla}.\vec{E}\right)-\nabla^2\vec{E}=-\mu\frac{\partial}{\partial t}\left[\vec{\nabla}\times\vec{H}\right]$$

$$\Rightarrow\vec{\nabla}.(0)-\nabla^2\vec{E}=-\mu\frac{\partial}{\partial t}\left[\sigma\vec{E}+\varepsilon\frac{\partial\vec{E}}{\partial t}\right] \qquad \text{(using eqn.(4.24))}$$

$$\Rightarrow-\nabla^2\vec{E}=-\mu\sigma\frac{\partial\vec{E}}{\partial t}-\varepsilon\mu\frac{\partial^2\vec{E}}{\partial t^2}$$

$$\Rightarrow\nabla^2\vec{E}-\mu\sigma\frac{\partial\vec{E}}{\partial t}-\varepsilon\mu\frac{\partial^2\vec{E}}{\partial t^2}=0 \qquad ...(4.28)$$

Similarly, taking curl of equation (5) we have,

$$\vec{\nabla}\times\left(\vec{\nabla}\times\vec{H}\right)=\vec{\nabla}\times\left[\sigma\vec{E}+\varepsilon\frac{\partial\vec{E}}{\partial t}\right]$$

$$\Rightarrow \vec{\nabla}.\left(\vec{\nabla}.\vec{H}\right)-\nabla^2\vec{H}=\left[\sigma\left(\vec{\nabla}\times\vec{E}\right)+\varepsilon\frac{\partial\left(\vec{\nabla}\times\vec{E}\right)}{\partial t}\right]$$

$$\Rightarrow \vec{\nabla}.(0)-\nabla^2\vec{H}=\left[\sigma\left(-\mu\frac{\partial\vec{H}}{\partial t}\right)+\varepsilon\frac{\partial}{\partial t}\left(-\mu\frac{\partial\vec{H}}{\partial t}\right)\right] \qquad \text{(using eqn.(4.25))}$$

$$\Rightarrow -\nabla^2\vec{H}=-\mu\sigma\frac{\partial\vec{H}}{\partial t}-\mu\varepsilon\frac{\partial^2\vec{H}}{\partial t^2}$$

$$\Rightarrow \nabla^2\vec{H}-\mu\sigma\frac{\partial\vec{H}}{\partial t}-\mu\varepsilon\frac{\partial^2\vec{H}}{\partial t^2}=0 \qquad \text{...(4.29)}$$

Eqns.(4.28) and (4.29) represent wave equations which govern the electromagnetic field in a homogeneous, linear medium independent of being conducting or non-conducting, and here the charge density is zero.

4.7 Plane Wave Equation in Free Space

Before Maxwell, there were two independent phenomena, light and electromagnetic effects. Maxwell was the pioneer of unification of these two. From his electromagnetic theory it was established for the first time. As said by famous physicist and Nobel laureate of all time Richard Feynmann " Maxwell had made one of the great unifications of physics. Before his time, there was light, and there was electricity and magnetism. The later two had been unified by the experimental work of Faraday, Oersted, and Ampere. Then, all of a sudden, light was no longer 'something else', but was only electricity and magnetism in this new form – little pieces of electric and magnetic fields which propagate through space on their own."

For free space we have,

$$\varepsilon=\varepsilon_0,\quad \mu=\mu_0,\quad \sigma=0\text{, and, }\rho=0 \qquad \text{...(4.30)}$$

Hence the wave eqns. (4.28) and (4.29) become

$$\nabla^2\vec{E}-\varepsilon_0\mu_0\frac{\partial^2\vec{E}}{\partial t^2}=0\text{, and,}$$

$$\nabla^2\vec{H}-\varepsilon_0\mu_0\frac{\partial^2\vec{H}}{\partial t^2}=0 \qquad \text{...(4.31)}$$

The above equations are similar to the wave equation,

$$\nabla^2 u-\frac{1}{v^2}\frac{\partial^2 u}{\partial t^2}=0 \qquad \text{...(4.32)}$$

Here, 'u' represents any mechanical wave and, 'v' is the velocity of the wave. Hence comparing eqns.(4.24) and (4.25) we have the velocity of the e.m. wave as,

$$v = \frac{1}{\sqrt{\mu_0 \varepsilon_0}} = \sqrt{\frac{4\pi}{\mu_0 .4\pi\varepsilon_0}} = \sqrt{\frac{4\pi}{4\pi \times 10^{-7}} \times 9 \times 10^9}$$

$$= 3 \times 10^8 \, meter / \sec$$

[using the values of $\mu_0 = 4\pi \times 10^{-7} H/m, \frac{1}{4\pi\varepsilon_0} = 9 \times 10^9 m/F$]

Hence, $\frac{1}{\sqrt{\mu_0 \varepsilon_0}} = c$, is the velocity of light.

So, using eqn.(4.24), we have,

$$\nabla^2 \vec{E}\left(or, \vec{H}\right) = \frac{1}{c^2} \frac{\partial^2 \vec{E}\left(or, \vec{H}\right)}{\partial t^2} = 0$$

- **A plane wave is defined as a wave whose amplitude is same at any point in a plane perpendicular to a specified direction.**

The unit of $\frac{1}{\sqrt{\mu_0 \varepsilon_0}}$

$$\frac{1}{\sqrt{\mu_0 \varepsilon_0}} = \frac{1}{\sqrt{\frac{Henry}{mt} \times \frac{Farad}{mt}}} = \frac{mt}{\sqrt{Henry \times Farad}}$$

Now, $|e| = L\frac{di}{dt} = L\frac{d^2 q}{dt^2}$

$$\Rightarrow L = |e| \Big/ \frac{d^2 q}{dt^2} = \frac{V}{q/t^2} = \frac{Vt^2}{q}$$

$$\Rightarrow Henry = \frac{Volt \times \sec^2}{Coul.}$$

Also, $C = \frac{q}{V} \Rightarrow Farad = \frac{Coul.}{Volt}$

Hence, $c = \frac{1}{\sqrt{\mu_0 \varepsilon_0}} = \frac{mt}{\sqrt{Henry \times Farad}} = \frac{mt}{\sqrt{\frac{Volt \times \sec^2}{Coul.} \times \frac{Coul.}{Volt}}} = \frac{mt}{\sec}$

4.8 Uniform Plane Wave Propagation

The free space wave equations for electric and magnetic fields as,

$$\nabla^2 \vec{E} = \varepsilon\mu \frac{\partial^2 \vec{E}}{\partial t^2} \qquad ...(4.33)$$

$$\nabla^2 \vec{H} = \varepsilon\mu \frac{\partial^2 \vec{H}}{\partial t^2} \qquad ...(4.34)$$

Here we have used the free space constants $\varepsilon = \varepsilon_0, \mu = \mu_0$.
For one dimensional wave equation along only X-axis for electric vector we have,

$$\frac{\partial^2}{\partial x^2}\vec{E} = \varepsilon\mu \frac{\partial^2 \vec{E}}{\partial t^2} \qquad ...(4.35)$$

The vector eqn.(4.35) is equivalent to three scalar equations, one for each of the scalar components of '$\vec{E}$'. In general, for uniform plane wave propagation along X-direction, '$\vec{E}$' have 'E_y, E_z' but not 'E_x'. This is shown in Fig.4.3. Here ABCD is a part of the plane wave moving along X-direction. We can solve the eqn.(4.35) now for Y-component and may extend to Z-component.

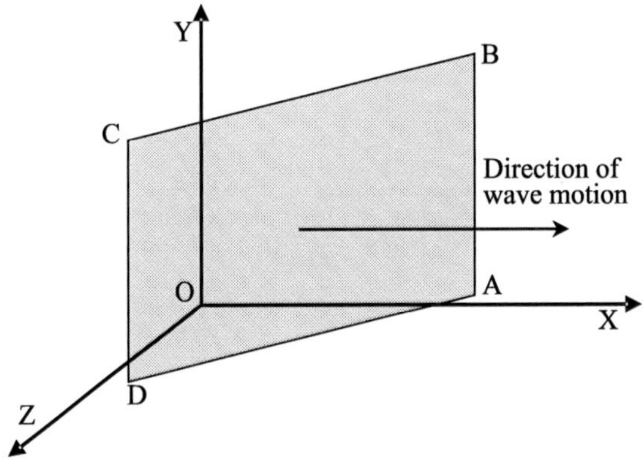

Fig. 4.3 Uniform plane wave motion with amplitude lying in plane ABCD.

Hence, the wave eqn. to be solved is

$$\frac{\partial^2}{\partial x^2}E_y = \varepsilon\mu \frac{\partial^2 E_y}{\partial t^2} \qquad ...(4.36)$$

Eqn.(4.36) is a second order partial differential equation. Its general solution is

$$E_y = f_1(x - v_0 t) + f_2(x + v_0 t) \qquad ...(4.37)$$

Here, $v_0 = \frac{1}{\sqrt{\mu\varepsilon}}$ and f_1, f_2 are any functions. f_1 is function of $(x - v_0 t)$ and f_2 is function of $(x + v_0 t)$.

Now we can also define wave. If a physical phenomenon that occurs at one place at a given time is reproduced at other places at later times, the time delay being proportional to the space separation from the first location, then the group of phenomena constitutes a 'wave'.

Here f_1, f_2 describe such wave mathematically. $f_1(x - v_0 t)$ and $f_2(x + v_0 t)$ represent waves traveling to positive X-direction and negative X-direction respectively. If there are no reflecting surface present to reflect the wave back to the source, the second term of eqn.(4.37) is zero and then the solution is

$$E_y = f_1(x - v_0 t) \qquad ...(4.38)$$

4.9 Uniform Plane Wave

Eqn.(4.38) is a solution of the wave equation for a particular case for which '$\vec{E}$' is independent of 'y & z', but only depends on 'x & t". Such a wave is called a uniform plane wave.

The plane wave equation is

$$\nabla^2 \vec{E} = \varepsilon\mu \frac{\partial^2 \vec{E}}{\partial t^2}$$

In a region where there is no free charge density, *i.e.*, $\rho = 0$, we have

$$\vec{\nabla}.\vec{E} = \vec{\nabla}.\left(\frac{\vec{D}}{\varepsilon}\right) = \frac{1}{\varepsilon}\left(\vec{\nabla}.\vec{D}\right) = \frac{\rho}{\varepsilon} = 0$$

$$\Rightarrow \frac{\partial E_x}{\partial x} + \frac{\partial E_y}{\partial y} + \frac{\partial E_z}{\partial z} = 0$$

For plane wave as stated earlier, $\dfrac{\partial E_x}{\partial x} = 0 \Rightarrow E_x =$ constant,

so its second derivative is also zero and thus

$$\frac{\partial^2 E_x}{\partial t^2} = 0 \qquad \text{(from wave equation).}$$

It indicates either $E_x = 0$ or constant with time, or, increasing uniformly with time. A field satisfying either of the last two conditions would not be a part of the wave motion and so $E_x = 0$. Therefore a uniform plane wave progressing along X-direction has no X-component of '$\vec{E}$'. Similarly, using same analogy for '$\vec{H}$', we get the same conclusion. Therefore, uniform plane e.m. waves are transverse and have components of '$\vec{E}$' and '$\vec{H}$' only in directions perpendicular to the direction of propagation. This is shown in Fig.4.4.

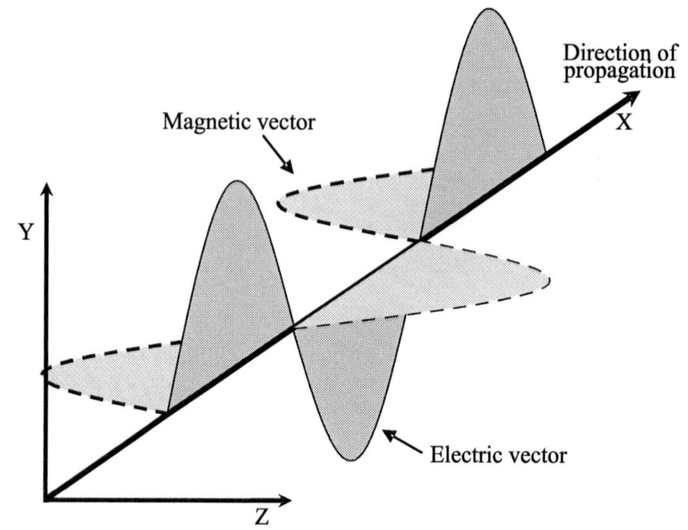

Fig. 4.4 Schematic diagram of transverse nature of light.

4.10 Relation between '$\vec{E}$' and '$\vec{H}$' in a Uniform Plane Wave

From earlier discussions it is clear that '$\vec{E}$' and '$\vec{H}$' are not having any X-component along the direction of propagation of e.m. wave, so we have $E_x = 0 = H_x$. Now,

$$\vec{\nabla}\times\vec{E} = \begin{vmatrix} 0 & \hat{j} & \hat{k} \\ \frac{\partial}{\partial x} & \frac{\partial}{\partial y} & \frac{\partial}{\partial z} \\ 0 & E_y & E_z \end{vmatrix}$$

$$= -\frac{\partial}{\partial x}E_z\hat{j} + \frac{\partial}{\partial x}E_y\hat{k} \qquad \text{(as } E_x \text{ is zero, so, } \hat{i} = 0\text{)} \qquad ...(4.39)$$

And,
$$\vec{\nabla}\times\vec{H} = -\frac{\partial}{\partial x}H_z\hat{j} + \frac{\partial}{\partial x}H_y\hat{k} \qquad ...(4.40)$$

Hence using Maxwell's fourth equation (eqn.(4.9)) with $\vec{J} = \sigma\vec{E} = 0$ (as $\sigma = 0$), we have,

$$\vec{\nabla}\times\vec{H} = \vec{J} + \varepsilon\frac{\partial\vec{E}}{\partial t}$$

$$\Rightarrow -\frac{\partial}{\partial x}H_z\hat{j}+\frac{\partial}{\partial x}H_y\hat{k}=\varepsilon\left[\frac{\partial}{\partial t}E_y\hat{j}+\frac{\partial}{\partial t}E_z\hat{k}\right]\text{(using eqn.(4.40))} \quad ...(4.41)$$

Also from Maxwell's 3rd equation,

$\left(\vec{\nabla}\times\vec{E}=\frac{\partial\vec{B}}{\partial t}\right)$ and eqn.(4.39) we have,

$$-\frac{\partial}{\partial x}E_z\hat{j}+\frac{\partial}{\partial x}E_y\hat{k}=-\mu\left[\frac{\partial}{\partial t}H_y\hat{j}+\frac{\partial}{\partial t}H_z\hat{k}\right] \quad ...(4.42)$$

Separating coefficients of unit vector from bothsides of eqn.(4.41),

$$-\frac{\partial}{\partial x}H_z=\varepsilon\frac{\partial}{\partial t}E_y \quad ...(4.45a)$$

$$\frac{\partial}{\partial x}H_y=\varepsilon\frac{\partial}{\partial t}E_z \quad ...(4.45b)$$

Same from eqn.(4.42), $\frac{\partial}{\partial x}E_z=\mu\frac{\partial}{\partial t}H_y$ ...(4.45c)

$$\frac{\partial}{\partial x}E_y=-\mu\frac{\partial}{\partial t}H_z \quad ...(4.45d)$$

Now considering the solution as $E_y=f_1\left(x-v_0t\right)$

So, we have

$$\frac{\partial}{\partial t}E_y=\frac{\partial}{\partial t}f_1=\frac{\partial f_1}{\partial\left(x-v_0t\right)}\frac{\partial\left(x-v_0t\right)}{\partial t}=-v_0\frac{\partial f_1}{\partial\left(x-v_0t\right)}=-v_0f_1'(x-v_0t)$$

Here,

$$f_1'=f_1'(x-v_0t)=\frac{\partial f_1}{\partial\left(x-v_0t\right)} \text{ (as } f_1 \text{ is a function of } \left(x-v_0t\right))$$

So, $\frac{\partial}{\partial t}E_y=-v_0f_1'$ ...(4.46)

Using eqn.(4.45a) and (4.46) we get,

$$-\frac{\partial}{\partial x}H_z=\varepsilon(-v_0f_1')$$

$$\frac{\partial}{\partial x}H_z=\varepsilon(v_0f_1')=\frac{1}{\sqrt{\mu\varepsilon}}.\varepsilon.f_1'=\left(\sqrt{\frac{\varepsilon}{\mu}}\right)f_1'$$

$$\Rightarrow H_z=\left(\sqrt{\frac{\varepsilon}{\mu}}\right)\int f_1'dx+K \quad ...(4.47)$$

Here 'K' is integration constant.

But, $$\frac{\partial}{\partial x} f_1 = \frac{\partial f_1}{\partial(x - v_0 t)} \frac{\partial(x - v_0 t)}{\partial x} = f_1 \times 1 = f_1'$$

Using it into eqn.(4.47) we have,

$$\Rightarrow H_z = \left(\sqrt{\frac{\varepsilon}{\mu}}\right)\int \frac{\partial}{\partial x} f_1 dx + K = \left(\sqrt{\frac{\varepsilon}{\mu}}\right) f_1 + K = \left(\sqrt{\frac{\varepsilon}{\mu}}\right) E_y + K \qquad ...(4.48)$$

'K' indicates that a field independent of 'x' may be present. We can easily neglect this field as it is not a part of wave motion. Hence eqn.(4.48) reduces to

$$H_z = \left(\sqrt{\frac{\varepsilon}{\mu}}\right) E_y \Rightarrow \frac{E_y}{H_z} = \left(\sqrt{\frac{\mu}{\varepsilon}}\right) \qquad ...(4.49)$$

Similarly, $$\frac{E_z}{H_y} = -\left(\sqrt{\frac{\mu}{\varepsilon}}\right) \qquad ...(4.50)$$

Since, $E = \sqrt{E_y^2 + E_z^2}$ and $H = \sqrt{H_y^2 + H_z^2}$, 'E and H' are the net strengths, then,

$$E = \sqrt{\left(\frac{\mu}{\varepsilon}\right) H_z^2 + \left(\frac{\mu}{\varepsilon}\right) H_y^2} = \sqrt{\left(\frac{\mu}{\varepsilon}\right)}\sqrt{H_y^2 + H_z^2} = \sqrt{\left(\frac{\mu}{\varepsilon}\right)} H$$

$$\Rightarrow \frac{E}{H} = \sqrt{\left(\frac{\mu}{\varepsilon}\right)} \qquad ...(4.51)$$

Eqn.(4.51) states that in a traveling plane wave there is a definite ratio between the amplitudes of $\vec{E}$ and $\vec{H}$, and that ratio is equal to the square root of the ratio of permeability to the dielectric constant of the medium.

Here the traveling wave progressing in one direction and there is no standing wave formation.

For free space, $$\frac{E}{H} = \sqrt{\left(\frac{\mu}{\varepsilon}\right)} = \sqrt{\left(\frac{\mu_0}{\varepsilon_0}\right)} = \sqrt{\frac{4\pi \times 10^{-7}}{1/(36\pi \times 10^9)}} \approx 120\pi = 377\,\Omega$$

'$\sqrt{\left(\frac{\mu}{\varepsilon}\right)}$' has the unit of Ω as 'E' is in Volt/m and 'H' is in Amp/m.

This ratio '$\sqrt{\left(\frac{\mu}{\varepsilon}\right)}$' is known as the 'Characteristic impedance, η' or the 'Intrinsic impedance' of the non-conducting medium.

Now, $\vec{E}.\vec{H} = E_y H_y + E_z H_z = (\eta H_z) H_y + (-\eta H_y) H_z = 0$

[substituting from eqn.(4.50), $E_z = -\sqrt{\frac{\mu}{\varepsilon}} = -(\eta) H_y$ and from eqn.(4.49), $E_y = (\eta) H_z$]

Hence for a uniform plane wave, $\vec{E}$ and $\vec{H}$ are right angles to each other.

Also,

$$\vec{E}\times\vec{H} = \begin{vmatrix} \hat{i} & \hat{j} & \hat{k} \\ 0 & E_y & E_z \\ 0 & H_y & H_z \end{vmatrix} = \hat{i}\left[E_y H_z - E_z H_y\right]$$

$$= \hat{i}\left[(\eta H_z)H_z - (-\eta H_y)H_y\right]$$

$$= \eta\hat{i}\left[H_z^2 + H_y^2\right] = \eta\hat{i}\left[H^2\right]$$

Thus the electric field vector crossed into the magnetic field vector gives the direction in which the wave travels.

4.11 The Wave Equations for a Conducting Medium

In free space we have solved Maxwell's equations. However, for a perfect dielectric like free space, there are neither charges nor conduction currents. We need to get the solution now for regions in which the conductivity is not zero and conduction currents may exist. This is the general case.

From Maxwell's 4th equation,

$$\vec{\nabla}\times\vec{H} = \vec{J} + \frac{\partial\vec{D}}{\partial t}$$

And, $\vec{J} = \sigma\vec{E}$, we get,

$$\vec{\nabla}\times\vec{H} = \sigma\vec{E} + \varepsilon\frac{\partial\vec{E}}{\partial t} \qquad \text{...(4.52)}$$

Taking curl of both sides of Maxwell's 3rd equation $\vec{\nabla}\times\vec{E} = -\mu\frac{\partial\vec{H}}{\partial t}$, we have,

$$\vec{\nabla}\times\vec{\nabla}\times\vec{E} = -\mu\frac{\partial}{\partial t}\left(\vec{\nabla}\times\vec{H}\right)$$

$$\Rightarrow \vec{\nabla}.\vec{\nabla}.\vec{E} - \nabla^2\vec{E} = -\mu\frac{\partial}{\partial t}\left[\sigma\vec{E} + \varepsilon\frac{\partial}{\partial t}\vec{E}\right] \qquad \text{(from eqn.(4.52))}$$

$$\Rightarrow \nabla^2 \vec{E} - \mu\varepsilon \frac{\partial^2}{\partial t^2}\vec{E} - \sigma\mu \frac{\partial}{\partial t}\vec{E} = \vec{\nabla}.\vec{\nabla}.\vec{E} \quad ...(4.53)$$

From Maxwell's 1st equation,

$$\vec{\nabla}.\vec{D} = \rho \Rightarrow \vec{\nabla}.\vec{E} = \rho / \varepsilon \quad ...(4.54)$$

Since there are no net charge within a conductor (although there may be a charge on the surface), $\rho = 0$. This is because within any macroscopic element of volume the positive and negative charges are equal in number (on the average).

Hence, from eqn.(4.54),

$$\vec{\nabla}.\vec{E} = 0 \Rightarrow \vec{\nabla}.\vec{D} = 0$$

Hence eqn.(4.53) becomes

$$\nabla^2 \vec{E} - \mu\varepsilon \frac{\partial^2}{\partial t^2}\vec{E} - \sigma\mu \frac{\partial}{\partial t}\vec{E} = 0 \quad ...(4.55)$$

Similarly for $\vec{H}$ we have,

$$\nabla^2 \vec{H} - \mu\varepsilon \frac{\partial^2}{\partial t^2}\vec{H} - \sigma\mu \frac{\partial}{\partial t}\vec{H} = 0 \quad ...(4.56)$$

These eqns.(4.55) and (4.56) are the wave equations for $\vec{E}$ and $\vec{H}$.

4.12 Poynting's Theorem

When an e.m.wave reaches to a point 'B' from a point 'A', the point 'B' receives some amount of energy which is flowing from point 'A'. When a source is sending a signal, the receiver receives energy from the source. Hence, some amount of energy is associated with an e.m.wave propagating from a point to another. J.H. Poynting in 1884 first postulated about this energy and his theorem is known as Poynting's theorem in electromagnetism.

While an e.m.wave propagates, transfer of energy takes place from one point to the other. A relationship between the rate of energy transfer and the amplitudes of $\vec{E}, \vec{H}$ associated with the e.m.wave exists and can be obtained by using Maxwell's equations.

From Maxwell's fourth equation (eqn.(4.9)), we have,

$$\vec{\nabla} \times \vec{H} = \vec{J} + \varepsilon \frac{\partial \vec{E}}{\partial t} \Rightarrow \vec{J} = \vec{\nabla} \times \vec{H} - \varepsilon \frac{\partial \vec{E}}{\partial t} \quad ...(4.57)$$

So, taking the 'dot product' with '$\vec{E}$' on bothsides we have,

$$\vec{E}.\vec{J} = \vec{E}.\left(\vec{\nabla} \times \vec{H}\right) - \varepsilon \vec{E}.\frac{\partial \vec{E}}{\partial t} \quad ...(4.58)$$

$$\Rightarrow \vec{E}.\vec{J} = \left[\vec{H}.\left(\vec{\nabla} \times \vec{E}\right) - \vec{\nabla}.\left(\vec{E} \times \vec{H}\right)\right] - \varepsilon \vec{E}.\frac{\partial \vec{E}}{\partial t} \quad ...(4.59)$$

(using $\vec{\nabla}.\left(\vec{E}\times\vec{H}\right)=\vec{H}.\left(\vec{\nabla}\times\vec{E}\right)-\vec{E}.\left(\vec{\nabla}\times\vec{H}\right)$)

From Maxwell's third equation (eqn.(4.17a)),

$$\vec{\nabla}\times\vec{E}=-\mu\frac{\partial\vec{H}}{\partial t}$$

Putting eqn.(4.59) into (4.58),

$$\vec{E}.\vec{J}=\left[\vec{H}.\left(\vec{\nabla}\times\vec{E}\right)-\vec{\nabla}.\left(\vec{E}\times\vec{H}\right)\right]-\varepsilon\vec{E}.\frac{\partial\vec{E}}{\partial t} \quad ...(4.60)$$

Now we have, $\vec{E}.\frac{\partial\vec{E}}{\partial t}=\frac{1}{2}\frac{\partial}{\partial t}(E)^2$ and, $\vec{H}.\frac{\partial\vec{H}}{\partial t}=\frac{1}{2}\frac{\partial}{\partial t}(H)^2$ ...(4.61)

So from eqns.(4.60) and (4.61),

$$\vec{E}.\vec{J}=-\mu.\frac{1}{2}\frac{\partial}{\partial t}(H)^2-\vec{\nabla}.\left(\vec{E}\times\vec{H}\right)-\varepsilon.\frac{1}{2}\frac{\partial}{\partial t}(E)^2$$

Integrating over a volume 'V', we have,

$$\int_V\vec{E}.\vec{J}dV=-\frac{\partial}{\partial t}\int_V\left[\frac{\mu}{2}(H)^2+\frac{\varepsilon}{2}(E)^2\right]dV-\int_V\vec{\nabla}.\left(\vec{E}\times\vec{H}\right)dV$$

$$\Rightarrow\int_V\vec{E}.\vec{J}dV=-\frac{\partial}{\partial t}\int_V\left[\frac{\mu}{2}(H)^2+\frac{\varepsilon}{2}(E)^2\right]dV-\oint_S\left(\vec{E}\times\vec{H}\right)dS \quad ...(4.62)$$

4.12.1. Physical Interpretation of eqn.(4.62)

(*i*) Term '$\int_V\vec{E}.\vec{J}dV$':

We consider a conductor of cross sectional area 'A' carrying a current 'I' and having an electric field 'E'. So a power loss is '*EI*' watts per unit length.

Power dissipated per unit volume is

$$\frac{EI}{A}=EJ \text{ Watt/vol. (as } EJ=\frac{EI}{A}=\frac{V}{d}.\frac{I}{A}=\frac{VI}{Ad}=\frac{Power}{Volume}\text{)}$$

Here $\vec{E},\vec{J}$ are in the same direction. However, in other cases also '$\vec{E}.\vec{J}$' gives the power dissipated per unit volume and so for the whole volume the total power dissipated is given by

$$\int_V\vec{E}.\vec{J}dV \quad ...(4.63)$$

This is the instantaneous power dissipated in volume 'V'. Hence eqn.(4.62) is a generalization of Joule's law.

(*a*) When '$\vec{E}$' is required to produce '$\vec{J}$' in the conducting medium, eqn.(4.62) represents ohmic loss or dissipation loss (I^2R)

(*b*) When ' $\vec{E}$ ' is due to a source of power, *e.g.*, battery, eqn.(4.62) would be used up in driving the current in the load against the battery voltage.

(*ii*) Term ' $\frac{\partial}{\partial t}\int_V\left[\frac{\mu}{2}(H)^2+\frac{\varepsilon}{2}(E)^2\right]dV$ ':

Here, ' $\frac{\varepsilon}{2}(E)^2$ ' is the energy density or stored electric energy per unit volume of the electric field, and, ' $\frac{\mu}{2}(H)^2$ 'is the stored energy density of the magnetic field.

These quantities continue to represent stored electric and magnetic energy densities for a time varying field. On integration we obtain the stored energy in the volume 'V'. Hence, these terms with a negative sign represents the rate at which the stored energy in the volume is decreasing.

(*iii*) Term ' $\oint_S\left(\vec{E}\times\vec{H}\right)dS$ ' :

From the law of conservation of energy, the rate of energy dissipation in the volume 'V' must equal the rate at which the stored energy in 'V' is decreasing, plus, the rate at which energy is entering the volume 'V' from outside.

Hence, '- $\oint_S\left(\vec{E}\times\vec{H}\right)dS$ ' must give the rate of flow of energy outward through the surface enclosing the volume 'V'.

The interpretation of eqn.(4.62) leads to the conclusion that ' $\left(\vec{E}\times\vec{H}\right)$' over any closed surface gives the rate of energy flow through that surface. This vector can be represented as

$$\vec{P}=\left(\vec{E}\times\vec{H}\right) \qquad \text{...(4.63a)}$$

This vector ' $\vec{P}$ ' is known as Poynting vector having the dimension of 'Watt/m^2'. **This is Poynting's Theorem.** It states that the vector product ' $\vec{P}$ ' at any point is a measure of the rate of energy flow per unit area at that point. The direction is perpendicular to both $\vec{E},\vec{H}$ in the direction of the vector ' $\left(\vec{E}\times\vec{H}\right)$' and is shown in Fig.4.5.

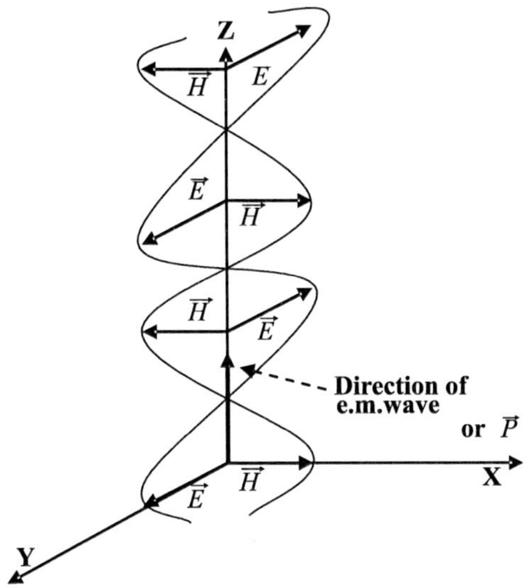

Fig. 4.5 Propagation of e.m. wave alongwith its electric and magnetic vector components.

4.12.2. Example: Power Flow for a Plane Wave: Here, velocity of e.m.wave propagating in space is $v_0 = \sqrt{\dfrac{1}{\mu\varepsilon}}$ and the total energy density is

$$\xi = \left[\frac{\mu}{2}(H)^2 + \frac{\varepsilon}{2}(E)^2\right].$$

So for a wave moving with a velocity 'v_0' the rate of flow of energy per unit area is given by

$$P = \frac{E}{At} = \frac{\xi V}{At} = \frac{\xi AL}{At} = \frac{\xi L}{t} = \xi v_0 = v_0\left[\frac{\mu}{2}(H)^2 + \frac{\varepsilon}{2}(E)^2\right] \quad ...(4.64)$$

But we know from eqn.(4.51), $\dfrac{E}{H} = \sqrt{\dfrac{\mu}{\varepsilon}}$

From eqn.(4.64) we have,

$$P = \frac{1}{2}v_0\left[\mu.\frac{H}{E}(EH) + \varepsilon.\frac{E}{H}(EH)\right]$$

$$= \frac{1}{2}v_0\left[\mu.\frac{1}{\sqrt{\dfrac{\mu}{\varepsilon}}}(EH) + \varepsilon.\sqrt{\frac{\mu}{\varepsilon}}(EH)\right] \quad \text{(using eqn.(4.51))}$$

$$=\frac{1}{2}v_0\left[\sqrt{\mu\varepsilon}\,(EH)+\sqrt{\mu\varepsilon}\,(EH)\right]$$

$$=2\times\frac{1}{2}\times\frac{1}{\sqrt{\mu\varepsilon}}\times\sqrt{\mu\varepsilon}\,(EH)=EH$$

Vectorically, $\vec{P}=\left(\vec{E}\times\vec{H}\right)$

4.12.3. Interpretation of $\left(\vec{E}\times\vec{H}\right)$

The interpretation of '$\left(\vec{E}\times\vec{H}\right)$' as the power flow per unit area is very important in radiation problems. An integration of '$\left(\vec{E}\times\vec{H}\right)$' over a surface enclosing an antenna transmitting signals gives the power radiated by the antenna. Eqn.(4.62) is calculated over the closed surface surrounding the volume. For any closed surface surrounding a bar magnet, '$\left(\vec{E}\times\vec{H}\right)$' integrated over the closed surface is always zero. So the net power flow outward from the magnet is zero and it should be.

Secondly, although outward power flow through any closed surface is correctly given by $\oint_S\left(\vec{E}\times\vec{H}\right)dS$, it does not necessarily follow that '$\vec{P}=\left(\vec{E}\times\vec{H}\right)$' represents correctly the power flow at each point. This can easily be understood mathematically. To the vector '$\left(\vec{E}\times\vec{H}\right)$', we can add any other vector, say, '$\vec{K}$', having zero divergence (*i.e.*, any vector having finite value of curl) without changing the value of the above expression.

Hence, the correct value of power flow is now

$$\vec{P}=\left(\vec{E}\times\vec{H}\right)+\vec{K}$$

Here, '$\vec{K}$' is the curl of some other vector, *i.e.*, $\vec{K}=\left(\vec{\nabla}\times\vec{C}\right)$, say, then the net power flow through any closed surface would be

$$\oint_S\left[\left(\vec{E}\times\vec{H}\right)+\vec{K}\right].\overrightarrow{dS}=\oint_S\left[\left(\vec{E}\times\vec{H}\right)\right].\overrightarrow{dS}+\oint_S\left[\vec{K}\right].\overrightarrow{dS}$$

$$=\oint_S\left[\left(\vec{E}\times\vec{H}\right)\right].\overrightarrow{dS}+\int_V\vec{\nabla}.\vec{K}dV$$

$$=\oint_S\left[\left(\vec{E}\times\vec{H}\right)\right].\overrightarrow{dS}+\int_V\vec{\nabla}.\left(\vec{\nabla}\times\vec{C}\right)dV$$

$$= \oint_S \left[\left(\vec{E} \times \vec{H} \right) \right] . \vec{dS} + 0$$

$$= \oint_S \left[\left(\vec{E} \times \vec{H} \right) \right] . \vec{dS}$$

So above expression again gives correctly the net flow of power through a closed surface, however, it is still not possible to say just where the energy is. This problem persists in other areas also. For example, total potential energy of the raised weight is a readily calculable quantity, but the distribution of this energy is not known. At which place the potential energy of a raised weight or a charged body lies is a question for philosophical speculation only.

4.13 Power Loss in a Plane Conductor

The power flow per unit area through the surface or the power loss in the conductor is given by the normal component of Poynting vector at the surface of a conductor.

We now consider a tangential component of magnetic field strength '$\overrightarrow{H_{\tan}}$' at the surface of a metallic conductor. The conductor is an infinitely large flat plate having thickness much larger than the skin depth 'δ'. The characteristic impedance of the metal is assumed to be 'η_m'.

From the continuity requirements across the boundary surface the tangential component of '$\vec{H}$' just inside the conductor, same value '$\overrightarrow{H_{\tan}}$' exists for magnetic field. Inside the conductor '$\overrightarrow{E_{\tan}}$', the tangential component of '$\vec{E}$' is given by

$$\frac{E_{\tan}}{H_{\tan}} = \eta_m,$$

and,

$$\eta_m = \sqrt{\frac{j\omega\mu_m}{\sigma_m + j\omega\varepsilon_m}} \approx \sqrt{\frac{j\omega\mu_m}{\sigma_m}} = \sqrt{\frac{\omega\mu_m}{\sigma_m}} \angle 45^\circ$$

$$\left[\sqrt{j} = \sqrt{\frac{1+2j-1}{2}} = \frac{\sqrt{(1+j)^2}}{\sqrt{2}} = \frac{1}{\sqrt{2}} + j.\frac{1}{\sqrt{2}} = \cos 45^\circ + j\sin 45^\circ = cis(45^\circ) = \angle 45^\circ \right]$$

The subscript 'm' is used to indicate the quantities for metals.

Just inside the surface of the conductor, we have, $E_{\tan} = \eta_m H_{\tan}$.

Again from the continuity requirements across the boundary, the tangential component of electric field just outside the surface will also be '$E_{\tan}$' and the power flow (normally) will be

$$P_n(real) = \frac{1}{2}\text{Re}\left[\overrightarrow{E_{\tan}} \times \overrightarrow{H^*_{\tan}}\right] \qquad ...(4.65)$$

When $\overrightarrow{E_{\tan}}$, $\overrightarrow{H_{\tan}}$ are at right angles and since for any good conductor $E_{\tan}$ leads $H_{\tan}$ by 45Ú in time phase, eqn.(4.65) becomes

$$P_n = \frac{1}{2}|E_{\tan}||H_{\tan}|\sin 45^\circ = \frac{1}{2\sqrt{2}}|E_{\tan}||H_{\tan}|$$

$$= \frac{1}{2\sqrt{2}}|\eta_m||H_{\tan}|^2 = \frac{1}{2\sqrt{2}}\frac{|E_{\tan}|^2}{|\eta_m|} \qquad ...(4.66)$$

Here bars indicate the absolute magnitude of the complex quantity.

For a conductor which has a thickness much larger than the skin depth 'δ', the surface impedance 'Z_s' is equal in magnitude to the intrinsic impedance 'η_m' of the conductor. So we have now,

$$P_n = \frac{1}{2\sqrt{2}}|Z_s||H_{\tan}|^2 = \frac{1}{2\sqrt{2}}\frac{|E_{\tan}|^2}{|Z_s|} \text{ W/sq. mt.} \qquad ...(4.67)$$

In a conductor we have already observed from Ampere's law that current density per unit length, linear current density '$\overrightarrow{J_S}$', is equal in magnitude to the tangential component of magnetic field, *i.e.*, $H_{\tan}$, at the surface, so,

$$P_n = \frac{1}{2\sqrt{2}}|Z_s||J_S|^2 \text{ W/m}^2 \qquad ...(4.68)$$

In eqns.(4.67) and (4.68), $E_{\tan}$, $H_{\tan}$ and J_S are peak values.

In terms of effective values,

$$P_n = \frac{1}{\sqrt{2}}\frac{1}{|Z_s|}\frac{|E_{\tan}|^2}{2}$$

$$= \frac{1}{\sqrt{2}}\frac{1}{|Z_s|}|E_{\tan(eff)}|^2$$

$$= \frac{1}{\sqrt{2}}|Z_s||H_{\tan(eff)}|^2$$

$$= \frac{1}{\sqrt{2}}|Z_s||J_{S(eff)}|^2$$

$$= R_S J^2_{S(eff)} \text{ W/sq. mt.} \qquad ...(4.69)$$

4.14 Maxwell's Equations Using Phasor Notation

Generally for e.m.wave both $\vec{E}$ and $\vec{H}$ vary sinusoidally with time (approximately). This can be expressed mathematically as

$$E = E_0 \sin \omega t \quad ...(4.70a)$$

and,

$$E = E_0 \cos \omega t \quad ...(4.70b)$$

Here, $f = \omega/2\pi$ and is the frequency of vibration. Eqns.(4.70) show that the attachment of the sinusoidal time factor to every term. The time factor may be suppressed through a new mathematical concept by the use of 'Phasor' notation.

In 'Phasor' notation the time varying electric field $\tilde{E}(\vec{r},t)$ may be expressed in terms of $\vec{E}(\vec{r})$ as

$$\tilde{E}(\vec{r},t) = \text{Re}\left\{\vec{E}\left(\vec{r}\right).e^{j\omega t}\right\}. \quad ...(4.71)$$

Here the symbol '~' has been placed over the time varying quantity to distinguish it from the phasor quantity and '$\vec{E}(\vec{r})$' is the phasor quantity free of any time dependent part.

4.14.1. Physical Interpretation

For simplicity we now consider one component at a time. For the X-component, the phasor 'E_x' is defined as

$$\tilde{E}_x(\vec{r},t) = \text{Re}\left\{\vec{E_x}\left(\vec{r}\right).e^{j\omega t}\right\}. \quad ...(4.72)$$

Generally $\vec{E_x}(\vec{r})$ is a complex number and thus at some fixed point $\vec{r}$ in space $\vec{E_x}$ may be written as a point 'A' in the complex plane with 'O' as origin and this is shown in Fig.4.6.

Here, $\quad E_x = |E_x| e^{j\phi}$

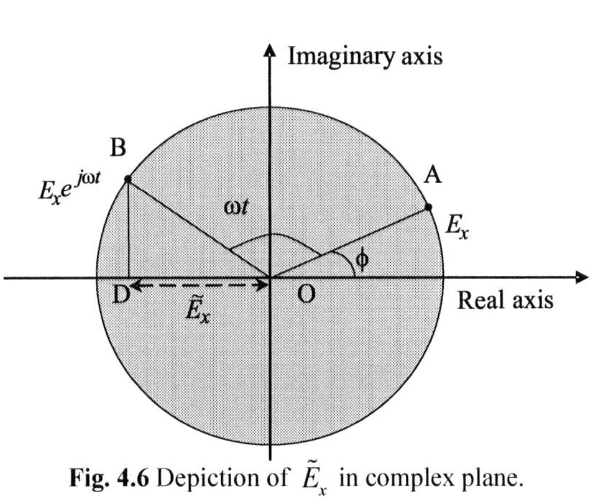

Fig. 4.6 Depiction of $\tilde{E}_x$ in complex plane.

Multiplying ' E_x ' by ' $e^{j\omega t}$ ', eqn.(4.72) becomes

$$E_x e^{j\omega t} = (|E_x| e^{j\phi}) e^{j\omega t} = |E_x| e^{j(\omega t + \phi)}$$

It results in a rotation through the angle ' ωt ' measured from the angle ' ϕ ' and is located at 'B' as in Fig.4.6. With time the point 'B' traces out a circle with center at the origin 'O'. Now taking the real part is the same as taking the projection on the real axis (as it is the 'sine part' of the form) and this projection varies sinusoidally with time. The phase of the sinusoidal is determined by the argument ' ϕ ' of the complex number $\overrightarrow{E_x}(\vec{r})$ and thus the time varying quantity may be expressed as

$$\tilde{E}_x = \text{Re}\left\{|E_x| e^{j\phi} e^{j\omega t}\right\}$$

$$= \text{Re}\left\{|E_x|\left[\cos(\omega t + \phi) + j\sin(\omega t + \phi)\right]\right\}$$

$$= |E_x|\cos(\omega t + \phi) \qquad \text{...(4.73)}$$

The phasor notation is one of the many possible definitions. We can also use the time factor ' $e^{-j\omega t}$ ' or make use of the imaginary part instead of the real part. Another possibility is to introduce a ' $\sqrt{2}$ ' factor on the right hand side of the phasor definition and thus making ' $|E_x|$ ' the rms value of the sinusoidal rather than the peak value.

4.15 Electromagnetic Equations in Phasor Notation

4.15.1. Maxwell's Equations: Now it is desirable now to find the corresponding set of phasor equations applicable for sinusoidal time variations for the Maxwell's equations.

(*i*) Fourth Equation: Using phasor notation in Maxwell's fourth equation we have

$$\vec{\nabla} \times \tilde{H} = \frac{\partial}{\partial t}\tilde{D} + \tilde{J}$$

$$\Rightarrow \vec{\nabla} \times \text{Re}\left\{\overrightarrow{H} e^{j\omega t}\right\} = \frac{\partial}{\partial t}\text{Re}\left\{\overrightarrow{D} e^{j\omega t}\right\} + \text{Re}\left\{\vec{J} e^{j\omega t}\right\}$$

$$\Rightarrow \vec{\nabla} \times \text{Re}\left\{\overrightarrow{H} e^{j\omega t}\right\} = \text{Re}\left\{j\omega \overrightarrow{D}\right\} + \text{Re}\left\{\vec{J} e^{j\omega t}\right\}$$

$$\Rightarrow \text{Re}\left[\left\{\vec{\nabla} \times \overrightarrow{H} - j\omega \overrightarrow{D} - \vec{J}\right\} e^{j\omega t}\right] = 0$$

The relation is valid for all 't' and hence,

$$\vec{\nabla} \times \overrightarrow{H} = j\omega \overrightarrow{D} + \vec{J} \qquad \text{...(4.74)}$$

This is the required differential equation in phasor form for 4th Maxwell's equation.

***(ii)* Third Equation:** Similar to eqn.(4.74), the 3rd Maxwell's equation can be written as

$$\vec{\nabla}\times\tilde{E} = -\frac{\partial}{\partial t}\tilde{B}$$

$$\Rightarrow \vec{\nabla}\times\mathrm{Re}\left\{\vec{E}e^{j\omega t}\right\} = -\frac{\partial}{\partial t}\mathrm{Re}\left\{\vec{B}e^{j\omega t}\right\} = -\mathrm{Re}\left\{j\omega\vec{B}e^{j\omega t}\right\}$$

$$\Rightarrow \mathrm{Re}\left\{\left(\vec{\nabla}\times\vec{E} + j\omega\vec{B}\right)e^{j\omega t}\right\} = 0$$

$$\Rightarrow \left(\vec{\nabla}\times\vec{E} + j\omega\vec{B}\right) = 0 \qquad \text{(for any 't')}$$

$$\Rightarrow \vec{\nabla}\times\vec{E} = -j\omega\vec{B} \qquad ...(4.75)$$

***(iii)* First and Second Equations:** Similar to eqn.(4.74), 1st and 2nd Maxwell's equations now become,

$$\vec{\nabla}.\vec{D} = \rho \qquad ...(4.76)$$

$$\vec{\nabla}.\vec{B} = 0 \qquad ...(4.77)$$

4.15.2. Equation of Continuity: For the equation of continuity in phasor notation we have,

$$\vec{\nabla}.\tilde{J} = -\frac{\partial}{\partial t}\tilde{\rho} = -\frac{\partial}{\partial t}\mathrm{Re}\left\{|\rho|.e^{j\omega t}\right\} \quad (\text{as } \rho = |\rho|.e^{j\omega t})$$

$$\Rightarrow \vec{\nabla}.\vec{J} = -j\omega\rho \qquad ...(4.78a)$$

4.15.3. Gauss's Divergence Theorem: For divergence theorem we have

$$\int_V \vec{\nabla}.\vec{J}dV = -j\omega\int_V \rho dV$$

$$\Rightarrow \oint \vec{J}.\vec{dS} = -\int_V j\omega\rho dV \qquad ...(4.78b)$$

4.15.4. Wave Equation

***(i)* Free Space:** For sinusoidal time variations, the free space wave equation for electric field becomes,

$$\nabla^2\tilde{E} = \mu\varepsilon\frac{\partial^2\tilde{E}}{\partial t^2}$$

$$= \mu\varepsilon \frac{\partial^2}{\partial t^2} \text{Re}\left[|E|.e^{j\omega t}\right] = (j\omega)^2 (\mu\varepsilon)\vec{E}$$

$$\Rightarrow \nabla^2 \vec{E} = -\omega^2 \mu\varepsilon \vec{E} \qquad \text{...(4.79)}$$

Similarly, the free space wave equation for magnetic field becomes,

$$\nabla^2 \vec{H} = -\omega^2 \mu\varepsilon \vec{H} \qquad \text{...(4.80)}$$

This is the vector Helmholtz equation.

(*ii*) Conducting Medium: For a conducting medium for sinusoidal time variations, the wave equation for electric field becomes,

$$\nabla^2 \tilde{E} - \mu\varepsilon \frac{\partial^2 \tilde{E}}{\partial t^2} - \mu\sigma \frac{\partial}{\partial t} \tilde{E} = 0$$

$$\Rightarrow \nabla^2 \vec{E} + \left(\omega^2 \mu\varepsilon - j\omega\mu\sigma\right)\vec{E} = 0 \quad \text{(as in eqn.(4.79))} \qquad \text{...(4.81)}$$

Similarly, the wave equation for magnetic field becomes,

$$\nabla^2 \vec{H} + \left(\omega^2 \mu\varepsilon - j\omega\mu\sigma\right)\vec{H} = 0 \qquad \text{...(4.82)}$$

4.16 Wave Propagation in a Conducting Medium

For sinusoidal time variations the phasor notation permits a straightforward solution of the wave equation in a conducting medium. Hence we can write eqn.(4.81) as

$$\nabla^2 \vec{E} - \gamma^2 \vec{E} = 0 \qquad \text{...(4.83)}$$

where, $\gamma^2 = -\left(\omega^2 \mu\varepsilon - j\omega\mu\sigma\right)$

$$= \left(j\omega\mu\sigma - \omega^2 \mu\varepsilon\right)$$

$$= \left(j\omega\mu\sigma + (j\omega)^2 \mu\varepsilon\right) = j\omega\mu\left[\sigma + j\omega\varepsilon\right]$$

Here, 'γ' is known as the 'Propagation Constant' and is a complex number.

Hence, $\gamma = \alpha + j\beta$

So, $\alpha = \text{Re}\{\gamma\} = \text{Re}\left\{\sqrt{j\omega\mu\left[\sigma + j\omega\varepsilon\right]}\right\}$

We have, $\gamma^2 = j\omega\mu\left[\sigma + j\omega\varepsilon\right] = (\alpha + j\beta)^2$

$$= \alpha^2 + 2j\alpha\beta - \beta^2$$

Equating the real and imaginary parts,

$$\alpha^2 - \beta^2 = -\omega^2 \mu\varepsilon \text{ and } 2\alpha\beta = \omega\mu\sigma \Rightarrow \beta = \frac{\omega\mu\sigma}{2\alpha}$$

So, $$\alpha^2 - \left(\frac{\omega\mu\sigma}{2\alpha}\right)^2 = -\omega^2\mu\varepsilon \Rightarrow 4\alpha^4 + \omega^2\mu\varepsilon\left(4\alpha^2\right) - \left(\omega\mu\sigma\right)^2 = 0$$

$$\Rightarrow \alpha^4 + \omega^2\mu\varepsilon\left(\alpha^2\right) - \frac{\left(\omega\mu\sigma\right)^2}{4} = 0$$

$$\Rightarrow \left(\alpha^2\right)^2 + 2.\frac{\omega^2\mu\varepsilon}{2}.\left(\alpha^2\right) + \left(\frac{\omega^2\mu\varepsilon}{2}\right)^2 = \left(\frac{\omega^2\mu\varepsilon}{2}\right)^2 + \frac{\left(\omega\mu\sigma\right)^2}{4}$$

$$\Rightarrow \left[\alpha^2 + \frac{\omega^2\mu\varepsilon}{2}\right]^2 = \left(\frac{\omega^2\mu\varepsilon}{2}\right)^2 \left[1 + \frac{\frac{\left(\omega\mu\sigma\right)^2}{4}}{\left(\frac{\omega^2\mu\varepsilon}{2}\right)^2}\right]$$

$$\Rightarrow \left[\alpha^2 + \frac{\omega^2\mu\varepsilon}{2}\right]^2 = \left(\frac{\omega^2\mu\varepsilon}{2}\right)^2 \left[1 + \frac{\sigma^2}{\omega^2\varepsilon^2}\right]$$

$$\Rightarrow \left[\alpha^2 + \frac{\omega^2\mu\varepsilon}{2}\right] = \left(\frac{\omega^2\mu\varepsilon}{2}\right) \sqrt{\left[1 + \frac{\sigma^2}{\omega^2\varepsilon^2}\right]}$$

$$\Rightarrow \alpha^2 = \left(\frac{\omega^2\mu\varepsilon}{2}\right) \sqrt{\left[1 + \frac{\sigma^2}{\omega^2\varepsilon^2}\right]} - \frac{\omega^2\mu\varepsilon}{2}$$

$$= \frac{\omega^2\mu\varepsilon}{2}\left[\sqrt{\left[1 + \frac{\sigma^2}{\omega^2\varepsilon^2}\right]} - 1\right]$$

$$\Rightarrow \alpha = \pm\sqrt{\frac{\omega^2\mu\varepsilon}{2}\left[\sqrt{\left[1 + \frac{\sigma^2}{\omega^2\varepsilon^2}\right]} - 1\right]}$$

The sign must be positive so that when $\gamma \to 0$, 'α' should be zero.

Hence, $$\alpha = \omega\sqrt{\frac{\mu\varepsilon}{2}\left[\sqrt{\left[1 + \frac{\sigma^2}{\omega^2\varepsilon^2}\right]} - 1\right]} \qquad \text{...(4.84)}$$

Same way we can form equation for 'β' as $\alpha = \dfrac{\omega\mu\sigma}{2\beta}$

So, $$\left(\frac{\mu\omega\sigma}{2\beta}\right)^2 - \beta^2 = -\omega^2\mu\varepsilon$$

$$\Rightarrow \beta^4 - \left(\omega^2\mu\varepsilon\right)\beta^2 - \left(\frac{\mu\omega\sigma}{2}\right)^2 = 0$$

On solving, $$\beta = \omega\sqrt{\frac{\mu\varepsilon}{2}\left[\sqrt{\left[1+\frac{\sigma^2}{\omega^2\varepsilon^2}\right]}+1\right]} \quad ...(4.85)$$

Here square root of 'γ^2' has two values, but for convenience we agree that value of the square root has a positive real part 'α' and if 'α' is positive, 'β' is also positive.

Now we have only for x-direction, the electric vector must satisfy

$$\frac{\partial^2}{\partial x^2}\vec{E} = \gamma^2\vec{E} \quad ...(4.86)$$

And have its solution as

$$\vec{E}(x) = \vec{E_0}.e^{-\gamma x} \quad ...(4.87)$$

In time varying form, it becomes,

$$\tilde{E}(x,t) = \text{Re}\left\{\left(\vec{E_0}e^{j\omega t}\right)e^{-\gamma x}\right\}$$

$$= \text{Re}\left\{\left(\vec{E_0}e^{j\omega t}\right)e^{-(\alpha+j\beta)x}\right\}$$

$$= e^{-\alpha x}.\text{Re}\left\{\vec{E_0}e^{j(\omega t-\beta x)}\right\} \quad ...(4.88)$$

This is the equation of a wave traveling in the X-direction and attenuated by the factor '$e^{-\alpha x}$'.

For lossless cases, the phase shift factor and the phase velocity is given by

$$\beta = \frac{2\pi}{\lambda}, \text{ and } v = f\lambda = 2\pi f.\frac{\lambda}{2\pi} = \frac{\omega}{\beta}.$$

4.17 Conductors and Dielectrics

In electromagnetism the division of two classes of materials, conductors and dielectrics, is not sharp. Some media like the earth is considered as conductors in one part of the radio frequency range and as dielectric in another part of the range.

From the fourth Maxwell equation in phasor notation by eqn.(4.75) we have,

$$\vec{\nabla}\times\vec{H} = \sigma\vec{E} + j\omega\varepsilon\vec{E}$$

The first term on the right hand side is conduction current density and the second part is displacement current density. The ratio '$\frac{\sigma}{\omega\varepsilon}$' is therefore just the ratio of the conduction current density to displacement current density in the medium.

Hence, '$\frac{\sigma}{\omega\varepsilon} = 1$' is the dividing line between conductors and dielectrics.

4.17.1. Good Conductors: Here '$\frac{\sigma}{\omega\varepsilon}$' is very much greater than '1' over the entire radio frequency (RF) spectrum. Like copper even at a high frequency of 30,000 MHz, $\frac{\sigma}{\omega\varepsilon} \approx 3.5\times10^8$. For good conductors, σ, ε are nearly independent of frequency.

4.17.2. Good Dielectrics: Here, $\frac{\sigma}{\omega\varepsilon} << 1$ in RF range. For an example, Mica at audio or radio frequency, we have,

$$\frac{\sigma}{\omega\varepsilon} \approx 0.0002 .$$

For dielectrics σ, ε are dependent on frequencies. However, '$\frac{\sigma}{\omega\varepsilon}$' is relatively constant over the frequency range of interest. Under these circumstances, '$\frac{\sigma}{\omega\varepsilon}$' is known as the 'dissipation factor, D' of the dielectric.

For good dielectrics, 'D' is small and it is same as the 'Power Factor, PF' of the dielectric. Actually,

$$PF = \sin\phi, \phi = \tan^{-1} D$$

So although they are not actually same, they differ by <1% when their values are <0.15.

Most materials used in radio are either to conduct conduction current or to stop it completely. Hence we use conductors or insulators. The important practical exception is the earth which occupies an in between position throughout most of the RF spectrum.

4.18 Wave Propagation in Good Dielectrics

Here, $\frac{\sigma}{\omega\varepsilon} << 1$, hence we can have by neglecting higher order terms of '$\frac{\sigma^2}{\omega^2\varepsilon^2}$' as

$$\sqrt{\left[1+\frac{\sigma^2}{\omega^2\varepsilon^2}\right]} = \left[1+\frac{1}{2}\frac{\sigma^2}{\omega^2\varepsilon^2}+....\right] \approx 1+\frac{1}{2}\frac{\sigma^2}{\omega^2\varepsilon^2} \qquad ...(4.89)$$

So,
$$\alpha = \omega\sqrt{\frac{\mu\varepsilon}{2}\left[\sqrt{\left[1+\frac{\sigma^2}{\omega^2\varepsilon^2}\right]}-1\right]}$$

$$\approx \omega\sqrt{\frac{\mu\varepsilon}{2}\left[\left[1+\frac{\sigma^2}{2\omega^2\varepsilon^2}\right]-1\right]} \qquad \text{(using eqn.(4.89))}$$

$$\Rightarrow \alpha = \omega\sqrt{\frac{\mu\varepsilon}{2}\times\frac{\sigma^2}{2\omega^2\varepsilon^2}} = \frac{\sigma}{2}\sqrt{\frac{\mu}{\varepsilon}} \qquad ...(4.90)$$

This expression may be compared with the expression for the attenuation factor of a low-loss transmission line having zero series resistance.

The expression of 'β' now becomes

$$\beta = \omega\sqrt{\frac{\mu\varepsilon}{2}\left[\sqrt{\left[1+\frac{\sigma^2}{\omega^2\varepsilon^2}\right]}+1\right]}$$

$$\approx \omega\sqrt{\frac{\mu\varepsilon}{2}\left[\left[1+\frac{\sigma^2}{2\omega^2\varepsilon^2}\right]+1\right]}$$

$$\Rightarrow \beta = \omega\sqrt{\frac{\mu\varepsilon}{2}\left[\left[2+\frac{\sigma^2}{2\omega^2\varepsilon^2}\right]\right]}$$

$$= \omega\sqrt{\mu\varepsilon}.\sqrt{\frac{\left[2+\frac{\sigma^2}{2\omega^2\varepsilon^2}\right]}{2}} = \omega\sqrt{\mu\varepsilon}\left[1+\frac{\sigma^2}{4\omega^2\varepsilon^2}\right]^{1/2}$$

$$\Rightarrow \beta \approx \omega\sqrt{\mu\varepsilon}\left[1+\frac{\sigma^2}{8\omega^2\varepsilon^2}\right] \qquad ...(4.91)$$

Here '$\omega\sqrt{\mu\varepsilon}$' is the phase shift factor for a perfect dielectric. The second term of the right hand side of 'β' is the small amount of loss as a correction factor.

The velocity of the wave in the dielectric is given by

$$v = \frac{\omega}{\beta} = \frac{\omega}{\omega\sqrt{\mu\varepsilon}\left[1+\frac{\sigma^2}{8\omega^2\varepsilon^2}\right]}$$

$$= \frac{1}{\sqrt{\mu\varepsilon}}\left[1+\frac{\sigma^2}{8\omega^2\varepsilon^2}\right]^{-1} \approx \frac{1}{\sqrt{\mu\varepsilon}}\left[1-\frac{\sigma^2}{8\omega^2\varepsilon^2}\right]$$

$$\Rightarrow v = v_0\left[1-\frac{\sigma^2}{8\omega^2\varepsilon^2}\right] \qquad ...(4.92)$$

Here '$v_0 = \frac{1}{\sqrt{\mu\varepsilon}}$' is the velocity of the wave in dielectric with zero conductivity.

The effect of the loss '$\frac{\sigma^2}{8\omega^2\varepsilon^2}$' reduce the velocity of propagation of the wave.

The general expression for the intrinsic or characteristic impedance of a medium is given by

$$\eta = \sqrt{\frac{j\omega\mu}{\sigma + j\omega\varepsilon}} = \sqrt{\frac{j\omega\mu / j\omega}{\frac{(\sigma + j\omega\varepsilon)}{j\omega}}} = \sqrt{\frac{\mu}{\left(\frac{\sigma}{j\omega}+\varepsilon\right)}}$$

$$= \sqrt{\frac{\mu}{\varepsilon}\left[\frac{1}{\left(\frac{\sigma}{j\omega\varepsilon}+1\right)}\right]} = \sqrt{\frac{\mu}{\varepsilon}\left(1+\frac{\sigma}{j\omega\varepsilon}\right)^{-1}}$$

$$\Rightarrow \eta = \sqrt{\frac{\mu}{\varepsilon}\left(1-\frac{j\sigma}{\omega\varepsilon}\right)^{-1}}$$

$$= \sqrt{\frac{\mu}{\varepsilon}}\left(1-\frac{j\sigma}{\omega\varepsilon}\right)^{-1/2} \approx \sqrt{\frac{\mu}{\varepsilon}}\left(1+\frac{j\sigma}{2\omega\varepsilon}\right)$$

For a perfect dielectric, $\sigma = 0$ and '$\sqrt{\frac{\mu}{\varepsilon}}$' is the intrinsic impedance. Again the effect of loss of a small amount is to add a small reactive component to the intrinsic impedance.

4.19 Wave Propagation in Good Conductor

Here, $\frac{\sigma}{\omega\varepsilon} \gg 1$ and $\gamma^2 = j\omega\mu[\sigma + j\omega\varepsilon]$

Hence, $\gamma = \sqrt{j\omega\mu\sigma[1+\frac{j\omega\varepsilon}{\sigma}]} \approx \sqrt{j\omega\mu\sigma[1+0]}$ (as $\frac{\omega\varepsilon}{\sigma} << 1$)

$$\Rightarrow \gamma = \sqrt{j\omega\mu\sigma} = \sqrt{\frac{2j\omega\mu\sigma}{2}}$$

$$= \sqrt{\frac{(1+2j-1)\omega\mu\sigma}{2}} = \sqrt{\frac{(1+j)^2\omega\mu\sigma}{2}}$$

$$\Rightarrow \gamma = \left[\frac{1+j}{\sqrt{2}}\right].\sqrt{\omega\mu\sigma} = (\frac{1}{\sqrt{2}} + j\frac{1}{\sqrt{2}}).\sqrt{\omega\mu\sigma}$$

$$\Rightarrow \gamma = \sqrt{\omega\mu\sigma}[\cos(45^o) + j\sin(45^o)] = \sqrt{\omega\mu\sigma}\angle 45^o \qquad ...(4.93)$$

Also,

$$\gamma = \sqrt{\frac{\omega\mu\sigma(1+j)}{2}} = \alpha + j\beta$$

So, $$\alpha = \sqrt{\frac{\omega\mu\sigma}{2}}; \beta = \sqrt{\frac{\omega\mu\sigma}{2}} \qquad ...(4.94)$$

The velocity of wave in the conductor then given by

$$v = \frac{\omega}{\beta} = \frac{\omega}{\sqrt{\frac{\omega\mu\sigma}{2}}} = \sqrt{\frac{2\omega}{\mu\sigma}}$$

And the intrinsic impedance is

$$\eta = \sqrt{\frac{j\omega\mu}{\sigma + j\omega\varepsilon}} = \sqrt{\frac{j\omega\mu}{\sigma}.\frac{1}{[1+j\frac{\omega\varepsilon}{\sigma}]}}$$

$$\approx \sqrt{\frac{j\omega\mu}{\sigma}} (as \frac{\omega\varepsilon}{\sigma} \langle\langle 1) \qquad \text{(as in eqn.(4.93))}$$

$$= \sqrt{\frac{\omega\mu}{\sigma}}.(\frac{1+j}{\sqrt{2}}) = \sqrt{\frac{\omega\mu}{\sigma}}.\angle 45^o \qquad ...(4.95)$$

For a good conductor 'σ' is very large and so both 'α, β' are also large. This means the wave is attenuated greatly as it progresses through it. The velocity of the wave, 'v', is thus small for the good conductor and is of the same order of magnitude as that of a sound wave in air. The characteristic impedance, 'η,' is also small and it has reactive component. The angle of this impedance is always 45° for good conductors.

Summery

(*i*) General Materials: $\eta = \sqrt{\dfrac{j\omega\mu}{\sigma + j\omega\varepsilon}}$

(*ii*) Good Conductors: $\eta = \sqrt{\dfrac{\omega\mu}{\sigma}}.\angle 45^o$

(*iii*) Good Dielectrics: $\eta = \sqrt{\dfrac{\mu}{\varepsilon}}$

(*iv*) Free Space: $\eta = \sqrt{\dfrac{\mu_0}{\varepsilon_0}} = 376.6\ \Omega$

4.20 Depth of Penetration or Skin Depth

For the good conductor at radio frequency range, $\dfrac{\sigma}{\omega\varepsilon} \rangle\rangle 1$, the wave is attenuated very fast and may penetrate only a very short distance before reduced to a minimum value. The depth of penetration or skin depth, δ, is defined as that depth in which the wave has been attenuated to '1/e' or approximately 37% of its original value. Normally the amplitude of the wave decreases by $e^{-\alpha x}$ with x. Then for $x = \delta$, we have, (as $a = a_o.e^{-\alpha x}$)

$$\Rightarrow \frac{a_o}{e} = a_o.e^{-\alpha\delta} \Rightarrow -1 = -\alpha\delta$$

$$\Rightarrow \delta = \frac{1}{\alpha}$$

Hence, $$\delta = \frac{1}{\alpha} = \frac{1}{\omega\sqrt{\dfrac{\mu\varepsilon}{2}\sqrt{1 + \dfrac{\sigma^2}{\omega^2\varepsilon^2}} - 1}}$$

For a good conductors, $\dfrac{\sigma}{\omega\varepsilon} \rangle\rangle 1$, hence

$$\delta = \frac{1}{\alpha} \approx \sqrt{\frac{2}{\omega\mu\sigma}} = \sqrt{\frac{2}{\omega\sigma\mu}} \qquad \text{(using eq}^n\text{.(4.94))} \qquad ...(4.96)$$

Example:

1. Copper: $\sigma = 5.8 \times 10^7\ mhos/mt, \mu = \mu_o = 4\pi \times 10^{-7}\ H/mt$

(*i*) At $f = 1 \times 10^6\ Hz$,

We have,

$$\delta = \sqrt{\frac{2}{(4\pi\times10^{-7})\times(5.8\times10^{7})\times(2\pi\times1\times10^{6})}}\ \text{m.}$$

$$\Rightarrow \delta = 0.0667\,mm$$

(*ii*) At $f = 100MHz$, $\delta = 0.00667$ mm

(*iii*) At $f = 60Hz$, $\delta = 8.67$ mm

2. In Fresh Water: $f = 1MHz$, $\delta = 7.1$.

3. In Sea Water: At $f = 1MHz$, $\delta = 25$ cm

4.21 Polarization

The polarization of a uniform plane wave refers to the time varying behavior of the electric field strength vector at some fixed point in space. The magnetic field variation is ignored for its negligibly small magnitude as compared to the electric field associated with e.m.wave. Polarization denotes the instantaneous orientation of its electric field vectors.

4.21.1. Theory of Production of Plane, Circularly and Elliptically Polarized Light: According to Maxwell's electromagnetic theory of light, a light wave consists of electric and magnetic vectors vibrating perpendicular to each other and as well as perpendicular to the direction of propagation of light. The electric vector is generally responsible for optical effect.

- For plane polarized light the orientation of light vector (electric vector) remains fixed, while its magnitude changes during vibration.
- When two plane polarized waves are allowed to superimpose in such a way that both electric vector vibration are of equal amplitude differ in phase by 90°, then, the resultant vector rotates about the direction of propagation of light. The magnitude of the resultant light vector remains constant, but its orientation varies continuously, the light is then said to be circularly polarized light. If the resultant electric vector rotation takes place in clockwise direction, the light is said to be right circularly polarized light. If the rotation is in anticlockwise direction then the light is said to be left circularly polarized light.
- When two plane polarized waves are allowed to superimpose in such a way that both electric vector vibration are of different amplitude and also differ in phase by 90°, then, the resultant electric vector start to rotate about the direction of propagation of light. In this condition both magnitude and orientation of resultant electric vector vary continuously, the light is then said to be elliptically polarized light. If the rotation of resultant electric vector takes place in clockwise direction then the light

is said to be right elliptically polarized light. If the rotation occurs anticlockwise then it is said to left elliptically polarized light.

4.21.2. Analytical Treatment

(*i*) The Electric Vectors of Waves are Vibrating Mutually Perpendicular to Each Other with Variable Phase Difference: Let us consider the case of two linearly polarized light vibrating in mutually perpendicular direction with the same frequency and traveling in the same direction, say Z-direction.

The two electric vectors are

$$X_1 = a\sin\omega t \quad \text{and,} \quad X_2 = b\sin(\omega t+\delta)$$

along X- and Y –axes respectively. Here 'a, b' are the amplitudes of waves and 'δ' be the phase difference between them.

Then the resultant wave becomes,

$$\begin{aligned} X &= X_1 + X_2 \\ &= a\sin\omega t + b\sin(\omega t+\delta) \\ &= a\sin\omega t + b\sin\omega t\cos\delta + b\sin\delta\cos\omega t \\ &= \sin\omega t(a+b\cos\delta) + b\cos\omega t\sin\delta \\ &= A\cos\phi\sin\omega t + A\sin\phi\cos\omega t \\ &= A\sin(\omega t+\phi) \end{aligned} \qquad ...(4.97)$$

Here, $A\cos\phi = a + b\cos\delta$

And, $A\sin\phi = b\sin\delta$.

Eqn.(4.99) represents the resultant of two waves. If the phase difference between two waves varies at random then the two waves will be incoherent and the direction of resultant vector 'X' varies randomly.

When $X_1 = X_2$, the resultant vector will give unpolarized light.

If $X_1 \neq X_2$, then the resultant electric vector will give partially polarized light.

(*ii*) The Electric Vectors of Waves are Vibrating Perpendicular to each other with Constant Phase Difference: Now the phase difference between two waves remains constant. In this case if the electric vector vibrations are along X-axis and Y-axis then the resultant electric vector will describe a certain closed curve in XY-plane. Here, the two electric vectors are along X-axis and Y-axis.

So along X-axis electric vector magnitude is given by

$$X = a\sin(\omega t+\delta) \qquad ...(4.98)$$

Along Y-axis electric vector magnitude of wave is given by

$$Y = b\sin\omega t \qquad ..(4.99)$$

From eqn.(4.99), $\sin\omega t = Y/b$

$$\Rightarrow \cos \omega t = \sqrt{1-\left(Y/_b\right)^2}\,.$$

Hence using above equation, eqn.(4.98) becomes ,

$$\frac{X}{a} = \sin \omega t \cos \delta + \cos \omega t \sin \delta$$

$$= \left(\frac{Y}{b}\right)\cos \delta + \sqrt{1-\left(\frac{Y}{b}\right)^2}.\sin \delta$$

$$\Rightarrow \left(\frac{X}{a} - \frac{Y}{b}.\cos \delta\right) = \sqrt{1-\left(\frac{Y}{b}\right)^2}.\sin \delta$$

$$\Rightarrow \left(\frac{X}{a} - \frac{Y}{b}.\cos \delta\right)^2 = \left[1-\left(\frac{Y}{b}\right)^2\right]\sin^2 \delta$$

$$\Rightarrow \frac{X^2}{a^2} + \frac{Y^2}{b^2}\cos^2 \delta - 2\frac{XY}{ab}\cos \delta = \sin^2 \delta - \frac{Y^2}{b^2}\sin^2 \delta$$

$$\Rightarrow \frac{X^2}{a^2} + \frac{Y^2}{b^2} - 2\frac{XY}{ab}\cos \delta = \sin^2 \delta \qquad ...(4.100)$$

Equation (4.100) is a general equation of an ellipse.

(*iii*) Special Cases:

(*a*) Plane Polarized Light: At $\delta = 0$ or $n\pi$, $\Rightarrow \sin\delta = 0, \cos\delta = 1$

Hence, using eqn.(4.100), we have,

$$\frac{X^2}{a^2} + \frac{Y^2}{b^2} - 2\frac{XY}{ab} = 0$$

$$\Rightarrow \pm Y = \pm \frac{b}{a} X \qquad ...(4.101)$$

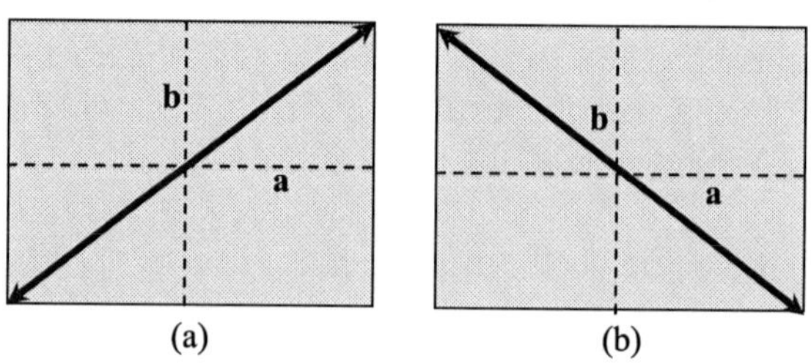

Fig. 4.7 Resultant electric vector of plane polarized light

Eqn.(4.101) is a straight line as shown in Fig.4.7(a). Hence the emergent light will be linearly plane polarized, vibrating along one direction. In both case of phase difference the resultant vector vibration will be as shown in the Fig.4.7. Fig.4.7(a) shown positive slope while Fig.4.7(b) shows negative slope.

(*b*) Elliptically Polarized Light: At $\delta = \left(\frac{2n+1}{2}\right)\pi$, here, $n = 0,1,2,...$, hence,

$$\Rightarrow \sin\delta = \pm 1, \cos\delta = 0 .$$

Hence, using eqn.(4.100), we have,

$$\frac{X^2}{a^2} + \frac{Y^2}{b^2} = 1 \qquad ...(4.102)$$

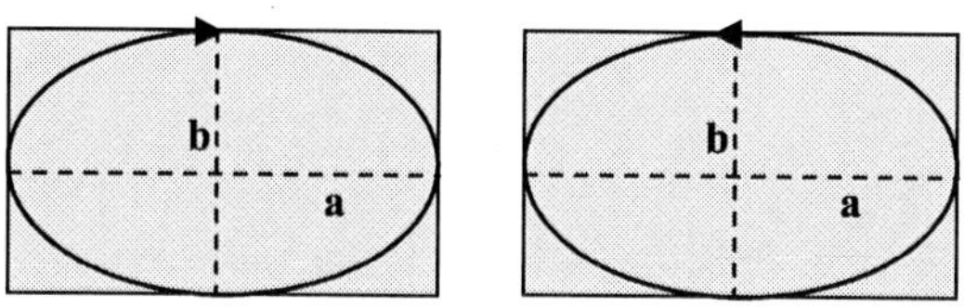

(a) (b)

Fig. 4.8 Elliptical rotation of resultant electric vector.

This is the equation of an ellipse. Hence the emergent light will be elliptically polarized. The resultant electric vector rotation about direction of propagation of light in elliptically polarized light is shown in Fig.4.8(a) and Fig.4.8(b).

(*iii*) Circularly Polarized Light: In eqn.(4.102), for $a = b$, and with the thickness of plate as

$$\left(\frac{2n+1}{2}\right)\pi, \qquad \text{here n=0,1,2.3}$$

So we have from eqn.(4.102),

$$X^2 + Y^2 = a^2$$

This is an equation of a circle of radius 'a'. Hence the emergent light is circularly polarized. The resultant electric vector rotation about direction of ropagation in circularly polarized light is shown in Fig.4.9 (a) and Fig.4.9 (b).

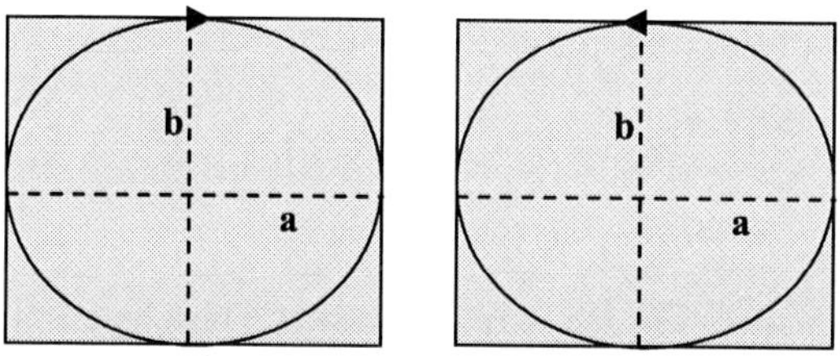

(a) (b)

Fig. 4.9 Circular rotation of resultant electric vector.

We now consider a uniform plane wave traveling in the Z-direction. So the $\vec{E}, \vec{H}$ vectors are lying in the XY-plane. If $\tilde{E}_y = 0$ and only $\tilde{E}_x$ is present, the wave is said to be polarized in the X-direction. If both $\tilde{E}_x$ and $\tilde{E}_y$ are present and are in phase, the resultant electric field has a direction depending on the magnitudes of $\tilde{E}_x$ and $\tilde{E}_y$. The angle which this direction makes with the X-axis is '$\theta = \tan^{-1}\left(\frac{\tilde{E}_y}{\tilde{E}_x}\right)$' and this angle will be constant with time and is shown in Fig.4.10.

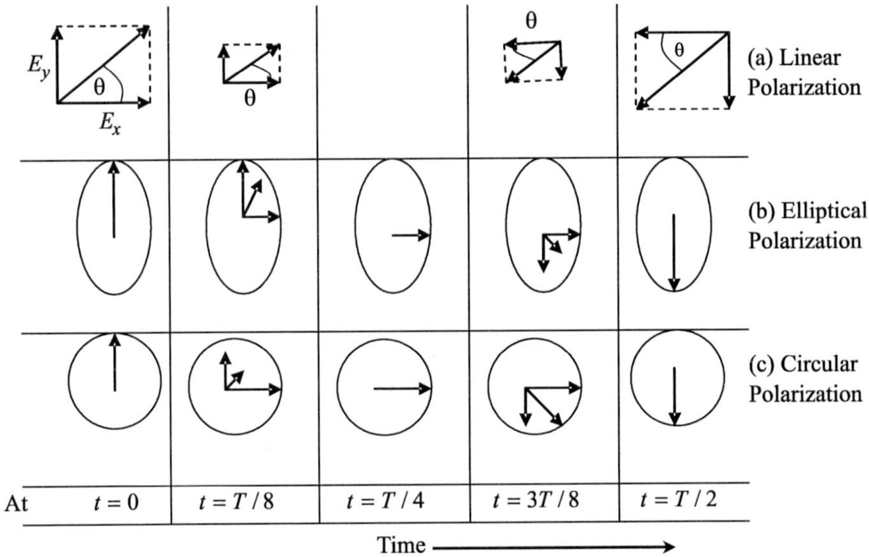

Fig. 4.10 Rotation of electric vector with time in various polarized light.

In this case the direction is constant, so the wave is said to be linearly polarized.

If $\tilde{E}_x$ and $\tilde{E}_y$ are not in phase, *i.e.*, they reach their maximum values at different instants of time, then the direction of the resultant electric vector will vary with time. If for a case when the locus of the end points of the resultant $\tilde{E}$ is in a ellipse, the wave is said to be elliptically polarized. When the locus is a circle, the wave is circularly polarized.

4.21.3. Polarization using Phasor Notation: The electric field of a uniform plane wave traveling in Z-direction may be expressed in phasor rotation following eqn.(4.72) as

$$\vec{E}(z) = \vec{E_0}.e^{-j\beta z} \quad \text{and in time varying form as}$$

$$\tilde{E}(z,t) = \text{Re}\left\{\tilde{E}_0 e^{-j\beta z}.e^{-j\omega t}\right\} \quad ...(4.103)$$

Here, $\tilde{E}$ lies in XY-plane as the wave travels along Z-direction. Generally, $\vec{E_0}$ is a complex vector and is given by

$$\vec{E_0} = \vec{E}_r + j\vec{E_i} \quad ...(4.104)$$

Here, $\vec{E_r}$, $\vec{E_i}$ are real and imaginary parts of 'E_0' respectively and are real vectors having different directions. So at some point in space for simplicity, let at $z = 0$, the resultant time varying field is

$$\tilde{E}(0,t) = \text{Re}\left\{\tilde{E}_0 e^{-j\omega t}.e^0\right\} \quad \text{(using eqn.(4.103))}$$

$$\Rightarrow \tilde{E}(0,t) = \text{Re}\left\{\left(\vec{E}_r + j\vec{E_i}\right)e^{-j\omega t}.1\right\}$$

$$= \text{Re}\left\{\left(\vec{E}_r + j\vec{E_i}\right)\left[\cos\omega t + j\sin\omega t\right]\right\}$$

$$\Rightarrow \tilde{E}(0,t) = \left\{\left(\vec{E}_r \cos\omega t - \vec{E_i}\sin\omega t\right)\right\} \quad ...(4.105)$$

Eqn.(4.105) indicates that in the resultant phasor part of '$\tilde{E}$', the magnitudes and directions of $\tilde{E}$ changes.

***(i)* Circular Polarization:** Here the X and Y-components of the electric field are equal in magnitude but differing in phase by 90^0 as shown in Fig.4.11. We consider the Y-component leading the X-component by 90^0 and the amplitudes of both are 'E_a', then the electric field at is given by

$$\vec{E_0} = \left(\hat{i}E_a + \hat{j}jE_a\right) = E_a\left(\hat{i} + \hat{j}j\right)$$

The time varying field is then given by

$$\tilde{E}(0,t) = \text{Re}\left\{\vec{E_0}.e^{j\omega t}\right\}$$

$$= E_a\left(\hat{i}\cos\omega t - \hat{j}\sin\omega t\right) \quad \text{(using eqn.(4.105))}$$

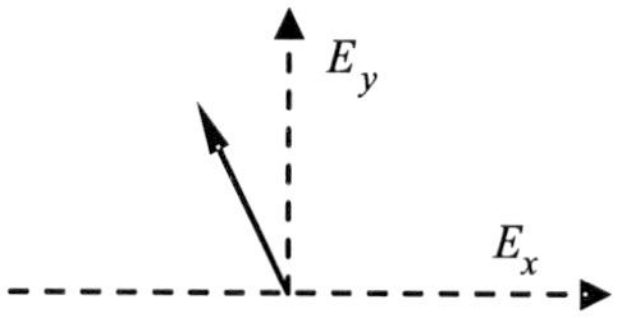

Fig. 4.11 Electric vector in circular polarization.

Hence we can get the components as

$$\tilde{E}_y = E_a \cos\omega t \quad \text{and} \quad \tilde{E}_x = -E_a \sin\omega t$$

Then, $$\left(\tilde{E}_x\right)^2 + \left(\tilde{E}_y\right)^2 = \left(-E_a \sin\omega t\right)^2 + \left(E_a \cos\omega t\right)^2 = \left(E_a\right)^2$$

It indicates clearly that the end point of $\tilde{E}(0,t)$ traces out a circle of radius 'E_a' as time progresses. The direction of rotation is that of a left handed screw advancing in Z-direction. So the wave is left circularly polarized. Similarly, for right circular polarization, the complex vector is given by

$$\overrightarrow{E_0} = E_a\left(\hat{i} - j\hat{j}\right)$$

***(ii)* Elliptical Polarization:** Here the X and Y-components of the electric field are not equal in magnitude but differing in phase by 90^0. We again consider the Y-component leads the X-component by 90^0 and the electric field is given by

$$\overrightarrow{E_0} = \left(\hat{i}A + j\hat{j}B\right)$$

Here A and B are positive real constants.

The corresponding time varying field on phasor notation is given by

$$\tilde{E}(0,t) = \text{Re}\left\{\overrightarrow{E_0}.e^{j\omega t}\right\}$$

$$= \text{Re}\left\{\left(\hat{i}A + j\hat{j}B\right)\left(\cos\omega t + j\sin\omega t\right)\right\} = \left(\hat{i}A\cos\omega t - \hat{j}B\sin\omega t\right)$$

Hence we can get the components as

$$\tilde{E}_x = A\cos\omega t \quad \text{and} \quad \tilde{E}_y = -B\sin\omega t$$

Hence, $$\frac{\left(\tilde{E}_x\right)^2}{A^2} + \frac{\left(\tilde{E}_y\right)^2}{B^2} = 1$$

Thus the end point of $\tilde{E}(0,t)$ vector traces out an ellipse and the wave is said to be elliptically polarized. Here the sense is again left handed.

Elliptical polarization is the most general form of polarization. The polarization is completely specified by the orientation and the axial ratio of the polarization ellipse and by the sense in which the end point of the electric field vector moves around the ellipse.

❑❑❑

CHAPTER 5

REFLECTION AND REFRACTION OF E.M.WAVES

5.1 Introduction

Till now the electromagnetic (EMI field interaction with different medium such as conductor, dielectric has been dealt to study the signal properties such as attenuation constant, velocity, impedance etc. When this EM field signal passes from one medium to another medium various phenomenon such as reflection, transmission etc. fakes place. This chapter deals with various optical phenomenon due to EM field interaction with the matter.

5.2 Reflection by a Perfect Conductor

5.2.1. Normal Incidence: When a plane e.m.wave in air is incident normally upon the surface of a perfect conductor, the wave is entirely reflected. For time varying fields, $\vec{E}, \vec{H}$ cannot exist within a perfect conductor; hence no part of incident energy can be transmitted. There can be no loss within a perfect conductor; none of the energy is absorbed. Hence, the amplitudes of $\vec{E}, \vec{H}$ in the reflected wave are the same as in the incident wave, except the oppositely directed flow of power.

We consider the electric field of the incident wave is:

$$E_i e^{-j\beta x}$$

and the surface of the perfect conductor is taken to be the $x = 0$ plane as shown in Fig.5.1. Hence, the expression of the reflected wave is $E_r e^{j\beta x}$.

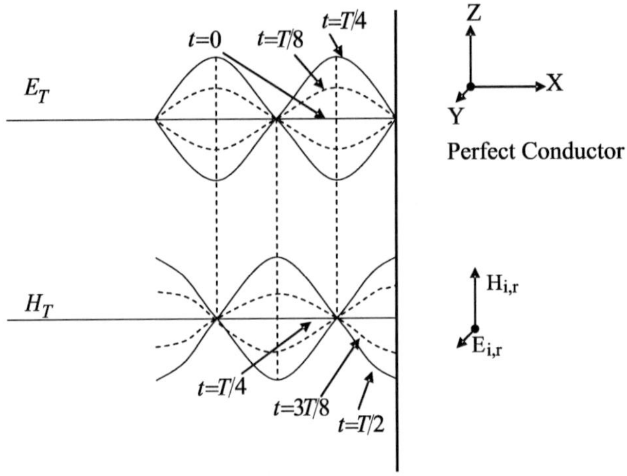

Fig. 5.1 Electric and magnetic field vectors on perfect conductor.

Here, E_r can be determined from the boundary conditions. We know that tangential component of $\vec{E}$ must be continuous across the boundary. As $E = 0$ within the conductor, the tangential component of E, just outside the conductor, must also be zero. Hence, the sum of the electric field strengths in the initial and the reflected waves must add to give zero resultant field strengths in the plane at $x = 0$. Therefore,

$$\vec{E}_r = -\vec{E}_i \qquad ...(5.1)$$

The amplitude of the reflected electric field strength is equal to that of the initial electric field strength; but its phase has been reversed on reflection. This is shown in Fig.5.1. The resultant electric field strength at any point a distance '$-x$' from '$x = 0$' plane will be the sum of the field strengths of the incident and reflected waves. Hence,

$$E_T(x) = E_i.e^{j\beta(-x)} + E_r.e^{j\beta x}$$

$$= E_i.e^{-j\beta x} - E_i.e^{j\beta x} \qquad \text{(using eqn.(5.1))}$$

$$= E_i[(\cos\beta x - j\sin\beta x) - (\cos\beta x + j\sin\beta x)]$$

$$\Rightarrow E_T(x) = -2jE_i.\sin\beta x \qquad ...(5.2)$$

In phasor notation, transmitted electric field is given by

$$\tilde{E}_T(x,t) = \text{Real part of } \{-2jE_i \sin(\beta x).e^{j\omega t}\}$$

If E_i is chosen to be real, then,

$$\Rightarrow \tilde{E}_T(x,t) = \text{Re}\{-2jE_i \sin(\beta x).(\cos\omega t + j\sin\omega t)\}$$

$$= 2E_i.\sin(\beta x).\sin\omega t$$

$$= (2E_i.\sin\beta x)\sin\omega t \qquad ...(5.3)$$

Hence eqn.(5.2) shows that the incident and reflected waves combine to produce a standing wave. Its properties are :

(*i*) Magnitude varies sinusoidally from the reflected plane due to presence of ' $\sin \beta x$ ' term,

(*ii*) Magnitude is zero at the surface and at multiple of λ/2 from the surface as then $\sin \beta x = 0$,

(iii) It has a maximum value of twice the electric field strength of the incident wave at distance from the surface that are odd multiple of λ/4, as then $\sin \beta x = 1$ and then amplitude becomes ' $2E_i$ '.

The electric field vector should be opposite in phase on reflection to produce zero resultant field at the surface. Similarly, the magnetic field vector must be reflected without any change in the phase. If both magnetic and electric field vectors are reversed, there will be no reversal of direction of energy propagation. Therefore, the phase of the reflected magnetic field strength ' H_r ' is same as that of the incident magnetic field strength ' H_i ' at surface of reflection $x = 0$. So, expression for the resultant magnetic field will be

$$H_T(x) = H_i.e^{-j\beta x} + H_r e^{j\beta x}$$

$$= H_i.e^{-j\beta x} + (H_i).e^{j\beta x} \qquad (\text{as } (H_r = H_i)$$

$$= H_i(e^{-j\beta x} + e^{j\beta x})$$

$$= 2H_i \cos \beta x \qquad ...(5.4)$$

However, ' H_i ' is real as it is in same phase with ' E_i '. So, for magnetic field of transmitted wave in phasor notation is

$$\tilde{H}_T(x,t) = \text{Re}\{2H_i \cos \beta x.e^{j\omega t}\}$$

$$= \text{Re}\{2H_i \cos \beta x.(\cos \omega t + j \sin \omega t)\}$$

$$= 2H_i.\cos \beta x.\cos \omega t$$

$$\Rightarrow \tilde{H}_T(x,t) = (2H_i.\cos \beta x).\cos \omega t \qquad ...(5.5)$$

Thus, the resultant magnetic field strength ' $\tilde{H}_T$ ' also has a standing wave distribution. Its properties are:

(*i*) It has maximum value at the surface of the conductor and at multiples of a half wave-length from the surface due to the presence of ' $\cos \beta x$ ' term,

(*ii*) The zero point occurs at odd multiples of ' $\lambda / 4$ ' from the surface as then $\cos \beta x = 0$.

From the boundary conditions for H, it follows that there must be a surface current of J_L Amp/mt, such that,

$$J_L = H_T \qquad \text{(at } x = 0\text{)}$$

[We have, $\vec{\nabla} \times \vec{H} = \vec{J}$, Dimensionally, $H = J \times L = \frac{I}{L^2} \times L = \frac{I}{L^2} = J_L$]

A comparison of eqns.(5.2) and (5.4) shows that E_T and H_T are 90° out of time phase due to the imaginary factor 'j' in eqn.(5.2). It indicates no average flow of power. This is the case when energy transmitted in forward direction is equal to the energy reflected back.

This can also be proved mathematically. From eqn.(5.2) we have,

$$E_T(x) = 2(-j).E_i \sin \beta x$$

$$(\text{as } -j = 0 + j.(-1) = \cos(-\pi/2) + j.\sin(-\pi/2) = e^{(-j\pi/2)})$$

$$\Rightarrow 2E_i.\sin \beta x.\left(e^{-j.(\pi/2)}\right)$$

Hence,

$$\tilde{E}_T(x,t) = \text{Re}\{2E_i.\sin \beta x.e^{-j(\pi/2)}.e^{j\omega t}\}$$

$$= 2E_i \sin \beta x.\cos(\omega t - \pi/2) \qquad ...(5.6)$$

Similarly, from eqn.(5.5)

$$H_T = 2H_i.\cos \beta x.\cos \omega t \qquad ...(5.7)$$

Comparing eqns.(5.6) and (5.7) we clearly found the time phase lag of '$\pi/2$' between them.

5.2.2. Oblique Incidence: For oblique incidence of an e.m.wave on the interface between two mediums, two cases are specifically possible.

First: The electric vector is parallel to the boundary surface or perpendicular to the plane of incidence. The plane of incidence is the plane containing the incident ray and the normal to the surface. This case is known as '**Horizontal Polarization'** as shown in Fig.5.2 (a).

Second: Here the magnetic vector is parallel to the boundary surface and the electric vector is parallel to the plane of incidence. This is known as '**Vertical Polarization'** and is shown in Fig.5.2 (b).

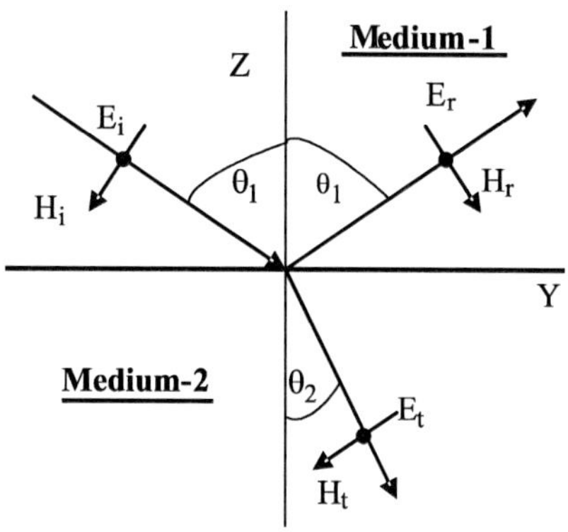

Fig. 5.2 (*a*) Horizontal polarization.

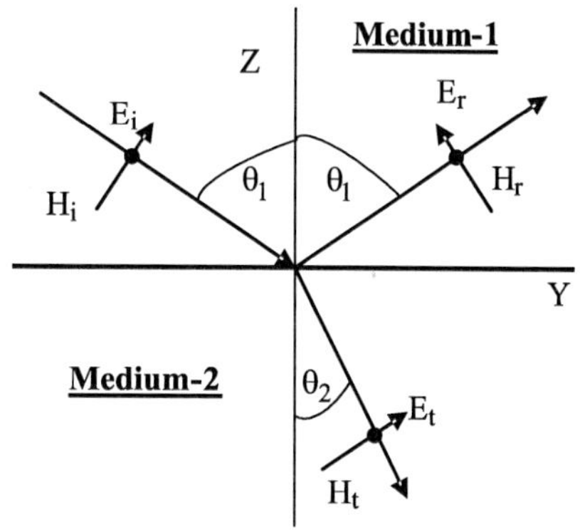

Fig. 5.2 (*b*) Vertical polarization.

In Fig.5.2 (a) and 5.2 (b), '**.**' represents the vector perpendicular to the plane of incidence (here along X-axis). 'θ_1, θ_2' are the angles of incidence and refraction respectively.

(*a*) The Electric Vector '$\vec{E}$' is Perpendicular to the Plane of Incidence: We consider here that the incident and reflected waves make an angle $\theta_1 = \theta_2 = \theta$ with the Z-axis and is shown in the Fig.5.3.

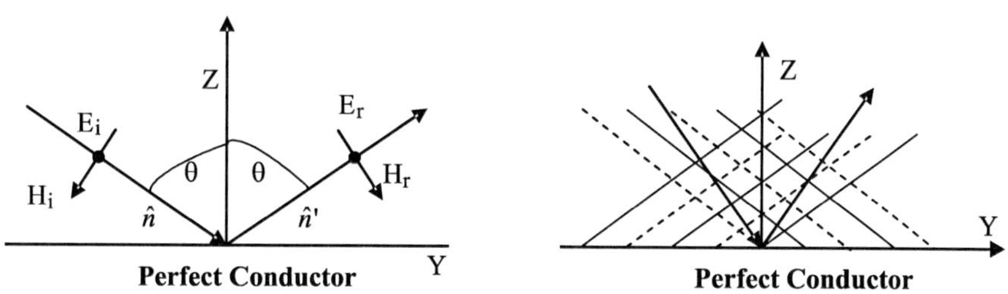

Fig. 5.3 Horizontal polarization on perfect conductor.

These two waves have equal wavelength and opposite directions. There must be a standing wave distribution along Z-axis. With both incident and reflected waves progressing to the right, there will be a traveling wave in the + Y-direction. This will be confirmed mathematically in the following.

From Fig.5.4 (a), the expression for the reflected wave is

$$E_{ref} = E_r.e^{-j\beta(\hat{n}'.\vec{r})} \Rightarrow E_r.e^{-j\beta(x\cos A + y\cos B + z\cos C)} \qquad ...(5.8)$$

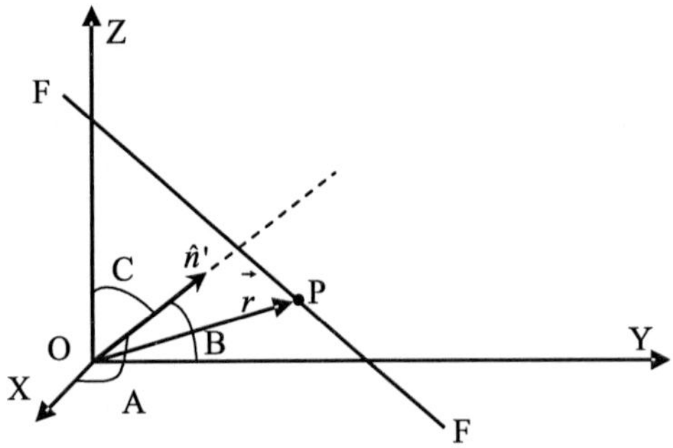

Fig. 5.4 (*a*) Reflected electric vector from XY-plane.

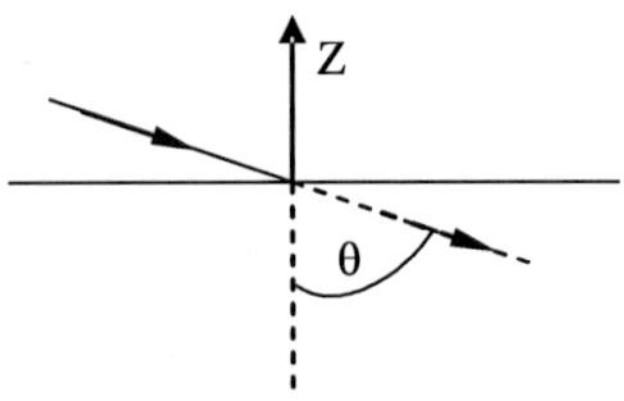

Fig. 5.4 (*b*) Transmitted electric vector in another medium.

Here, '$\hat{n}'$' is the wave normal, *i.e.*, unit vector normal to the plane 'FF' containing point 'P' as shown in Fig.5.4(a), '$\vec{r}$' is radius vector from origin 'O' to 'P', '$\vec{E}_r$' is the amplitude of the reflected wave at the origin, $C = \pi - \theta$, as 'C' is the angle made with positive Z-axis as in Fig.5.4(b).

For the wave normal to the reflected wave, we have,

$$\hat{n}'.\vec{r} = x.\cos(\pi/2) + y.\cos(\pi/2 - \theta) + z\cos\theta$$

$$= 0 + y\sin\theta + z\cos\theta \qquad ...(5.9)$$

Hence, from eqns.(5.8) and (5.9), we have

$$\vec{E}_{ref} = \vec{E}_r.e^{-j\beta(y\sin\theta + z\cos\theta)} \qquad ...(5.10)$$

For the incident wave,

$$\hat{n}.\vec{r} = x\cos\left(\frac{\pi}{2}\right) + y.\cos\left(\frac{\pi}{2} - \theta\right) + z\cos(\pi - \theta)$$

$$\Rightarrow \hat{n}.\vec{r} = 0 + y\sin\theta - z\cos\theta \qquad ...(5.11)$$

So,

$$\vec{E}_{incident} = \vec{E}_i.e^{-j\beta(\hat{n}.\vec{r})}$$

$$\Rightarrow \vec{E}_{incident} = \vec{E}_i.e^{-j\beta(y\sin\theta - z\cos\theta)} \quad \text{(using eqn.(5.11))} \qquad ...(5.12)$$

From the boundary condition we have,

$$E_r = -E_i \qquad ..(5.13)$$

So, combining eqns.(5.10), (5.12) with (5.13),we have the total electric field strength is,

$$\vec{E} = \vec{E}_{in} + \vec{E}_{ref} = E_i.e^{-j\beta(y\sin\theta - z\cos\theta)} + (-E_i).e^{-j\beta(y\sin\theta + z\cos\theta)}$$

$$\Rightarrow \vec{E} = E_i[e^{-j\beta(y\sin\theta - z\cos\theta)} - e^{-j\beta(y\sin\theta + z\cos\theta)}]$$

$$\Rightarrow \vec{E} = E_i\left[e^{-j\beta.y\sin\theta}.e^{j\beta z\cos\theta} - e^{-j\beta y\sin\theta}.e^{-j\beta z\cos\theta}\right]$$

$$\Rightarrow \vec{E} = E_i.\left[e^{j\beta z\cos\theta} - e^{-j\beta z\cos\theta}\right].e^{-j\beta.y\sin\theta}$$

$$\Rightarrow \vec{E} = 2jE_i.\sin\left(\beta z\cos\theta\right).e^{-j\beta y\sin\theta}$$

$$\Rightarrow \vec{E} = 2jE_i.\sin\left(\beta_z z\right).e^{-j(\beta_z.y)} \qquad ...(5.14)$$

Here, $\beta_y = \beta\sin\theta$ and $\beta_z = \beta\cos\theta$ ...(5.15)

'$\beta = \frac{2\pi}{\lambda}$' is phase shift constant of the incident wave with '$\beta_z = \beta\cos\theta$' is phase shift constant in the Z-direction and '$\beta_y = \beta\sin\theta$' is phase shift constant in the Y-direction. Eqn.(5.14) shows a standing wave distribution of 'E' along Z-direction. Its wavelength 'λ_z' measured along this axis is greater than 'λ' of the incident wave and is given by

$$\lambda_z = \frac{2\pi}{\beta_z} \qquad \left(\text{as } \beta = \frac{2\pi}{\lambda} \Rightarrow \lambda = \frac{2\pi}{\beta}\right)$$

$$\lambda_z = \frac{2\pi}{\beta\cos\theta} = \frac{\lambda}{\cos\theta}$$

Hence as $\cos\theta \le 1$, we have $\lambda_z \ge \lambda$.

The plane of zero electric field strength occurs at multiples of '$\lambda_Z/2$' *i.e.*, 'nodal planes', from the reflecting surface. So the plane of maximum 'E' occur at odd multiples '$\lambda_Z/4$' from the surface.

The complete standing wave distribution of 'E' is traveling with a speed 'v_y' along Y-axis as $v_y = \frac{\omega}{\beta_y} = \frac{\omega}{\beta\sin\theta} = \frac{v}{\sin\theta}$.

This is the velocity with which a crest of the incident wave moves along Y-axis. So the wavelength in the direction is $\lambda_y = \frac{\lambda}{\sin\theta}$.

(*b*) Here $\vec{E}$ is Parallel to the Plane of Incidence: Here, instantaneous directions of 'E_i' and 'E_r' are shown in the Fig.5.5. Here the components

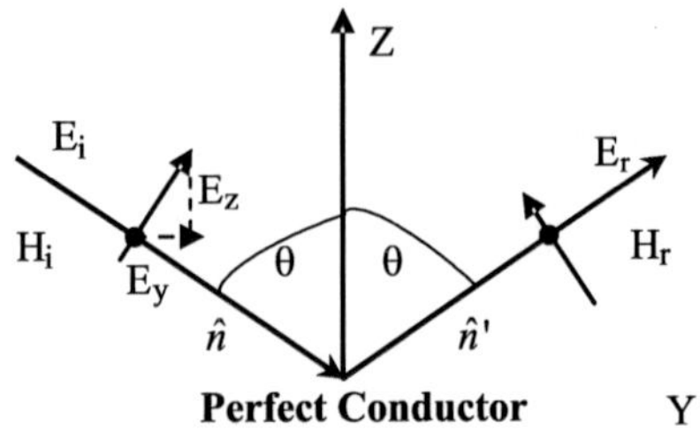

Fig. 5.5 Horizontal polarization on perfect conductor.

parallel to the perfectly boundary must be equal and opposite. The magnetic field vector '$\vec{H}$' will be reflected without phase reversal. The magnitude of $\vec{E},\vec{H}$ is related by

$$\frac{E_i}{H_i}=\frac{E_r}{H_r}=\eta\ .$$

For the incident wave the expression for magnetic field strength would be

$$H_{in}=H_i.e^{-j\beta(y\sin\theta-z\cos\theta)}$$

For the reflected wave, we have,

$$H_{ref}=H_r.e^{-j\beta(y\sin\theta+z\cos\theta)}$$

As '$H_i=H_r$', the total magnetic field strength is given by

$$H=H_{in}+H_{ref}=H_i.e^{-j\beta(y\sin\theta-z\cos\theta)}+(H_i).e^{-j\beta(y\sin\theta+z\cos\theta)}$$

$$=H_i.\left[e^{j\beta z\cos\theta}+e^{-j\beta z\cos\theta}\right].e^{-j\beta y\sin\theta}$$

$$=2H_i.\cos(\beta z\cos\theta).e^{-j\beta y\sin\theta}$$

$$=2H_i.\cos(\beta_z z).e^{-j\beta y\sin\theta}$$

$$\Rightarrow H=2H_i.\cos(\beta_z z).e^{-j(\beta_y y)}\quad\text{(from eqn.(5.15))}\qquad ...(5.16)$$

The magnetic field strength has a standing wave distribution along Z-direction with the planes at maximum H located at the conducting surface and at multiple of '$\lambda/2$' from the surface. The planes of zero magnetic field strength occurs at odd multiple of '$\lambda/4$' from the surface.

Now, $E_i=\eta H_i$

Hence, $E_z=E_i\sin\theta=\eta H_i\sin\theta$

And, $E_y=E_i\cos\theta=\eta H_i.\cos\theta$

For the reflected wave, $H_r=H_i$

Hence, $E_z = E_r \sin\theta = \eta H_r \sin\theta$

And, $E_y = -E_r \cos\theta = -\eta H_r .\cos\theta$

The total Z-component of electric field strength is

$$E_z = \eta H_z = \eta.(H\sin\theta)$$

$$= \eta\sin\theta\left(2H_i.\cos(\beta_z z).e^{-j(\beta_y y)}\right) \qquad \text{(using eqn.(5.16))}$$

$$= 2\eta H_i.\sin\theta.\cos(\beta_z z).e^{-j(\beta_y y)} \qquad ...(5.17)$$

Similarly the total Y-component of 'E' is given by

$$E_y = \eta H_y = 2j\eta\cos\theta.H_i.\sin(\beta_z Z).e^{-j\beta_y .y} \qquad ...(5.18)$$

Both components of the electric field strength have standing wave distributions above the reflecting plane. However, for the normal and Z-component of 'E', maxima occurs at the plane and multiple of '$\lambda_Z/2$' from the plane. Whereas, for the component of 'E' parallel to the reflecting plane, minima occurs at the plane and at multiple of '$\lambda_Z/2$' from the plane.

5.3 Reflection by a Perfect Dielectric

5.3.1. Normal Incidence: A perfect dielectric has zero conductivity so that there is no absorption of power during propagation of the wave through the dielectric. Generally, when a plane e.m.wave is incident normally on the surface of it, a part of energy is transmitted and the rest is reflected. We consider here a plane wave traveling in the X-direction, incident on a boundary that is parallel to the '$x = 0$' plane.

Let, 'E_i', 'E_r' and 'E_t' are the electric field strength of the incident wave striking the boundary, of the reflected wave leaving the boundary in the first medium and of the transmitted wave propagating into the second medium respectively. Similar subscripts are applied to the magnetic field strength 'H' also.

Let 'ε_1, μ_1' and 'ε_2, μ_2' are the constants of the first medium and the second medium respectively.

Hence, $\eta_1 = \sqrt{\dfrac{\mu_1}{\varepsilon_1}}$; $\eta_2 = \sqrt{\dfrac{\mu_2}{\varepsilon_2}}$

and $E_i = \eta_1 H_i$, $E_r = -\eta_1 H_r$, $E_t = \eta_2 H_t$ ...(5.19)

The continuity of the tangential components of 'E' and 'H' requires that

$$H_i + H_r = H_t \qquad E_i + E_r = E_t \qquad ...(5.20)$$

Combining eqns.(5.19) and (5.20) we have,

$$H_i + H_r = H_t$$

$$\Rightarrow \frac{1}{\eta_1}E_i - \frac{1}{\eta_1}E_r = \frac{1}{\eta_2}E_t = \frac{1}{\eta_2}(E_i + E_r)$$

$$\Rightarrow \eta_2\left(E_i - E_r\right) = \eta_1\left(E_i + E_r\right)$$

$$\Rightarrow E_i\left(\eta_2 - \eta_1\right) = \left(\eta_1 + \eta_2\right)E_r$$

$$\Rightarrow \frac{E_r}{E_i} = \frac{\eta_2 - \eta_1}{\eta_2 + \eta_1} = r \qquad \text{...(5.21)}$$

Here, 'r' is the reflection coefficient or reflectivity.

Also, the transmission coefficient or transmittivity 't' is given by

$$t = \frac{E_t}{E_i} = \frac{E_i + E_r}{E_i} \qquad \text{(from eqn.(5.20))}$$

$$= 1 + \frac{E_r}{E_i} = 1 + \frac{\eta_2 - \eta_1}{\eta_2 + \eta_1} \qquad \text{(from eqn.(5.21))}$$

$$\Rightarrow t = \frac{2\eta_2}{\eta_1 + \eta_2} \qquad \text{...(5.22)}$$

Similarly, using eqn.(5.19), we have,

$$\frac{E_i}{E_r} = \frac{\eta_1 H_i}{-\eta H_r}$$

$$\Rightarrow {}^{H_r}\!\!\diagup_{H_i} = -\frac{E_r}{E_i} \Rightarrow \frac{H_r}{H_i} = \frac{\eta_1 - \eta_2}{\eta_1 + \eta_2} \quad \text{(using eqn.(5.21))} \qquad \text{...(5.23)}$$

and

$$\frac{H_t}{H_i} = \frac{\eta_1 E_t}{\eta_2 E_i} = \frac{2\eta_1}{\eta_1 + \eta_2} \qquad \text{...(5.24)}$$

However, the permeability of all known insulator have approximately same value as for free space, so,

$$\mu_1 = \mu_2 = \mu_0 \qquad \text{...(5.25)}$$

Hence, using eqn.(5.21), we have,

$$\frac{E_r}{E_i} = \frac{\eta_2 - \eta_1}{\eta_2 + \eta_1} = \frac{\sqrt{\mu_0/\varepsilon_2} - \sqrt{\mu_0/\varepsilon_1}}{\sqrt{\mu_0/\varepsilon_2} + \sqrt{\mu_0/\varepsilon_1}}$$

$$\Rightarrow \frac{E_r}{E_i} = \frac{\sqrt{1/\varepsilon_2} - \sqrt{1/\varepsilon_1}}{\sqrt{1/\varepsilon_2} + \sqrt{1/\varepsilon_1}} = \frac{\sqrt{\varepsilon_1} - \sqrt{\varepsilon_2}}{\sqrt{\varepsilon_2} + \sqrt{\varepsilon_1}}$$

Hence, $$r = \frac{\sqrt{\varepsilon_1} - \sqrt{\varepsilon_2}}{\sqrt{\varepsilon_2} + \sqrt{\varepsilon_1}} \qquad ...(5.26)$$

Similarly, from eqn.(5.22) we have,

$$\frac{E_t}{E_i} = \frac{\frac{2}{\sqrt{\varepsilon_2}}}{\frac{1}{\sqrt{\varepsilon_1}} + \frac{1}{\sqrt{\varepsilon_2}}} = \frac{2\sqrt{\varepsilon_1}}{\sqrt{\varepsilon_1} + \sqrt{\varepsilon_2}}$$

Hence, $$t = \frac{2\sqrt{\varepsilon_1}}{\sqrt{\varepsilon_1} + \sqrt{\varepsilon_2}} \qquad ...(5.27)$$

Similarly using eqns.(5.23) and (5.24), we have,

$$\frac{H_r}{H_i} = \frac{\frac{1}{\sqrt{\varepsilon_1}} - \frac{1}{\sqrt{\varepsilon_2}}}{\frac{1}{\sqrt{\varepsilon_1}} + \frac{1}{\sqrt{\varepsilon_2}}} = \frac{\sqrt{\varepsilon_2} - \sqrt{\varepsilon_1}}{\sqrt{\varepsilon_1} + \sqrt{\varepsilon_2}} \qquad ...(5.28)$$

$$\frac{H_t}{H_i} = \frac{\frac{2}{\sqrt{\varepsilon_1}}}{\frac{1}{\sqrt{\varepsilon_1}} + \frac{1}{\sqrt{\varepsilon_2}}} = \frac{2\sqrt{\varepsilon_2}}{\sqrt{\varepsilon_1} + \sqrt{\varepsilon_2}} \qquad ...(5.29)$$

5.3.2. Oblique Incidence: SNELL'S LAW: Here the boundary conditions are complex ones and the transmitted wave will also be refracted. This is shown in Fig.5.6. It shows two rays of the incident wave. Incident ray-1 incident at point

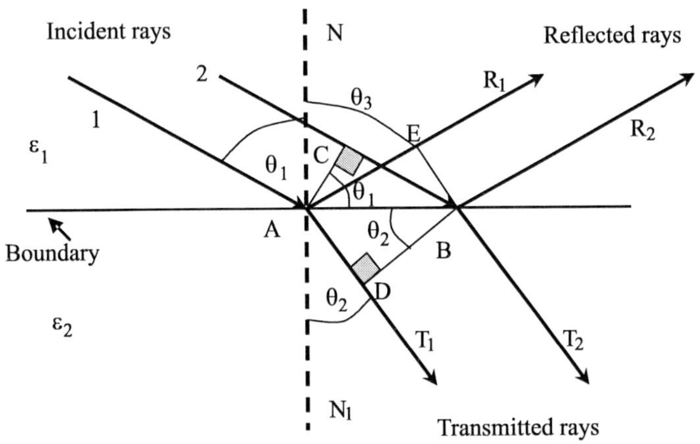

Fig. 5.6 Light incident from one medium to another medium.

'A' of the interface between the two mediums and then is transmitted as ray 'T_1' and reflected as ray 'R_1'. For incident ray-2, 'B' is the point of incidence on the interface between the two mediums with transmitted ray as ray 'T_2' and reflected as ray 'R_2'. During the time duration when incident ray-2 travels a distance 'CB', the ray 'T_1' travels distance 'AD' and reflected ray 'R_1' travels a distance 'AE'.

If 'v_1' and 'v_2' are the velocity of the wave in medium-1 and medium-2 respectively, then,

$$\frac{CB}{AD} = \frac{v_1 t}{v_2 t} = \frac{v_1}{v_2}$$

Now, in ΔABC, $\angle ABC = 90^0 - \theta_1$

So, $\angle CAB = 90^o - (90^o - \theta_1) = \theta_1$

Hence, from ΔABC,

$$\frac{CB}{AB} = \sin\theta_1 \Rightarrow CB = AB\sin\theta_1 \quad \text{...(5.30a)}$$

Now, $\angle CA1 = 90^\circ$, $\therefore \angle CAN = 90^\circ - \theta_1$

Thus, $\angle BAC = 90^\circ - \angle CAN = \theta_1$

and $\angle ABD = 90^\circ - \angle DAB = 90^\circ - (90^\circ - \angle DAN_1) = \theta_2$

In ΔABD, $\angle ABD = \theta_2$,

So, $AD / AB = Sin\theta_2 \Rightarrow AD = (AB)Sin\theta_2$ ...(5.30b)

So, using eqns.(5.30a) and (5.30b),

$$\frac{CB}{AD} = \frac{v_1}{v_2} \Rightarrow \frac{(AB)\sin\theta_1}{(AB)\sin\theta_2} = \frac{v_1}{v_2}$$

Hence, $$\frac{\sin\theta_1}{\sin\theta_2} = \frac{v_1}{v_2} \quad \text{...(5.31)}$$

However, we know, $$v_1 = \frac{1}{\sqrt{\mu_1\varepsilon_1}} = \frac{1}{\sqrt{\mu_o\varepsilon_1}}$$

$$v_2 = \frac{1}{\sqrt{\mu_2\varepsilon_2}} = \frac{1}{\sqrt{\mu_o\varepsilon_2}}$$

Hence using these into eqn.(5.31) we have,

$$\frac{\sin\theta_1}{\sin\theta_2} = \frac{\dfrac{1}{\sqrt{\mu_o\varepsilon_1}}}{\dfrac{1}{\sqrt{\mu_o\varepsilon_2}}} = \sqrt{\frac{\varepsilon_2}{\varepsilon_1}} \qquad ...(5.32)$$

Furthermore, $AE = CB$ (Both are distances from A and B on incident rays)

From, $\Delta ABC \,\&\, \Delta AEB$,

AB is a common,

$\angle C = \angle E = 90^o; AE = BC$

Hence, $\Delta ACB \cong \Delta AEB$ and thereby,

$\angle EAB = \angle CBA \quad \Rightarrow 90^\circ - \theta_1 = 90^\circ - \theta_3$

$$\Rightarrow \theta_1 = \theta_3 \qquad ...(5.33)$$

Thus the angle of incidence is equal to the angle of reflection.

Also the angle of incidence is related to the angle of refraction by eqn.(5.32) and is known as Snell's Law.

From chapter-IV we know that '$\vec{E}, \vec{H}$' are at right angle to each other, the power transmitted per square meter is equal to 'E^2/η'. The power in the incident wave striking AB will be proportional to '$\left(1/\eta_1\right)E_i^2\cos\theta_1$', the reflected wave will be '$\left(1/\eta_1\right)E_r^2\cos\theta_1$' and, that transmitted through the boundary will be '$\left(1/\eta_2\right)E_t^2\cos\theta_2$'.

From the principle of conservation of energy,

$$\left(1/\eta_1\right)E_i^2\cos\theta_1 = \left(1/\eta_1\right)E_r^2\cos\theta_1 + \left(1/\eta_2\right)E_t^2\cos\theta_2$$

$$\Rightarrow E_i^2 = E_r^2 + \frac{\eta_1}{\eta_2}.E_t^2.\frac{\cos\theta_2}{\cos\theta_1}$$

$$\Rightarrow \frac{E_r^2}{E_i^2} + \frac{\eta_1}{\eta_2}.\frac{E_t^2}{E_i^2}.\frac{\cos\theta_2}{\cos\theta_1} = 1$$

$$\Rightarrow \frac{E_r^2}{E_i^2} = 1 - \frac{\eta_1}{\eta_2}.\frac{E_t^2}{E_i^2}.\frac{\cos\theta_2}{\cos\theta_1}$$

$$= 1 - \frac{\sqrt{\mu_o}/\sqrt{\varepsilon_1}}{\sqrt{\mu_o}/\sqrt{\varepsilon_2}} \cdot \frac{E_t^2 \cos\theta_2}{E_i^2 \cos\theta_1}$$

$$\Rightarrow \frac{E_r^2}{E_i^2} = 1 - \frac{\sqrt{\varepsilon_2}}{\sqrt{\varepsilon_1}} \cdot \frac{E_t^2 \cos\theta_2}{E_i^2 \cos\theta_1} \qquad ...(5.34)$$

(*a*) Perpendicular (Horizontal) Polarization

Here, '$\vec{E}$' is perpendicular to the plane of incidence and parallel to reflecting surface. Let the electric field strength 'E_i' of the incident wave be in the '+' X-direction and let the assumed reflected ('E_r') and transmitted ('E_t') waves also be in the '+' X-direction.

Than applying the boundary condition that the tangential component '$\vec{E}$' is continuous across the boundary.

$$E_i + E_r = E_t$$

$$\Rightarrow \frac{E_t}{E_i} = 1 + \frac{E_r}{E_i} \qquad ...(5.35)$$

Putting this into eqn.(5.34),

$$\frac{E_r^2}{E_i^2} = 1 - \frac{\sqrt{\varepsilon_2}}{\sqrt{\varepsilon_1}} \left(1 + \frac{E_r}{E_i}\right)^2 \cdot \frac{\cos\theta_2}{\cos\theta_1}$$

$$\Rightarrow 1 - \frac{E_r^2}{E_i^2} = \frac{\sqrt{\varepsilon_2}}{\sqrt{\varepsilon_1}} \left(1 + \frac{E_r}{E_i}\right)^2 \cdot \frac{\cos\theta_2}{\cos\theta_1}$$

$$\Rightarrow \left(1 + \frac{E_r}{E_i}\right) \cdot \left(1 - \frac{E_r}{E_i}\right) = \frac{\sqrt{\varepsilon_2}}{\sqrt{\varepsilon_1}} \left(1 + \frac{E_r}{E_i}\right)^2 \cdot \frac{\cos\theta_2}{\cos\theta_1}$$

$$\Rightarrow 1 - \frac{E_r}{E_i} = \frac{\sqrt{\varepsilon_2}}{\sqrt{\varepsilon_1}} \left(1 + \frac{E_r}{E_i}\right) \cdot \frac{\cos\theta_2}{\cos\theta_1}$$

$$\Rightarrow \frac{E_r}{E_i} \left(1 + \frac{\sqrt{\varepsilon_2}}{\sqrt{\varepsilon_1}} \cdot \frac{\cos\theta_2}{\cos\theta_1}\right) = 1 - \left(\sqrt{\frac{\varepsilon_2}{\varepsilon_1}} \frac{\cos\theta_2}{\cos\theta_1}\right)$$

$$\Rightarrow \frac{E_r}{E_i} = \frac{\left(\sqrt{\varepsilon_1}\cos\theta_1 - \sqrt{\varepsilon_2}\cos\theta_2\right)\Big/\sqrt{\varepsilon_1}\cos\theta_1}{\left(\sqrt{\varepsilon_1}\cos\theta_1 + \sqrt{\varepsilon_2}\cos\theta_2\right)\Big/\sqrt{\varepsilon_1}\cos\theta_1}$$

$$\Rightarrow \frac{E_r}{E_i} = \frac{\left(\sqrt{\varepsilon_1}\cos\theta_1 - \sqrt{\varepsilon_2}\cos\theta_2\right)}{\left(\sqrt{\varepsilon_1}\cos\theta_1 + \sqrt{\varepsilon_2}\cos\theta_2\right)} \qquad ...(5.36)$$

Using eqn.(5.32),

$$\sqrt{\varepsilon_2}\cos\theta_2 = \sqrt{\varepsilon_2}.\sqrt{1-\sin^2\theta_2}$$

$$= \sqrt{\varepsilon_2 - \varepsilon_2\sin^2\theta_2} = \sqrt{\varepsilon_2 - \varepsilon_1\sin^2\theta_1} \qquad \left(\because \sin\theta_1 = \sqrt{\frac{\varepsilon_2}{\varepsilon 1}}\sin\theta_2\right)$$

Hence,
$$\frac{E_r}{E_i} = \frac{\sqrt{\varepsilon_1}\cos\theta_1 - \sqrt{\varepsilon_2 - \varepsilon_1\sin^2\theta_1}}{\sqrt{\varepsilon_1}\cos\theta_1 + \sqrt{\varepsilon_2 - \varepsilon_1\sin^2\theta_1}} \qquad ...(5.37)$$

$$= \frac{\cos\theta_1 - \sqrt{\left(\frac{\varepsilon_2}{\varepsilon_1}\right) - \sin^2\theta_1}}{\cos\theta_1 + \sqrt{\left(\varepsilon_2/\varepsilon_1\right) - \sin^2\theta_1}}$$

So,
$$r = \frac{\cos\theta_1 - \sqrt{\left(\frac{\varepsilon_2}{\varepsilon_1}\right) - \sin^2\theta_1}}{\cos\theta_1 + \sqrt{\left(\varepsilon_2/\varepsilon_1\right) - \sin^2\theta_1}} \qquad ...(5.38)$$

Eqn.(5.37) gives the ratio of reflected to incident electric field strength for the case of a perpendicularly polarized wave.

(*b*) Parallel (Vertical) Polarization: Here '$\vec{E}$' is parallel to the plane of incidence and '$\vec{H}$' is parallel to the reflecting surface. Again applying the boundary condition that the tangential component of '$\vec{E}$' is continuous across the boundary, which gives

$$\left(E_i - E_r\right)\cos\theta_1 = E_t\cos\theta_2$$

$$\Rightarrow E_t.\frac{\cos\theta_2}{\cos\theta_1} = E_i - E_r$$

$$\Rightarrow \frac{E_t}{E_i} = \left(1 - \frac{E_r}{E_i}\right)\frac{\cos\theta_1}{\cos\theta_2} \qquad ...(5.39)$$

Using eqn.(5.34) and eqn.(5.39),

$$\frac{E_r^{\,2}}{E_i^{\,2}} = 1 - \frac{\sqrt{\varepsilon_2}}{\sqrt{\varepsilon_1}}.\frac{\cos\theta_2}{\cos\theta_1}.\left(\frac{E_t}{E_i}\right)^2$$

$$= 1 - \frac{\sqrt{\varepsilon_2}}{\sqrt{\varepsilon_1}}.\frac{\cos\theta_2}{\cos\theta_1}\left[\left(1 - \frac{E_r}{E_i}\right)\frac{\cos\theta_1}{\cos\theta_2}\right]^2$$

$$\Rightarrow 1 - \frac{E_r^{\,2}}{E_i^{2}} = \sqrt{\frac{\varepsilon_2}{\varepsilon_1}}\left(1 - \frac{E_r}{E_i}\right)^2.\frac{\cos\theta_1}{\cos\theta_2}$$

$$\Rightarrow \left(1 + \frac{E_r}{E_i}\right).\left(1 - \frac{E_r}{E_i}\right) = \sqrt{\frac{\varepsilon_2}{\varepsilon_1}}\left(1 - \frac{E_r}{E_i}\right)^2.\frac{\cos\theta_1}{\cos\theta_2}$$

$$\Rightarrow \left(1 + \frac{E_r}{E_i}\right).\left(1 - \frac{E_r}{E_i}\right) = \sqrt{\frac{\varepsilon_2}{\varepsilon_1}}\left(1 - \frac{E_r}{E_i}\right)^2.\frac{\cos\theta_1}{\cos\theta_2}$$

$$\Rightarrow 1 + \frac{E_r}{E_i} = \sqrt{\frac{\varepsilon_2}{\varepsilon_1}}\left(1 - \frac{E_r}{E_i}\right).\frac{\cos\theta_1}{\cos\theta_2}$$

$$\Rightarrow \frac{E_r}{E_i}\left[1 + \sqrt{\frac{\varepsilon_2}{\varepsilon_1}}.\frac{\cos\theta_1}{\cos\theta_2}\right] = \sqrt{\frac{\varepsilon_2}{\varepsilon_1}}.\frac{\cos\theta_1}{\cos\theta_2} - 1$$

$$\Rightarrow \frac{E_r}{E_i} = \frac{\left(\sqrt{\varepsilon_2}\cos\theta_1 - \sqrt{\varepsilon_1}\cos\theta_2\right)\Big/\left(\sqrt{\varepsilon_1}\cos\theta_2\right)}{\left(\sqrt{\varepsilon_1}\cos\theta_2 + \sqrt{\varepsilon_2}\cos\theta_1\right)\Big/\left(\sqrt{\varepsilon_1}\cos\theta_2\right)}$$

$$= \frac{\sqrt{\varepsilon_2}\cos\theta_1 - \sqrt{\varepsilon_1}\cos\theta_2}{\sqrt{\varepsilon_2}\cos\theta_1 + \sqrt{\varepsilon_1}\cos\theta_2} \qquad ...(5.40)$$

$$= \frac{\left(\sqrt{\varepsilon_2}\cos\theta_1 - \sqrt{\varepsilon_1}\sqrt{1 - \sin^2\theta_2}\right)}{\sqrt{\varepsilon_2}\cos\theta_1 + \sqrt{\varepsilon_1}\sqrt{1 - \sin^2\theta_2}}$$

$$= \frac{\sqrt{\varepsilon_2}\cos\theta_1 - \sqrt{\varepsilon_1}.\sqrt{1-\frac{\varepsilon_1}{\varepsilon_2}\sin^2\theta_1}}{\sqrt{\varepsilon_2}\cos_1 + \sqrt{\varepsilon_1}.\sqrt{1-\frac{\varepsilon_1}{\varepsilon_2}\sin^2\theta_1}} \quad \left[\because \sin\theta_2 = \sqrt{\frac{\varepsilon_1}{\varepsilon_2}}\sin\theta_1\right] \quad \text{(from eqn.(5.32))}$$

$$= \frac{\sqrt{\varepsilon_2}\cos\theta_1 - \sqrt{\frac{\varepsilon_1}{\varepsilon_2}}\sqrt{\varepsilon_2 - \varepsilon_1\sin^2\theta}}{\sqrt{\varepsilon_2}\cos\theta_1 + \sqrt{\frac{\varepsilon_1}{\varepsilon_2}}.\sqrt{\varepsilon_2 - \varepsilon_1\sin^2\theta_1}}$$

$$= \frac{\left(\varepsilon_2\cos\theta_1 - \sqrt{\varepsilon_1}.\sqrt{\varepsilon_2 - \varepsilon_1\sin^2\theta_1}\right)\Big/\sqrt{\varepsilon_2}}{\left(\varepsilon_2\cos\theta_1 + \sqrt{\varepsilon_1}.\sqrt{\varepsilon_2 - \varepsilon_1\sin^2\theta_1}\right)\Big/\sqrt{\varepsilon_2}}$$

$$= \frac{\left(\varepsilon_2\cos\theta_1 - \varepsilon_1\sqrt{\varepsilon_2/\varepsilon_1 - \sin^2\theta_1}\right)}{\left(\varepsilon_2\cos\theta_1 + \varepsilon_1\sqrt{\varepsilon_2/\varepsilon_1 - \sin^2\theta_1}\right)}$$

$$= \frac{\left(\left(\varepsilon_2/\varepsilon_1\right).\cos\theta_1 - \sqrt{\varepsilon_2/\varepsilon_1 - \sin^2\theta_1}\right).\varepsilon_1}{\left(\left(\varepsilon_2/\varepsilon_1\right).\cos\theta_1 + \sqrt{\varepsilon_2/\varepsilon_1 - \sin^2\theta_1}\right).\varepsilon_1}$$

$$= \frac{\left(\left(\varepsilon_2/\varepsilon_1\right).\cos\theta_1 - \sqrt{\varepsilon_2/\varepsilon_1 - \sin^2\theta_1}\right)}{\left(\left(\varepsilon_2/\varepsilon_1\right).\cos\theta_1 + \sqrt{\varepsilon_2/\varepsilon_1 - \sin^2\theta_1}\right)}$$

So,

$$r = \frac{\left(\left(\varepsilon_2/\varepsilon_1\right).\cos\theta_1 - \sqrt{\varepsilon_2/\varepsilon_1 - \sin^2\theta_1}\right)}{\left(\left(\varepsilon_2/\varepsilon_1\right).\cos\theta_1 + \sqrt{\varepsilon_2/\varepsilon_1 - \sin^2\theta_1}\right)} \quad ...(5.41)$$

5.4 Brewster's Law and Brewster's Angle

Possibility of no reflection $(r = 0)$ at a particular angle can also be determined by using eqn.(5.38). Putting $r = 0$ in eqn.(5.38), we have,

$$\cos\theta_1 = \sqrt{\frac{\varepsilon_2}{\varepsilon_1} - \sin^2\theta_1}$$

$$\Rightarrow \cos^2\theta_1 + \sin^2\theta_1 = \frac{\varepsilon_2}{\varepsilon_1}$$

$$\Rightarrow \frac{\varepsilon_2}{\varepsilon_1} = 1$$

Hence, $\varepsilon_1 = \varepsilon_2$. This is not possible as then there is no change in medium properties, *i.e.*, $\varepsilon_1 \neq \varepsilon_2$. Hence this occurs only when the numerator of eqn.(5.41) becomes zero, *i.e.*, $E_r = 0$. So from eqn.(5.41) we have now,

$$\frac{\varepsilon_2}{\varepsilon_1}.\cos\theta_1 - \sqrt{\left(\varepsilon_2/\varepsilon_1\right) - \sin^2\theta_1} = 0$$

$$\Rightarrow \left(\frac{\varepsilon_2}{\varepsilon_1}\right)^2 .\cos^2\theta_1 = \left(\varepsilon_2/\varepsilon_1\right) - \sin^2\theta_1$$

$$\Rightarrow \left(\frac{\varepsilon_2}{\varepsilon_1}\right)^2 .\left(1 - \sin^2\theta_1\right) = \left(\varepsilon_2/\varepsilon_1\right) - \sin^2\theta_1$$

$$\Rightarrow \varepsilon_2^2.\left(1 - \sin^2\theta_1\right) = \left(\varepsilon_2 - \varepsilon_1\sin^2\theta_1\right)\varepsilon_1$$

$$\Rightarrow \left(\varepsilon_1^2 - \varepsilon_2^2\right)\sin^2\theta_1 = \left(\varepsilon_1\varepsilon_2 - \varepsilon^2_2\right) = \varepsilon_2\left(\varepsilon_1 - \varepsilon_2\right)$$

$$\Rightarrow \sin^2\theta_1 = \frac{\varepsilon_2\left(\varepsilon_1 - \varepsilon_2\right)}{\left(\varepsilon_1 + \varepsilon_2\right)} = \frac{\varepsilon_2}{\varepsilon_1 + \varepsilon_2}$$

So, $$\cos^2\theta_1 = 1 - \sin^2\theta_1$$

$$= 1 - \frac{\varepsilon_2}{\varepsilon_1 + \varepsilon_2} = \frac{\varepsilon_1}{\varepsilon_1 + \varepsilon_2}$$

Hence, $$\tan^2\theta_1 = \frac{\sin^2\theta_1}{\cos^2\theta_1} = \frac{(\varepsilon_2)/(\varepsilon_1 + \varepsilon_2)}{(\varepsilon_1)/(\varepsilon_1 + \varepsilon_2)} = \frac{\varepsilon_2}{\varepsilon_1}$$

$$\Rightarrow \tan\theta_1 = \sqrt{\frac{\varepsilon_2}{\varepsilon_1}} \qquad ...(5.42)$$

This angle 'θ_1' is known as the Brewster's angle. At this angle there is no reflected wave when the incident wave is parallel (vertically) polarized. If the incident wave is not entirely polarized (parallel), then there will be some reflection, but the reflected wave will be entirely of perpendicularly (horizontal) polarization. For perpendicular polarization, eqn.(5.37) shows that there is no corresponding Brewster's angle for this polarization. Quartz windows of gas-laser in the gas discharge tube are inclined to the 'Brewster's angle' to minimize reflection losses. Because of these windows the laser output is almost completely linearly polarized.

5.5 Total Internal Reflection

When light traveling from a denser medium is incident to a rarer medium with the angle of incidence more than the critical angle corresponding to the mediums, the incident light is reflected back to the incident medium without any refraction. This phenomenon is known as 'total internal reflection'.

Here, $\varepsilon_1 \rangle \varepsilon_2$, so $\sin\theta_1 \rangle \sqrt{\dfrac{\varepsilon_2}{\varepsilon_1}}$

The reflection is total provided that medium-1 is denser than medium-2.

In the rarer medium (medium-2 with reference to Fig.5.6) the fields are of the form $e^{-j\beta_2(y\sin\theta_2 - z\cos\theta_2)}$.

From Snell's law,

$$\frac{\sin\theta_1}{\sin\theta_2} = \sqrt{\frac{\varepsilon_2}{\varepsilon_1}} \Rightarrow \sin\theta_2 = \sqrt{\frac{\varepsilon_1}{\varepsilon_2}}\sin\theta_1$$

So, the Y-variation is given by

$$e^{-j\beta_2 y\sin\theta_2} = e^{-j\beta_2 y\sqrt{\frac{\varepsilon_1}{\varepsilon_2}}\sin\theta_1}$$

and the Z-variation is

$$e^{j\beta_2 z\cos\theta_2} = e^{j\beta_2 z\left[\pm\sqrt{1-\sin^2\theta_2}\right]} = e^{j\beta_2 z\left[\pm\sqrt{-\left[\left(\varepsilon_1/\varepsilon_2\right)\sin^2\theta_1 - 1\right]}\right]} \quad \left(\text{as } \left(\frac{\varepsilon_1}{\varepsilon_2}\right)\sin^2\theta_1 \rangle 1\right)$$

$$= e^{j\beta_2 z\left[\pm j\sqrt{\left(\varepsilon_1/\varepsilon_2\right)\sin^2\theta_1 - 1}\right]}$$

$$= e^{\pm\beta_2 z\left[\sqrt{\left(\varepsilon_1/\varepsilon_2\right)\sin^2\theta_1 - 1}\right]} \qquad ...(5.43)$$

In eqn.(5.43) lower sign must be chosen so that the fields decrease exponentially with 'z' becoming more and more negative, hence,

$$\cos\theta_2 = -\sqrt{1-\sin^2\theta_2}$$

$$= -\sqrt{-\left[\sin^2\theta_2 - 1\right]} = -j\sqrt{\frac{\varepsilon_1}{\varepsilon_2}\sin^2\theta_1 - 1}$$

$$= -j\sqrt{\frac{\varepsilon_1}{\varepsilon_2}}.\sqrt{\sin^2\theta_1 - \frac{\varepsilon_2}{\varepsilon_1}} \qquad ...(5.44)$$

So for the total internal reflection, a field exists in the denser medium. This phase of the field is propagating along the boundary with decreasing in an exponential value away from it. Hence it is a non-uniform plane wave.

The resultant phase velocity along the interface of the mediums is given by

$$\frac{\omega}{\beta_2.\sqrt{\frac{\varepsilon_1}{\varepsilon_2}}.\sin\theta_1}$$

For the total internal reflection, this phase velocity is less than the phase velocity '$\frac{\omega}{\beta_2}$' of a uniform plane wave in medium-2 in absence of medium-1. Hence the resultant non-uniform plane wave in medium-2 is slow wave. So both medium-1 and 2 are necessary with their common interface to support this wave and hence this wave is also known as 'surface wave'.

The reflection coefficient for perpendicular polarization is

$$r = \frac{E_r}{E_i} = \frac{\sqrt{\varepsilon_2}\cos\theta_1 - \sqrt{\varepsilon_2}\cos\theta_2}{\sqrt{\varepsilon_1}\cos\theta_1 + \sqrt{\varepsilon_2}\cos\theta_2} \qquad \text{(From eqn.(5.36))}$$

For parallel polarization we also have the reflection coefficient as,

$$r = \frac{E_r}{E_i} = \frac{\sqrt{\varepsilon_2}\cos\theta_1 - \sqrt{\varepsilon_1}\cos\theta_2}{\sqrt{\varepsilon_2}\cos\theta_1 + \sqrt{\varepsilon_1}\cos\theta_2} \qquad \text{(From eqn(5.40))}$$

For the total internal reflection for perpendicular polarization, we have from eqn.(5.36)

$$r = \frac{E_r}{E_i} = \frac{\sqrt{\varepsilon_1}\cos\theta_1 - \sqrt{\varepsilon_2}\left[-j.\frac{\sqrt{\varepsilon_1}}{\sqrt{\varepsilon_2}}.\sqrt{\sin^2\theta_1 - \frac{\varepsilon_2}{\varepsilon_1}}\right]}{\sqrt{\varepsilon_1}\cos\theta_1 + \sqrt{\varepsilon_2}.\left[-j.\frac{\sqrt{\varepsilon_1}}{\sqrt{\varepsilon_2}}.\sqrt{\sin^2\theta_1 - \frac{\varepsilon_2}{\varepsilon_1}}\right]} \qquad \text{(using eqn.(5.44))}$$

$$= \frac{\sqrt{\varepsilon_1}\left[\cos\theta_1 + j.\sqrt{\sin^2\theta_1 - \frac{\varepsilon_2}{\varepsilon_1}}\right]}{\sqrt{\varepsilon_1}\left[\cos\theta_1 - j.\sqrt{\sin^2\theta_1 - \frac{\varepsilon_2}{\varepsilon_1}}\right]} \qquad ...(5.45)$$

And for parallel polarization, the reflection coefficient is

$$r = \frac{E_r}{E_i} = \frac{\sqrt{\varepsilon_2}\cos\theta_1 - \sqrt{\varepsilon_1}\cos\theta_2}{\sqrt{\varepsilon_2}\cos\theta_1 + \sqrt{\varepsilon_1}\cos\theta_2} \qquad \text{(using eqn.(5.40))}$$

$$= \frac{\sqrt{\varepsilon_2}\cos\theta_1 - \sqrt{\varepsilon_1}\left[-j.\sqrt{\frac{\varepsilon_1}{\varepsilon_2}}.\sqrt{\sin^2\theta_1 - \frac{\varepsilon_2}{\varepsilon_1}}\right]}{\sqrt{\varepsilon_2}\cos\theta_1 + \sqrt{\varepsilon_1}\left[-j.\sqrt{\frac{\varepsilon_1}{\varepsilon_2}}.\sqrt{\sin^2\theta_1 - \frac{\varepsilon_2}{\varepsilon_1}}\right]} \qquad \text{(using eqn.(5.44))}$$

$$= \frac{\dfrac{\left(\varepsilon_2\cos\theta_1 + j\varepsilon_1.\sqrt{\sin^2\theta_1 - \frac{\varepsilon_2}{\varepsilon_1}}\right)}{\sqrt{\varepsilon_2}}}{\dfrac{\left(\varepsilon_2\cos\theta_1 - j\varepsilon_1.\sqrt{\sin^2\theta_1 - \frac{\varepsilon_2}{\varepsilon_1}}\right)}{\sqrt{\varepsilon_2}}}$$

$$= \frac{\left(\left\{\frac{\varepsilon_2}{\varepsilon_1}\right\}\cos\theta_1 + j\sqrt{\sin^2\theta_1 - \frac{\varepsilon_2}{\varepsilon_1}}\right)}{\left(\left\{\frac{\varepsilon_2}{\varepsilon_1}\right\}\cos\theta_1 - j\sqrt{\sin^2\theta_1 - \frac{\varepsilon_2}{\varepsilon_1}}\right)} \qquad ...(5.46)$$

Total internal reflection is widely used in optics to make binocular. There glass prisms are employed to shorten the length of the instrument to make it portable.

5.6 Reflection at the Surface of a Conducting Medium

We have here a medium with constants '$\varepsilon_1, \mu_1, \sigma_1$', where the uniform plane wave is traveling and it then incident normally upon an infinitely deep second medium having constants '$\varepsilon_2, \mu_2, \sigma_2$'. At the interface between the two mediums, the continuity of the tangential component of the fields gives

$$E_i + E_r = E_t \qquad ...(5.47a)$$

And

$$H_i + H_r = H_t \qquad ...(5.47b)$$

However, we know,

$$\eta_1 = \frac{E_i}{H_i}, \quad \eta_1 = -\frac{E_r}{H_r} \quad \text{and} \quad \eta_2 = \frac{E_t}{H_t}$$

Hence, from eqn.(5.47a) $E_r - E_t = -E_i$ ...(5.48a)

Also from eqn.(5.47b) $H_r - H_t = -H_i$

$$\Rightarrow -\frac{E_r}{\eta_1} - \frac{E_t}{\eta_2} = -\frac{E_i}{\eta_1} \quad ...(5.48b)$$

On solving eqns.(5.48a) and 5.48b),

$$E_r\left[\frac{1}{\eta_1} + \frac{1}{\eta_2}\right] = E_i\left[\frac{1}{\eta_1} - \frac{1}{\eta_2}\right]$$

$$\Rightarrow \frac{E_r}{E_i} = \frac{(\eta_2 - \eta_1)/\eta_1\eta_2}{(\eta_2 + \eta_1)/\eta_1\eta_2} = \frac{(\eta_2 - \eta_1)}{(\eta_2 + \eta_1)} \quad ...(5.49)$$

Similarly, $$\frac{E_t}{E_i} = \frac{2\eta_2}{(\eta_2 + \eta_1)} \quad ...(5.50)$$

For magnetic field, we can have from eqn.(5.48a),

$$E_r - E_t = -E_i$$

$$\Rightarrow -\eta_1 H_r - \eta_2 H_t = -\eta_1 H_i$$

$$\Rightarrow \eta_1 H_r + \eta_2 H_t = \eta_1 H_i \quad ...(5.51a)$$

Also from eqn.(5.48b),

$$H_r - H_t = -H_i \quad ...(5.51b)$$

Adding eqns.(5.51a) and (5.51b) and multiplying by 'η_2' we have,

$$(\eta_1 H_r + \eta_2 H_t) + (\eta_2 H_r - \eta_2 H_t) = \eta_1 H_i - \eta_2 H_i$$

$$\Rightarrow \frac{H_r}{H_i} = \frac{\eta_1 - \eta_2}{\eta_1 + \eta_2} \quad ...(5.52)$$

Similarly, $$\frac{H_t}{H_i} = \frac{2\eta_1}{\eta_1 + \eta_2} \quad ...(5.53)$$

Example

For Copper with following specifications at $f = 1MHz$

$$\mu_1 = \mu_o, \varepsilon_1 = \varepsilon_o, \sigma_1 = 0$$

$\mu_2 = \mu_0, \varepsilon_2 = \varepsilon_0, \sigma_2 = 5.8\times10^7$ mhos/m and $\eta_1 = \sqrt{\frac{\mu_o}{\varepsilon_o}} = 377\Omega$

Hence, characteristic impedance for medium-2 is

$$\eta_2 = \sqrt{\frac{j\omega\mu_2}{\sigma_2 + j\omega\varepsilon_2}} = \sqrt{\frac{j.2\pi\times10^6\times4\pi\times10^{-7}}{5.8\times10^7 + j.2\pi\times10^6\times8.854\times10^{-12}}} = 0.000369.\angle45^o\,\Omega$$

Then the ratio of reflected to incident electric field strengths from eqn.(5.49),

$$r = \frac{E_r}{E_i} = \frac{\eta_2 - \eta_1}{\eta_2 + \eta_1}$$

$$= \frac{3.69\times10^{-4}\angle45^o - 377}{3.69\times10^{-4}\angle45^o + 377} = -0.9999986\angle-0.000079^o = -\frac{H_r}{H_i}$$

The values of these reflection coefficients for copper for 'E' and 'H' are very close to '-1' and '+1' respectively, which are the values for a perfect reflector and are negligible. For most practical purposes copper can be considered a perfect reflector of radio waves.

The relative strengths of the transmitted fields for this case are

$$\frac{E_t}{E_i} = \frac{2\times3.69\times10^{-4}\angle45^o}{3.69\times10^{-4}\angle45^o + 377}$$

$$= 0.00000196\angle45^o \approx \left(2\times10^{-6}\right)\angle45^o$$

And,
$$\frac{H_t}{H_i} = \frac{2\times377}{377 + 3.69\times10^{-4}\angle45^o}$$

$$= 1.9999986\angle-0.00004^o \approx 2\angle-0.00004^o$$

So, the electric field strength just inside the metal is nearly 2×10^{-6} times of that of the initial wave. The magnetic field strength just inside the metal is approximately twice the magnetic field strength of the initial wave.

5.7 Surface Impedance

For a conductor at high frequency the current is confined almost entirely to very thin sheet at its surface, *i.e.*, at the 'skin' of the metal. This movement of e.m.wave through the metal surface is controlled by 'surface impedance' and can be defined as

$$Z_s = \frac{E_{\tan}}{J_{sh}} \qquad ...(5.54)$$

Here, '$E_{\tan}$' is electric field strength parallel to and at the surface of the conductor, and, 'J_{sh}' is the linear current density that flows due to' $E_{\tan}$'. It also represents the total conduction current flowing in the thin sheet per meter width. We have assumed a flat plate conductor with its surface at '$y = 0$' plane as shown in Fig.5.7a, the current distribution along Y-direction is given by

$$J = J_o.e^{-\gamma y}$$

Here, 'J_o' is current density at the surface, 'γ' is the rate at which 'J' is decaying from the surface of the conductor and is the propagation constant. Normally the thickness of the conductor is much larger than the skin depth. So there is no possibility of any reflection from the back surface of the conductor. The current density variation along YZ-plane is shown in Fig.5.7b.

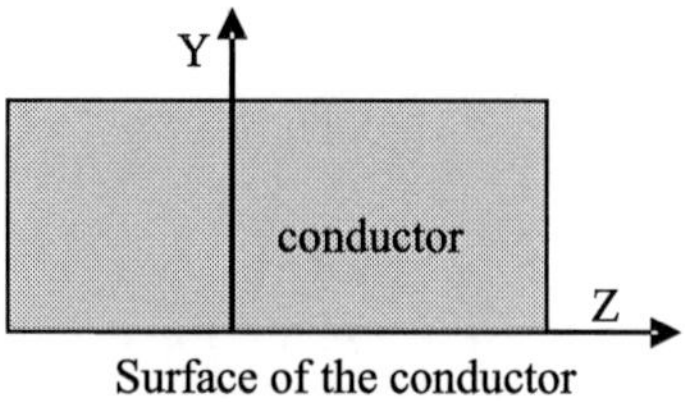

Fig. 5.7 (*a*) A conductor surface.

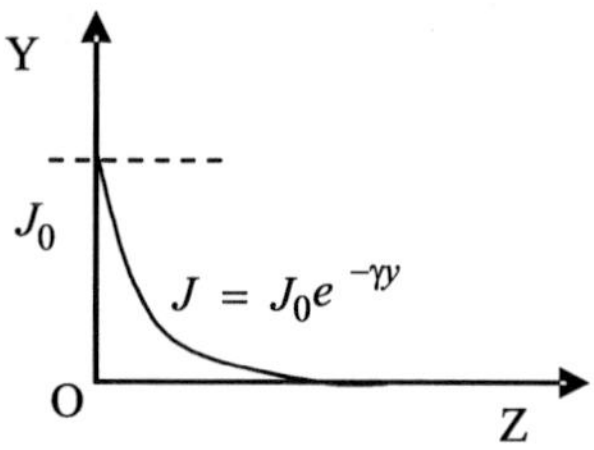

Fig. 5.7 (*b*) Current density variation along YZ-plane.

The total conduction current per meter width, *i.e.*, the linear current density is given by

$$J_{sh} = \int_0^\infty J.dy$$

$$= J_0.\int_0^\infty e^{-\gamma y}.dy = -\frac{J_o}{\gamma}[0-1]$$

$$\Rightarrow J_{sh} = \frac{J_0}{\gamma} \qquad ...(5.55)$$

'J_0' is the current density at the surface, hence,

$$J_0 = \sigma E_{tan} \qquad ...(5.56)$$

From eqn.(5.54),

$$Z_s = \frac{E_{tan}}{J_s} = \frac{E_{tan}}{J_0/\gamma}$$

$$= \left(\frac{\gamma}{J_0}\right)E_{tan} = \frac{\gamma.E_{tan}}{\sigma E_{tan}} \qquad \text{(from eqn.(5.56))}$$

$$\Rightarrow Z_s = \frac{\gamma}{\sigma} \qquad ...(5.57)$$

The propagation constant for conducting medium is given by

$$\gamma = \sqrt{j\omega\mu(\sigma + j\omega\varepsilon)} \approx \sqrt{j\omega\mu\sigma} \quad \text{(as for conductor, } \sigma \rangle\rangle \omega\varepsilon\text{)} \qquad ...(5.58)$$

Hence from eqns.(5.57) and (5.58),

$$Z_s = \frac{\sqrt{j\omega\sigma\mu}}{\sigma} = \sqrt{\frac{j\omega\mu}{\sigma}} = \eta \qquad ...(5.59)$$

So for good conductors, the surface impedance of a plane conductor (much thicker than the skin depth) is just equal to the characteristic impedance of the conductor. When the thickness of it is not sufficient, reflection of the wave occurs at the back surface of the conductor.

5.7.1. Surface Impedance of Good Conductor: For material with $\sigma \rangle\rangle \omega\varepsilon$ and very thick conductor comparatively much thicker than the skin depth we have,

$$Z_s \approx \sqrt{\frac{j\omega\mu}{\sigma}} = \sqrt{\frac{\omega\mu}{\sigma}} \angle 45^0$$

$$= \sqrt{\frac{\omega\mu}{\sigma}} \left[\cos 45^0 + j \sin 45^0 \right]$$

$$= \sqrt{\frac{\omega\mu}{\sigma}} \left[\frac{1}{\sqrt{2}} + j \frac{1}{\sqrt{2}} \right] \qquad ...(5.60)$$

But, $\quad Z_S = R_S + jX_S$

The surface resistance is then,

$$R_S = \sqrt{\frac{\omega\mu}{2\sigma}} \qquad ...(5.61)$$

The surface reactance has the same magnitude as 'R$_s$' at all frequencies as

$$X_s = \sqrt{\frac{\mu\omega}{2\sigma}} \qquad ...(5.62)$$

The surface resistance 'R$_s$' is the high frequency or skin effect resistance per unit length of a flat conductor of unit width.

The penetration or skin depth for a conductor from eqn.(4.96) is given by

$$\delta = \sqrt{\frac{2}{\omega\mu\sigma}} \qquad ...(5.63)$$

Hence,

$$R_S = \sqrt{\frac{\omega\mu}{2\sigma}} = \sqrt{\frac{\omega\mu\sigma}{2\sigma^2}}$$

$$= \sqrt{\frac{\omega\mu\sigma}{2}} \Big/ \sigma = \frac{1}{\sigma\delta} \qquad \left(\text{as } \delta = \sqrt{\frac{2}{\omega\sigma\mu}}\right) \qquad (5.64)$$

The surface resistance of a flat conductor at any frequency is thus related to the dc resistance of a thickness of skin depth 'δ' of the same conductor. This means that the conductor having a thickness very much greater than 'δ' and having the exponential current distribution throughout its depth, has the same resistance as would a thickness 'δ' of the conductor with the current distributed uniformly throughout this thickness. So, the power loss per unit area of the plane conductor will be given by

$$J_{S_{eff}}{}^2 R_s$$

Here '$J_{S_{eff}}$' is the average value of linear current density.

❑❑❑

CHAPTER 6

TRANSMISSION LINE

6.1 Transmission Line Theory

A device with minimum energy losses, used for the transfer of radio frequency energy to some radiator is called transmission line. Transmission lines are used to transfer the energy or signal or power from the transmitter to the receiver. The distance between them is generally appreciable.

The most usual forms of transmission line are as follows.

(*i*) A pair of conducting lines in the form of parallel wires (parallel wire lines),

(*ii*) A pair of concentric tubular conductor *i.e.*, coaxial line.

A transmission line consists of a conductor and a return conductor. A hundred mile wire used to bring power from a door to a city, parallel wire lines connecting telephones and the coaxial lines from the transmitter to TV antenna, etc. are the various examples of the transmission lines. In radio broad casting, transmission line are used to transfer radio frequency (R.F) power from the transmission to the radiating antenna without any power loss. Here, shall restrict our discussion to the RF transmission line.

Knowledge of the values of electric current parameters associated with these forms of line is necessary to understand for designing. The resistance, R, arises due to the finite resistivity of the material of the conductor and it causes power loss in them as the current flows. The magnetic flux which links the currents responsible for the leakage flux and this gives rise to inductance, L. Equal and opposite current flows in thin slices of the conductor and these are nothing but two moving charges. These charges and potential difference between the slices account for the capacitance, C. If the dielectric material is placed between the conductors, there is a leakage conductance, G between the conductors. In a smooth line these parameters are uniformly distributed over the length of the line.

The electric field remains associated with potential difference between the two conductors. As the electric and magnetic fields are at right angle to each other, the plane containing both the fields is at right angle to the axis of the conductor. Thus, the electric energy flows at right angle to the plane containing the electric and magnetic vectors. This type of transmission is technically known as transverse electric and magnetic mode (TEM). A simplest transmission line as a pair of parallel wires insulated from each other is shown in Fig.6.1(a).

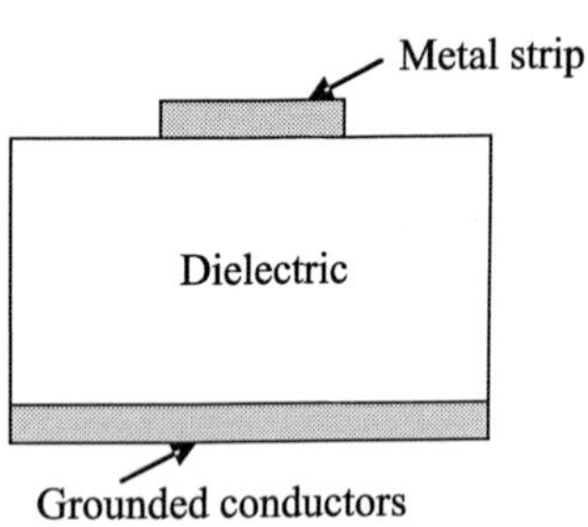

Fig. 6.1 (*a*) An ordinary transmission line.

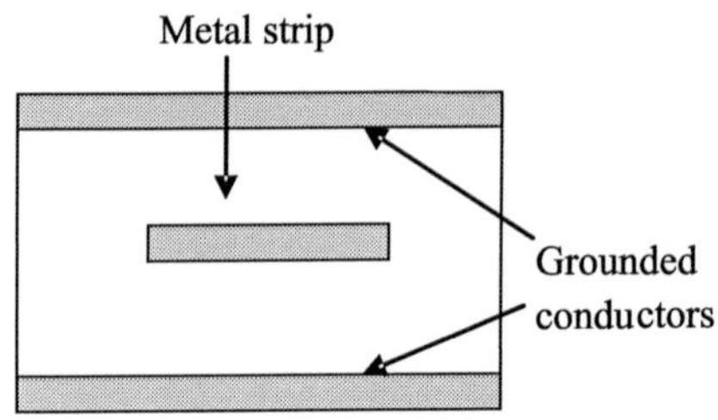

Fig. 6.1 (*b*) A coaxial transmission line.

Two wire line, coaxial line, strip line etc are the examples of transmission line and is shown in Fig.6.1(b). This transfer of signal from transmitter to receiver through transmission line is called wire line connection. It supports TEM mode of propagation. Here as the input voltage is applied at the input terminals, it takes a finite time for the voltage and current to travel the length of the transmission line as e.m wave has a finite velocity in space. Voltage and current traveling along are accompanied by an e.m wave in space between conductors and transmission line problems are analyzed in terms of this field rather in terms of voltage and current. The transmission line can thus be regarded as means of guiding the field so that it is confined near the line rather than spreading in space spherically. As the wave is confined, it does not suffer inverse square law decrease of power density with distance unlike waves in free space.

6.2 Transmission Line as a Distributed Circuit

The equivalent circuit of a transmission line is shown in Fig.6.2.

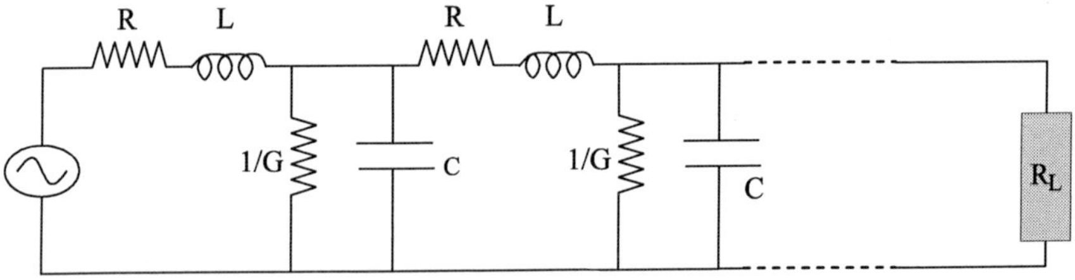

Fig. 6.2 Equivalent circuit of a transmission line.

Here, inductance, resistance, conductance and capacitance are distributed uniformly along the entire length 'l' of the transmission line, so it is said to be a uniform transmission line with each conductor of the line has a certain length and diameter. We thus consider 'L' is inductance per unit length of the conductor (H/m), 'C' is capacitance between the conductors per unit length (F/m), 'R' is resistance of conductor per unit length (Ω/m) and 'G' is shunt or leakage conductance per unit length (mhos /m). The analysis based on this model is known as 'Distributed Parameter' model of transmission line.

6.2.1. At Radiofrequencies: Here as frequency 'ω' is very large, so the inductive reactance (ωL) is much larger than the 'R', *i.e.*, $\omega L >> R$. Also, the capacitance susceptance (ωC) is larger to the shunt conductance 'G', *i.e.*, $\omega C >> G$. Here we can write the simplified equivalent circuit representation of a transmission line.

We consider two ideal cases for any transmission line as

(*i*) Infinite length ($l \to \infty$) of it, and,

(*ii*) Lossless transmission line (*i.e.*, $R = 0, G = \infty$)

These parameters 'R,L,C and G' are referred to primary constants of the transmission line.

6.3 Basic Transmission Line Equations

A transmission line can be analyzed either by Maxwell's equation or by using the distributed circuit parameter theory. They have following advantages or disadvantages as in the followings.

Distributed Parameter Theory	Field Theory
1. It involves only one space variable along with time variables.	1. It uses the three space variables along with the time variable.
2. So we can use one dimensional differential equations.	2. We use here three dimensional equation.

6.3.1. Derivation of Transmission Line Equation: A voltage drop occurs across each series increment of line, so the voltage applied to each increment of shunt admittance is a variable and thus the shunted current is variable along the line. Hence the line current around the loop is not a constant, but varies point to point along the line. Differential circuit equation that describes the action can be written for the steady state from which general circuit equation can be obtained.

An a.c source is connected at the sending end of a smooth transmission line of length 'l' and load impedance 'Z_R'is connected at the other end *i.e.*, the receiving end. The Fig.6.3(a) shows a transmission line circuit. Let a thin slice of the line having a very short length 'Δx' and taken at a distance 'x' measured from the receiving end be enlarged and is shown in Fig.6.3(b). The distributed parameters of 'Δx' is expanded in Fig.6.3(b).

Let, R is the resistance in ohm per unit length of the line,

L is the series inductance in henry per unit length of the line,

C is the capacitance between two conductor in farad per unit length of the line,

G is the shunt leakage conductance between two conductors in mhos per unit length of the line.

Hence,

$Z = R + j\omega L$; This is series impedance in ohm per unit length of the line, and,

$Y = G + j\omega C$; This is shunt admittance in mho per unit length of the line.

'I' and 'V' are the current and voltage at any point of the line respectively.

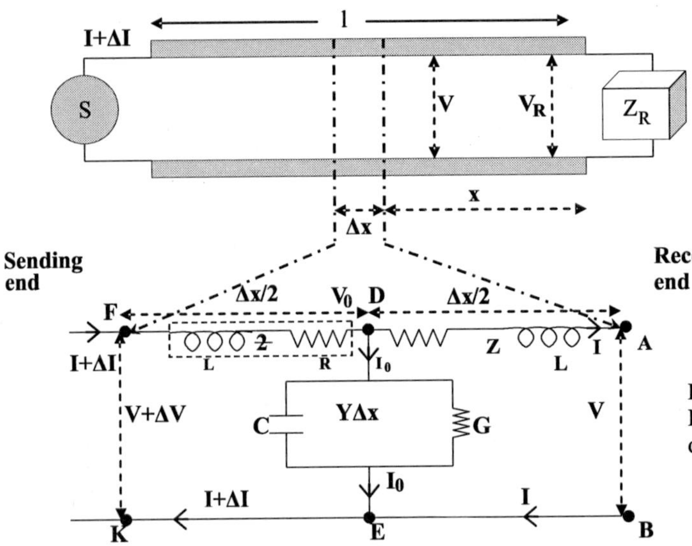

Fig. 6.3(*a*). A transmission line

Fig. 6.3 (b). Expanded form of elemental line

Fig. 6.3 Equivalent circuit diagram of elemental segment of the transmission line.

From Fig.6.3(b), the voltage at 'DE' is given by

$$V_o = V + \frac{1}{2} Z.\Delta x.I \qquad ...(6.1)$$

and current there is given by

$$I_o = V_o Y\Delta x = (V + \frac{1}{2} Z\Delta x.I)Y\Delta x = VY\Delta x + \frac{1}{2} ZYI(\Delta x)^2 \qquad ...(6.2)$$

Now, from Fig.6.3(b) observed at 'F' we have,

$$I + \Delta I = I_o + I$$

$$\Rightarrow \Delta I = I_o = VY\Delta x + \frac{1}{2} ZYI(\Delta x)^2 \quad \text{(using eqn.(6.2))} \qquad ...(6.3)$$

Also, from Fig.6.3(b) voltage at 'FK' is given by

$$V+\Delta V=V_o+(I+\Delta I)(\frac{1}{2}Z\Delta x)$$

$$=V+\frac{1}{2}Z\Delta x.I+\left[VY\Delta x+I\left(\frac{1}{2}ZY\left(\Delta x\right)^2+1\right)\right]\frac{1}{2}Z\Delta x \quad \text{(from eqn.(6.3))}$$

$$=V+\frac{1}{2}Z\Delta xI+\frac{1}{2}VY(\Delta x)^2+\frac{1}{4}Z^2YI(\Delta x)^3+\frac{1}{2}Z\Delta xI$$

$$\Rightarrow \Delta V=Z\Delta x.I+\frac{1}{2}VY(\Delta x)^2+\frac{1}{4}Z^2YI(\Delta x)^3 \qquad ...(6.4)$$

Now as $\Delta x\rightarrow 0$, $(\Delta x)^2$ and $(\Delta x)^3$ can be neglected,
Hence from eqn.(6.3),

$$\therefore \frac{\Delta I}{\Delta x}=VY \qquad ...(6.5)$$

and, from eqn.(6.4),

$$\frac{\Delta V}{\Delta x}=ZI \qquad ...(6.6)$$

So, $$\frac{\partial I}{\partial x}=VY;\frac{\partial V}{\partial x}=ZI \qquad ...(6.7)$$

These two are the transmission line equations. These are first order differential equation but they are not homogeneous, since equations contain both 'V' and 'I' as a function of 'x' of the parameters Z and Y.

Now, $$\frac{\partial^2 V}{\partial x^2}=Z\frac{\partial I}{\partial x}=ZVY=\gamma^2 V \qquad ...(6.8)$$

Also, $$\frac{\partial^2 I}{\partial x^2}=Y\frac{\partial V}{\partial x}=YZI=\gamma^2 I \qquad ...(6.9)$$

where $\gamma^2=ZY$.

So, $$\gamma=\sqrt{ZY}=\sqrt{(R+j\omega L)(G+j\omega C)}=\alpha+j\beta\text{, let,} \qquad ...(6.10)$$

γ is known as propagation constant, α is attenuation constant and β is phase shift constant.

This is a complex constant for a given frequency and is known as the propagation constant.

These eqns.(6.8) and (6.9) are the transmission line equations.

6.3.2. Solution of Transmission Line Equations: The solution of voltage equation (eqn.(6.8)) is in exponential form and is given by

$$V = Ae^{\gamma x} + Be^{-\gamma x} \qquad ...(6.11)$$

The two constants A and B can be evaluated by the boundary conditions.

Now, from eqn.(6.6), $I = \frac{1}{Z}.\frac{dV}{dx}$

$$= \frac{\gamma}{Z}.\left[Ae^{\gamma x} - Be^{-\gamma x}\right] = \frac{\sqrt{ZY}}{Z}.\left[Ae^{\gamma x} - Be^{-xz}\right]$$

$$= \sqrt{\frac{Y}{Z}}.\left[Ae^{\gamma x} - Be^{-\gamma x}\right] = \frac{1}{Z_0}\left[Ae^{\gamma x} - Be^{-\gamma x}\right] = \frac{A}{Z_0}e^{\gamma x} - \frac{B}{Z_0}e^{-\gamma x} \qquad ...(6.12)$$

Here, $Z_0 = \sqrt{\frac{Z}{Y}} = \sqrt{\frac{R + j\omega L}{G + j\omega C}}$ and is known as the Characteristic Impedance of the line.

Also, $Z_0 = R_0 + jX_0$, ...(6.13)

and R_0, X_0 are the resistive and reactive parts of the impedance.

The boundary condition is given by,

At $x = 0$, *i.e.*, at the receiving end, $V = V_R, I = I_R$.

Hence, from eqn.(6.11), $V_R = A + B$ ...(6.14)

Also, from eqn.(6.12), $I_R = \frac{1}{Z_0}[A - B]$ ...(6.15)

On solving, $A = \frac{V_R + I_R Z_0}{2}; B = \frac{V_R - I_R Z_0}{2}$ ...(6.16)

Hence using eqns.(6.11) and (6.16), we have,

$$V = \left[\frac{V_R + I_R Z_0}{2}\right]e^{\gamma x} + \left[\frac{V_R - I_R Z_0}{2}\right]e^{-\gamma x}$$

$$= \left[\frac{V_R + \left(\frac{V_R}{Z_R}\right)Z_0}{2}\right]e^{\gamma x} + \left[\frac{V_R - \left(\frac{V_R}{Z_R}\right)Z_0}{2}\right]e^{-\gamma x} \quad \left[\because V_R = I_R Z_R \Rightarrow I_R = \left(\frac{V_R}{Z_R}\right)\right]$$

$$\Rightarrow V = V_R\left[\frac{Z_R + Z_0}{2Z_R}\right]e^{\gamma x} + V_R\left[\frac{Z_R - Z_0}{2Z_R}\right]e^{-\gamma x} \qquad ...(6.17)$$

$$\Rightarrow V = V_R^{+}e^{\gamma x} + V_R^{-}e^{-\gamma x} \qquad ...(6.18)$$

Here, $$V_R^+ = \left[\frac{Z_R + Z_0}{2Z_R}\right] V_R \text{ and } V_R^- = \left[\frac{Z_R - Z_0}{2Z_R}\right] V_R \quad ...(6.19)$$

Similarly, using eqn.(6.15) and the values of A and B, we have,

$$I = I_R^+ e^{\gamma x} - I_R^- e^{-\gamma x} \quad ...(6.20)$$

Here, $$I_R^+ = \left[\frac{Z_R + Z_0}{2Z_0}\right] I_R \text{ and } I_R^- = \left[\frac{Z_R - Z_0}{2Z_0}\right] I_R \quad ...(6.21)$$

It may be observed that for the most general case in which Z_R is not equal to Z_0, each equation consists of two terms, one of which varies exponentially with '$+x$'. A wave travels from the sending end to the receiving end of the line, there is a decrease in amplitude as it approaches the receiving end. In a direction back along this wave from the receiving end, the amplitude of the wave would increase as intensity of the source increases, so that the wave that travels from the sending end to the receiving end can be identified as the component varying with '$e^{-\gamma x}$'. This wave of voltage or current is known as the incident wave.

Hence the 2nd term, varying with '$e^{-\gamma x}$'must represent a wave of voltage or current progressing from the receiving end towards the sending end, and decreasing in amplitude with increased distance from the load. Such a wave of voltage or current is called the reflected wave.

6.4 Line Terminated in its Characteristic Impedance

Here, the situation is represented in Fig.6.4 (a) and so $Z_R = Z_o$.

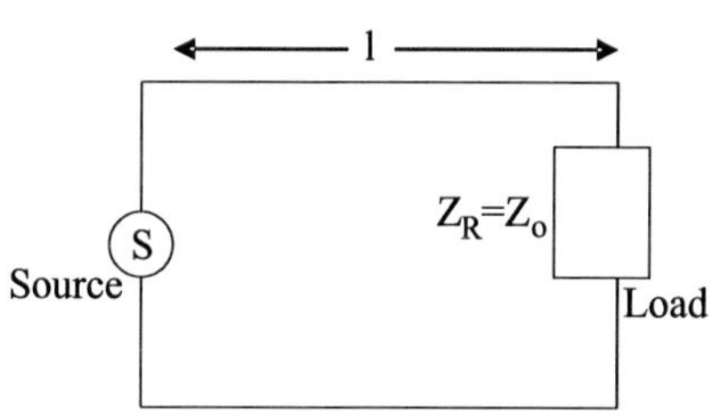

Fig. 6.4 (*a*) A transmission line of length 'l'.

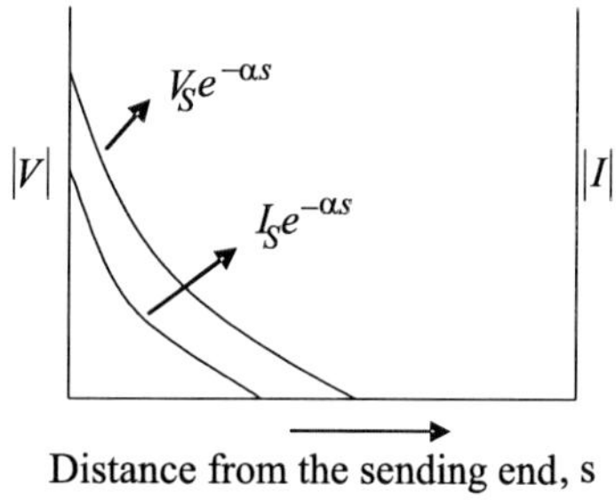

Fig. 6.4 (*b*) Variation of voltage or current with distance.

Then we have from eqns.(6.18) and (6.19),

$$V = V_R . e^{\gamma x} \quad ...(6.22)$$

And of eqns.(6.20) and (6.21),

$$I = \frac{V_R}{Z_o}.e^{\gamma x} \qquad ...(6.23)$$

The impedance is then given by

$$Z = \frac{V}{I} = Z_o$$

Now at source end, $x = l$, we have, $V = V_S; I = I_S$

So, using eqns.(6.22) and (6.23),

$$V_S = V_R e^{\gamma l} \Rightarrow V_R = V_S e^{-\gamma l}$$

$$I_S = \frac{V_R}{Z_o} e^{\gamma l} \Rightarrow V_R = Z_o.I_S.e^{-\gamma l}$$

So, from eqn.(6.22), we have,

$$V = V_R e^{\gamma x} = V_S e^{\gamma(x-l)} = V_S.e^{-\gamma s} \qquad ...(6.24)$$

Here, $s = l - x$

Also, from eqn.(6.23),

$$I = \frac{V_R}{Z_o} e^{\gamma x} = I_S.e^{-\gamma(l-x)} = I_S.e^{-\gamma(x-l)} = I_S.e^{-\gamma s} \qquad ...(6.25)$$

Hence using eqn.(24) and eqn.(25) with $\gamma = \alpha + j\beta$ (from eqn.(6.10)), we have,

$$V = V_S.e^{-\alpha s}.e^{-j\beta s}; \qquad I = I_S.e^{-\alpha s}.e^{-j\beta s} \qquad ...(6.26)$$

Thus propagation takes place along the line in wave motion, the amplitude of voltage or current being constantly reduced due to attenuation factor '$e^{-\alpha s}$', the phase of the voltage or current constantly changing because of the phase factor '$e^{-j\beta s}$'. This is shown in Fig.6.4(b).

The power is given by

$$P = \frac{1}{2}|V||I| = \frac{1}{2}V_S I_S e^{-2\alpha s} = \frac{1}{2}\frac{V_S^2}{Z_o} e^{-2\alpha s} \qquad ...(6.27)$$

So the rate of change of power with distance is given by

$$p_L = \frac{dP}{ds} = -2\alpha \times \frac{1}{2}\frac{V_S^2}{Z_o} e^{-2\alpha s} = -2\alpha P \qquad \text{(using eqn.(6.27))}$$

$$\Rightarrow \alpha = -\frac{p_L}{2P} \qquad ...(6.28)$$

6.5 Input Impedance (Hyperbolic Function Solution) of Transmission Line

We have from eqn.(6.12) and the values of A and B in eqn.(6.16),

$$I = \frac{V_R}{Z_o}.\frac{Z_R + Z_o}{2Z_R}.e^{\gamma x} - \frac{V_R}{Z_o}.\frac{Z_R - Z_o}{2Z_R}.e^{-\gamma x} \qquad ...(6.29)$$

And from eqn.(6.17),

$$V = V_R.\frac{Z_R + Z_o}{2Z_R}.e^{\gamma x} + V_R.\frac{Z_R - Z_o}{2Z_R}.e^{-\gamma x}$$

$$= \frac{V_R}{2}\left(e^{\gamma x} + e^{-\gamma x}\right).+\frac{V_R}{2}.\frac{Z_o}{Z_R}.\left(e^{\gamma x} - e^{-\gamma x}\right)$$

$$= V_R \cosh \gamma x + I_R.Z_o.\sinh \gamma x \qquad ...(6.30)$$

Also, from eqn.(6.29),

$$I = \frac{V_R}{2Z_o}.\left(e^{\gamma x} + e^{-\gamma x}\right) + \frac{V_R}{2Z_R}\left(e^{\gamma x} + e^{-\gamma x}\right)$$

$$= \frac{V_R}{Z_o}.\sinh \gamma x + I_R \cosh \gamma x \qquad ...(6.31)$$

Now the input impedance of the line is

$$Z = \frac{V}{I} = \frac{V_R \cosh \gamma x + I_R Z_o \sinh \gamma x}{I_R \cosh \gamma x + \frac{V_R}{Z_o} \sinh \gamma x}$$

$$= \frac{Z_R \cosh \gamma x + Z_o \sinh \gamma x}{\cosh \gamma x + \frac{Z_R}{Z_o} \sinh \gamma x}$$

$$= Z_o \frac{Z_R \cosh \gamma x + Z_o \sinh \gamma x}{Z_o \cosh \gamma x + Z_R \sinh \gamma x} \qquad ...(6.32)$$

6.5.1. Short Circuited Line: Here, $Z_R = 0$ and hence using eqn.(6.32), we have,

$$Z = Z_{SC} = Z_o.\frac{\sinh \gamma x}{\cosh \gamma x} = Z_o \tanh \gamma x \qquad ...(6.33)$$

The variation of current or voltage along the short circuited line is shown in Fig.6.5.

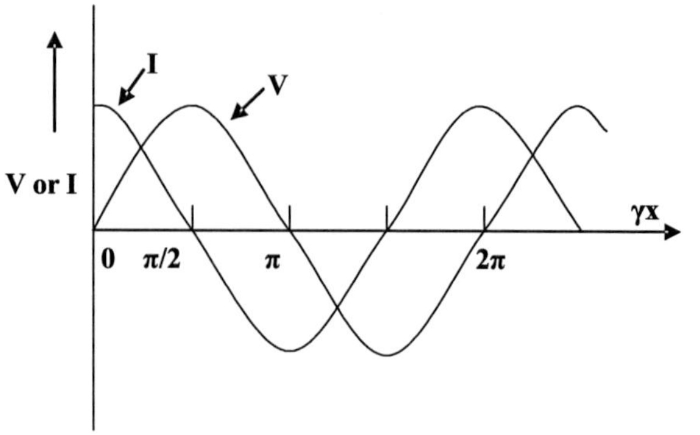

Fig. 6.5 Variation of current or voltage along a short circuited line.

6.5.2. Open Circuit Line: Here, $Z_R = \infty$, So again from eqn.(6.32), we get,

$$Z = Z_{OC} = \underset{Z_R \to \infty}{Lt} Z_o . \frac{\cosh \gamma x + \frac{Z_o}{Z_R} \sinh \gamma x}{\frac{Z_o}{Z_R} \cosh \gamma x + \sinh \gamma x}$$

$$= Z_o . \coth \gamma x \qquad ...(6.34)$$

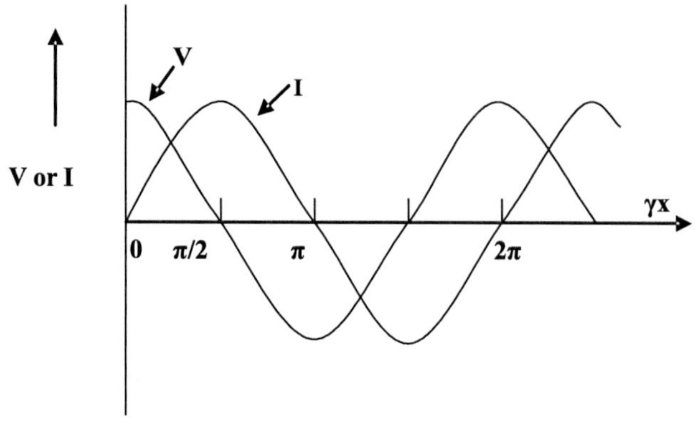

Fig. 6.6 Variation of current or voltage along a open circuited line.

The variation of current or voltage along the open circuited line is shown in Fig. 6.6.

The value of reactance is a repetitive function of length with a period of '$x = \lambda/2$' as a result of the presence of 'tangent' term. For the first quarter wavelength, a short circuited line acts as an inductance, whereas, an open circuited line appears as a capacitance. These reactances reverse each quarter wavelength. The variations of 'reactance' with 'γx' for the short and open circuited lines are shown in Figs.6.7 and 6.8 respectively.

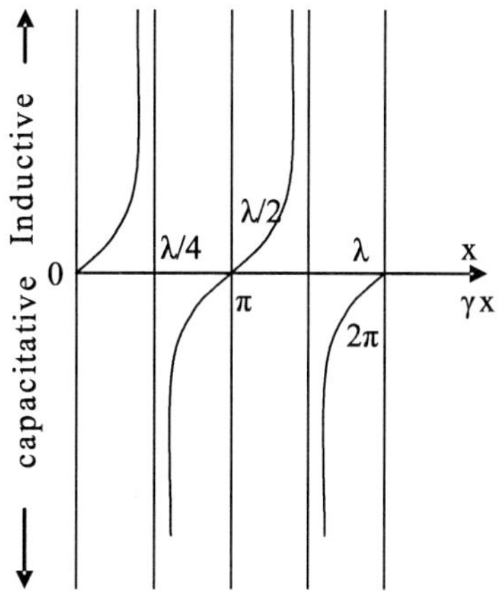

Fig. 6.7 Short circuited loss-less line.

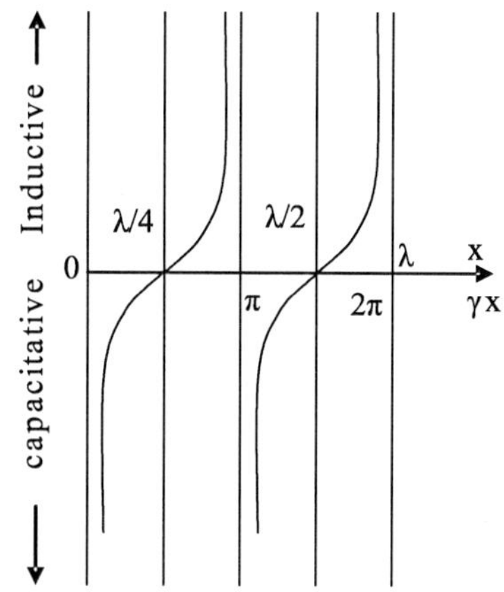

Fig. 6.8 Open circuited loss-less line.

So, from eqns.(6.33) and (6.34),

$$Z_{SC}.Z_{OC} = Z_0^2 \Rightarrow Z_o = \sqrt{Z_{OC}.Z_{SC}} \quad ..(6.35)$$

Also,

$$\frac{Z_{SC}}{Z_{OC}} = \tan^2 h\gamma x$$

$$\Rightarrow \tanh \gamma x = \sqrt{\frac{Z_{SC}}{Z_{OC}}} \Rightarrow \gamma x = \tanh^{-1}\sqrt{\frac{Z_{SC}}{Z_{OC}}}$$

$$\therefore \gamma = \frac{1}{x}\tanh^{-1}\sqrt{\frac{Z_{SC}}{Z_{OC}}} \quad ...(6.36)$$

This is the relationship between 'γ' with short and open circuited line impedances.

6.6 Characteristic Impedance (Z_o)

Characteristic impedance 'Z_o' of the transmission line is defined as the ratio of traveling voltage wave to the current wave at any point on the line. This is the value of input impedance under certain standard condition and is taken as the reference. This is also called as surge impedance.

$$Z_o = \sqrt{\frac{R + j\omega L}{G + j\omega C}}$$

Special Cases

6.6.1. Loss Less Line: No Resistance and No Leakage Through Dielectric

Here, $R = 0$ and $\frac{1}{G} \to \infty \Rightarrow G \to 0$

So, $Z_o = \sqrt{\frac{R + j\omega L}{G + j\omega C}} \approx \sqrt{\frac{L}{C}}$

As $Z_o = R_o + iX_o, R_o$ is the resistive part and X_o is the reactive part of the impedance.

Here, $R_o = \sqrt{\frac{L}{C}}$ and $X_o = 0$

Hence, here 'Z_o' is purely resistive.

6.6.2. Distortion Less Line

Here, $\frac{R}{L} = \frac{G}{C}$

Hence, $Z_o = \sqrt{\frac{R + j\omega L}{G + j\omega C}} = \sqrt{\frac{R\left(1 + j\omega \frac{L}{R}\right)}{G\left(1 + j\omega \frac{C}{G}\right)}} = \sqrt{\frac{R}{G} \cdot \frac{1 + j\omega \frac{C}{G}}{1 + j\omega \frac{C}{G}}}$ (using $\frac{R}{L} = \frac{G}{C}$)

$$\approx \sqrt{\frac{R}{G}} = \sqrt{\frac{L}{C}}$$

Here also, $R_o = \sqrt{\frac{L}{C}}$ and $X_o = 0$.

So, the distortionless lines are also the lossless lines.

6.6.3. Low Loss Lines: Resistance and Leakage through Dielectric is very Small

Here, $R \langle\langle \omega L; G \langle\langle \omega C$

Hence, $Z_o = \sqrt{\frac{j\omega L\left(1 + \frac{R}{j\omega L}\right)}{j\omega C\left(1 + \frac{G}{j\omega C}\right)}} = \sqrt{\frac{L}{C}} \cdot \left[\left(1 + \frac{R}{j\omega L}\right)^{1/2} \cdot \left(1 + \frac{G}{j\omega C}\right)^{-1/2}\right]$

$$= \sqrt{\frac{L}{C}}.\left(1+\frac{R}{2j\omega L}\right).\left(1-\frac{G}{2j\omega C}\right) = \sqrt{\frac{L}{C}}.\left[1+\frac{1}{2}.\left(\frac{R}{j\omega L}-\frac{G}{j\omega C}\right)-\frac{1}{4}\frac{GR}{(j\omega L)(j\omega C)}\right]$$

$$\approx \sqrt{\frac{L}{C}}\left[1+\frac{1}{2}\left(\frac{R}{j\omega L}-\frac{G}{j\omega C}\right)\right] \qquad \text{(as '}\omega\text{' is very large)}$$

$$= \sqrt{\frac{L}{C}}+\frac{1}{2}\left[\sqrt{\frac{L}{C}}\times\frac{R}{j\omega L}-\sqrt{\frac{L}{C}}\times\frac{G}{j\omega C}\right]$$

$$= \sqrt{\frac{L}{C}}+j\frac{1}{2}\sqrt{\frac{L}{C}}\left[\frac{G}{\omega C}-\frac{R}{\omega L}\right]$$

Here, $R_o = \sqrt{\frac{L}{C}}$

And $X_0 = \frac{1}{2}\sqrt{\frac{L}{C}}\left[\frac{G}{\omega C}-\frac{R}{\omega L}\right]$

6.7 Propagation Constant

Here, $\gamma = \sqrt{(R+j\omega L)(G+j\omega C)}$

Also, $\gamma = \alpha + j\beta$

Special Case

6.7.1. Loss Less Line: No Resistance and no Leakage through Dielectric

Here, $R = 0$ and $\frac{1}{G} \to \infty \Rightarrow G \to 0$

So $\gamma \approx \sqrt{j\omega L \times j\omega C} = j\omega\sqrt{LC}$

Hence, $\alpha = 0, \beta = \omega\sqrt{LC}$

Phase velocity $= v_p = \frac{\omega}{\beta} = \frac{1}{\sqrt{LC}}$

6.7.2. Distortion Less Line:

Here, $\frac{R}{L} = \frac{G}{C}$

Hence, $\gamma = \sqrt{(j\omega L)(j\omega C)(1+R/j\omega L)(1+G/j\omega C)} \approx j\omega\sqrt{LC}.\sqrt{(1+G/j\omega C)^2}$

$$= j\omega\sqrt{LC} + j\omega.\sqrt{LC}.\frac{G}{j\omega C} = j\omega\sqrt{LC} + G.\sqrt{\frac{L}{C}}$$

Thus $\alpha = G.\sqrt{\frac{L}{C}}$ and $\beta = \omega\sqrt{LC}$

And $v_p = \frac{1}{\sqrt{LC}}$

6.7.3. Low Loss Line: Resistance and Leakage through Dielectric is Very Small

Here, $R \langle\langle \omega L; G \langle\langle \omega C$

Hence, $\gamma = \sqrt{\left(1+\frac{R}{j\omega L}\right)\left(1+\frac{G}{j\omega C}\right)} \times \sqrt{j\omega L \times j\omega C}$

$$\approx j\omega\sqrt{LC}\left[1+\frac{1}{2}\left(\frac{R}{j\omega L}+\frac{G}{j\omega C}\right)\right]$$

$$= j\omega\sqrt{LC} + \frac{1}{2}\left[\frac{R}{j\omega L}\times j\omega\sqrt{LC} + \frac{G}{j\omega C}\times j\omega\sqrt{LC}\right]$$

$$= j\omega\sqrt{LC} + \frac{1}{2}\left[R\sqrt{\frac{C}{L}} + G.\sqrt{\frac{L}{C}}\right]$$

So, $\alpha = \frac{1}{2}.\left[R.\sqrt{\frac{C}{L}} + G.\sqrt{\frac{L}{C}}\right]$ and $\beta = \omega\sqrt{LC}$

$$v_p = \frac{\omega}{\omega\sqrt{LC}} = \frac{1}{\sqrt{LC}}$$

6.8 Reflection Coefficient

In solving transmission line equations, the traveling wave along the line contains the components that are traveling in '+X' and '-X' directions. It is convenient to solve the extension line problem at the load end, rather than at the source end, as the ratio of voltage to the current at the load end is fixed by the 'Z_R' (load impedance).

Following eqn.(6.18), the incident voltage and current wave along the transmission line is given by

$$V = V_R^{+}e^{\gamma x} + V_R^{-}e^{-\gamma x}$$

Here, the reflected voltage at the receiving end (*i.e.*, at $x = 0$) $= V_R^-$

And, incident voltage at the receiving end $= V_R^+$.

Reflection coefficient at the receiving end is given by

$$k_R = \frac{V_R^-}{V_R^+} = \frac{Z_R - Z_0}{Z_R + Z_0}$$

Case-I:

When $Z_R = Z_0$, then $k_R = 0$.

It implies the fact that there will not be any reflections.

Case-II: General Case

If Z_R and Z_0 are the complex quantities, then k_R is also complex quantity and is given by

$$k_R = |k_R| e^{j\varphi}; \text{ where } |k_R \le 1|.$$

Here, 'φ' is phase angle between the incident and reflected voltage at the receiving end, which is the phase angle of reflection coefficient.

6.8.1. Input Impedance

Now,
$$V = V_R^+ e^{\gamma x} + V_R^- e^{-\gamma x} = V_R^+ e^{\gamma x}\left[1 + \frac{V_R^-}{V_R^+} e^{-2\gamma x}\right]$$

$$= V_R^+ e^{\gamma x}\left[1 + k_R e^{-2\gamma x}\right]$$

$$= V_R^+ e^{\gamma x}\left[1 + |k_R| e^{j\phi} e^{-2\gamma x}\right]$$

Similarly for current, we have

$$I = I_R^+ e^{\gamma x} - I_R^- e^{-\gamma x}$$

$$= I_R^+ e^{\gamma x}\left[1 - |k_R| e^{j\phi} e^{-2\gamma x}\right]$$

Input impedance as a function of reflection coefficient is thus given by

$$Z = \frac{V}{I} = \frac{V_R^+ e^{\gamma x}\left[1 + |k_R| e^{j\phi} e^{-2\gamma x}\right]}{I_R^+ e^{\gamma x}\left[1 - |k_R| e^{j\phi} e^{-2\gamma x}\right]} = \frac{V_R^+\left[1 + |k_R| e^{j\phi} e^{-2\gamma x}\right]}{I_R^+\left[1 - |k_R| e^{j\phi} e^{-2\gamma x}\right]}$$

6.8.2. Refection Coefficient: The general solution of the reflection coefficient at any length for the transmission line at any point $x = d$ is given by

$$R = \frac{V_R^- e^{-\gamma d}}{V_R^+ e^{\gamma d}} = \frac{V_R^-}{V_R^+} e^{-2\gamma d}$$

$$= k_R e^{-2\gamma d} = k_R e^{-2(\alpha + j\beta)d}$$

$$= k_R e^{-2\alpha d} e^{-2j\beta d}$$

Hence when load reflection impedance is equal to the characteristic impedance of the line, *i.e.*, $Z_R = Z_0$, there won't be any reflections. On the other hand, when $Z_R \neq Z_0$, then there will be reflection from the receiving end to the source end. The reflected wave upon reaching the sending end will be reflected back to the receiving end when the source impedance is not equal to the characteristic impedance of the line.

6.9 Transmission Coefficient

Transmission coefficient is the ratio of the transmitted voltage to the incident voltage and is given by

$$T = \frac{V_{tr}}{V_{in}} = \frac{V_{in} - V_{refl}}{V_{in}}$$

$$= 1 - \frac{V_{refl}}{V_{in}} = 1 - \frac{V_R^-}{V_R^+}$$

$$= 1 - k_R$$

$$\Rightarrow T = 1 - \frac{Z_R - Z_0}{Z_R + Z_0} = \frac{2Z_0}{Z_R + Z_0}$$

6.10 Standing Wave Ratio

The superposition of both forward and reflected wave give rise to sinusoidal or co-sinusoidal distribution of 'βx', which is nothing but standing wave or non-progressive wave.

The ratio between the maximum and the minimum amplitude is called standing wave ratio (SWR). Hence,

Voltage standing wave ratio (VSWR) $= \dfrac{V_{\max}}{V_{\min}}$, and,

Current standing wave ratio (ISWR) $= \dfrac{I_{\max}}{I_{\min}}$

If voltage magnitudes are measured along the length of a line terminated in a load other than Z_0, the plotted values will appear as in Fig.6.9.

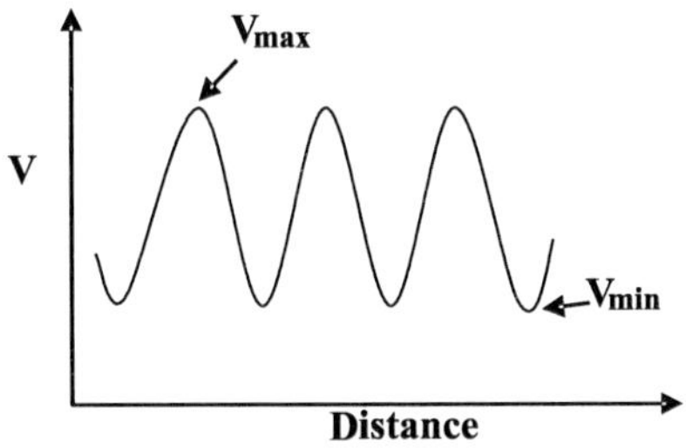

Fig. 6.9 (*a*) Variation of voltage wave. with distance for a resistive load of value not equal to R_0.

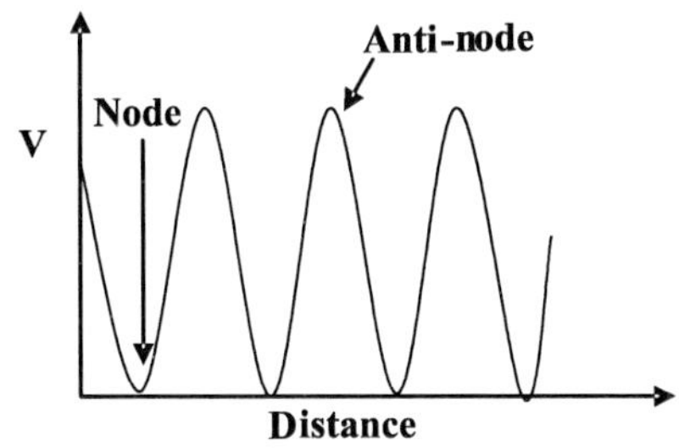

Fig. 6.9 (*b*) Variation of voltage wave. with distance for short or open circuit condition.

Fig.6.9 (a) is drawn for a resistive load of value not equal to R_0, and Fig.6.9(b) is the case for either open or short circuit. Maximum and minimum values on a line are labeled as in Fig.6.9(a), whereas, the nodes and anti-nodes are indicated in Fig.6.9(b).

For **open circuit**, voltage nodes occur at distances $\frac{\lambda}{4},\frac{3\lambda}{4},\frac{5\lambda}{4},\dots,$ from the open end of the line. Under the same conditions, current nodes occur at distances $0,\frac{\lambda}{2},\lambda,\frac{3\lambda}{2},\dots,$ from the voltage nodes occur at open termination.

For **short circuit**, these nodal points shift by a distance of $\lambda/4$, and the voltage nodes occur at $0,\frac{\lambda}{2},\lambda,\frac{3\lambda}{2},\dots,$ with current nodes at $\frac{\lambda}{4},\frac{3\lambda}{4},\frac{5\lambda}{4},\dots$.

For resistive loads greater than R_0, the voltage and current minima occur at the voltage and current nodal points for an open circuited line. For resistive loads smaller than R_0, the voltage and current minima occur at the voltage and current nodal points for a short circuited line.

6.11 Determination of Amplitude and Phase Angle of the Voltage Wave

The voltage equation of standing wave is given by $V = V_o e^{j\varphi}$ ...(6.37)

Here, 'V_0,ϕ' are the amplitude and phase angle of the voltage wave respectively.

We know from eqn.(6.11),

$$V = Ae^{+\gamma x} + Be^{-\gamma x} = Ae^{\alpha x}e^{j\beta x} + Be^{-\alpha x}e^{-j\beta x}$$

$$= Ae^{\alpha x}(\cos\beta x + j\sin\beta x) + Be^{\alpha x}(\cos\beta x + j\sin\beta x)$$

$$= (Ae^{\alpha x} + Be^{-\alpha x})\cos\beta x + j(Ae^{\alpha x} - Be^{-\alpha x})\sin\beta x \qquad ...(6.38)$$

From eqn.(6.37) we have,

$$V = V_o\left(\cos\phi + j\sin\phi\right) \qquad ...(6.38a)$$

Hence from eqns.(6.38) and (6.38a),

$$V_o\cos\phi + jV_o\sin\phi = (Ae^{\alpha x} + Be^{-\alpha x})\cos\beta x + j(Ae^{\alpha x} - Be^{-\alpha x})\sin\beta x \qquad ...(6.39)$$

Solving above equation for 'V_0' and 'ϕ' values by equating real and imaginary parts of eqn.(6.39), we have,

$$V_o\cos\phi = (Ae^{\alpha x} + Be^{-\alpha x})\cos\beta x \qquad ...(6.40)$$

$$V_o\sin\phi = \sin\beta x(Ae^{\alpha x} - Be^{-\alpha x}) \qquad ...(6.41)$$

$$\Rightarrow V_o^2 = (Ae^{\alpha x} + Be^{-\alpha x})^2\cos^2\beta x + (Ae^{\alpha x} - Be^{-\alpha x})^2\sin^2\beta x$$

$$\Rightarrow V_o = \sqrt{(Ae^{\alpha x} + Be^{-\alpha x})^2\cos^2\beta x + (Ae^{\alpha x} - Be^{-\alpha x})^2\sin^2\beta x} \qquad ...(6.42)$$

Here V_0 is required amplitude of standing wave pattern.
Also using eqns.(6.38) and (6.38a),

$$\tan\phi = \tan\beta x \times \frac{Ae^{\alpha x} - Be^{-\alpha x}}{Ae^{\alpha x} + Be^{-\alpha x}}$$

$$\Rightarrow \phi = \tan^{-1}\left(\tan\beta x \times \frac{Ae^{\alpha x} - Be^{-\alpha x}}{Ae^{\alpha x} + Be^{-\alpha x}}\right) \qquad ...(6.43)$$

Here ϕ is known as the phase pattern of standing wave.

6.12 Important Points about SWR

6.12.1. Maximum Amplitude of Standing Wave

From eqn.(6.42) it is clear that V_0 is maximum when $\beta x = n\pi$,where $n = 0,1,2,3..$

Thus using eqn.(6.42), we have, $V_{\max} = V_0\big|_{Max} = Ae^{\alpha x} + Be^{-\alpha x}$

$$= Ae^{\alpha x}\left(1 + \frac{Be^{-\alpha x}}{Ae^{\alpha x}}\right)$$

$$= Ae^{\alpha x}\left(1 + R\right)$$

6.12.2. Minimum Amplitude of Standing Wave

From eqn.(6.42) it is clear that V_0 is minimum when $\beta x = \left(\frac{2n+1}{2}\right)\pi$,where $n = 0,1,2,3..$

Thus using eqn.(6.42), we have, $V_{\min} = V_0\big|_{Min} = Ae^{\alpha x} - Be^{-\alpha x}$

$$= Ae^{\alpha x}\left(1-\frac{Be^{-\alpha x}}{Ae^{\alpha x}}\right)$$

$$= Ae^{\alpha x}(1-R)$$

6.12.3. (*i*) Distance Between Two Successive Maxima or Minima

For maxima: $\beta x = n\pi$

$$\Rightarrow x = \frac{n\pi}{\beta} = \frac{n\pi}{2\pi/\lambda} = \frac{n\lambda}{2}.$$

Hence, distance between two consecutive maxima is $\frac{(n+1)\lambda}{2} - \frac{n\lambda}{2} = \frac{\lambda}{2}$

For minima: $\beta x = \left(\frac{2n+1}{2}\right)\pi$

$$\Rightarrow x = \left(\frac{2n+1}{2\beta}\right)\pi = \left(\frac{2n+1}{2(2\pi/\lambda)}\right)\pi = \frac{(2n+1)\lambda}{4}.$$

Hence, distance between two consecutive minima is

$$\frac{(2(n+1)+1)\lambda}{4} - \frac{(2n+1)\lambda}{4} = \frac{\lambda}{2}$$

(*ii*) When $A \neq 0, B = 0$:

Here the equation of the standing wave pattern becomes $V_o = Ae^{\alpha x}$

(*iii*) When A=0 and B $\neq 0$:

Here the equation of the standing wave pattern becomes $V_o = Be^{-\alpha x}$

(*iv*) When $|Ae^{\alpha x}| = |Be^{-\alpha x}| = S$:

Here $V_o = 2Se^{\alpha x}\cos\beta x$, which is the equation of pure standing wave.

(*v*) SWR of pure traveling wave is unity. The line with SWR =1 is called a flat line.

(*vi*) SWR of pure standing wave is infinite.

(*vii*) Relationship Between the Reflection Coefficient and VWSR

From the definition of VWSR we have,

$$VSWR(S) = \frac{V_{\max}}{V_{\min}} = \frac{Ae^{\alpha x}(1+R)}{Ae^{\alpha xz}(1-R)}$$

$$\Rightarrow S = \frac{(1+R)}{(1-R)} \Rightarrow S(1-R) = (1+R) \Rightarrow R = \frac{S-1}{S+1}$$

$$\text{Reflection coefficient} = \frac{VSWR-1}{VSWR+1}$$

The variation of reflection coefficient with VWSR is shown in Fig.6.10.

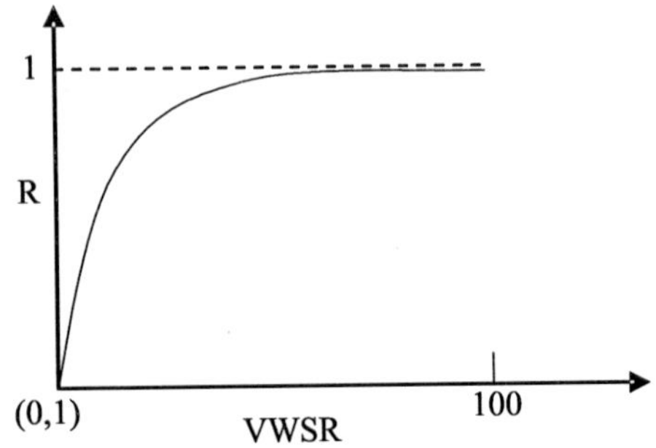

Fig. 6.10 Variation of Reflection coefficient with VWSR.

6.13 The Transmission Line Analogy

It is interesting to note that a close analogy is observed between the propagation of plane waves in a homogeneous medium and the propagation of voltage and current along a uniform transmission line. We observe that when an e.m.wave propagate through a medium, its electric and magnetic field components propagate and attenuate through the medium. For a transmission line, the voltage and current of input a.c. source propagate through a solid conducting medium. This analogy can be used not only as an aid in obtaining an understanding of a new subject, but also to obtain the solutions to actual problems. We are discussing them in details.

For a uniform transmission line with R, L, C and G per unit length, the voltage and current equations are written in differential form as

$$\frac{\partial \tilde{V}}{\partial x} + L\frac{\partial \tilde{I}}{\partial t} + R\tilde{I} = 0 \text{, and,}$$

$$\frac{\partial \tilde{I}}{\partial x} + C\frac{\partial \tilde{V}}{\partial t} + G\tilde{V} = 0 \quad \text{...(6.44)}$$

For a homogeneous medium Maxwell's equations are

$$\left(\vec{\nabla} \times \vec{E}\right) = -\mu\frac{\partial \vec{H}}{\partial t} \text{, and,}$$

$$\vec{\nabla} \times \vec{H} = \sigma \vec{E} + \varepsilon \frac{\partial \vec{E}}{\partial t}$$

For a uniform plane wave propagating in the X-direction with only components E_y, H_z, the equations of E, H are,

$$\frac{\partial \tilde{E}_y}{\partial x} + \mu \frac{\partial \tilde{H}_z}{\partial t} = 0$$

$$\frac{\partial \tilde{H}_z}{\partial x} + \varepsilon \frac{\partial \tilde{E}_y}{\partial t} + \sigma \tilde{E}_y = 0 \quad \text{...(6.45)}$$

Comparing above equations we get following analogous quantities.

(*i*) V (Volt) is with E (Volt/mt)
(*ii*) I (Amp) is with H (Amp/mt)
(*iii*) C (F/mt) is with ε (F/mt)
(*iv*) L (H/mt) is with μ (H/mt)
(*v*) G (Mho/mt) is with σ (Mho/mt)
(*vi*) R (Ohm/mt) : Here nothing is found in e.m.wave which is analogous to R in transmission line.

The voltage and current, electric and magnetic field strengths are assumed to vary sinusoidally with time. So we have for a transmission line,

$$\frac{\partial V}{\partial x} + (R + j\omega L)I = 0$$

$$\frac{\partial I}{\partial x} + (G + j\omega C)V = 0 \quad \text{...(6.46)}$$

Using the phasor notation for an e.m.wave, the electric and magnetic components become,

$$\frac{\partial E_y}{\partial x} + (0 + j\omega\mu)H_z = 0$$

$$\frac{\partial H_z}{\partial x} + (\sigma + j\omega\varepsilon)E_y = 0 \quad \text{...(6.47)}$$

On differentiating eqn.(6.46) with respect to 'x' we have,

$$\frac{\partial^2 V}{\partial x^2} + (R + j\omega L)\frac{\partial I}{\partial x} = 0$$

$$\Rightarrow \frac{\partial^2 V}{\partial x^2} - (R + j\omega L)(G + j\omega C)V = 0 \quad \text{...(6.48)}$$

Similarly, $$\frac{\partial^2 I}{\partial x^2} - (R + j\omega L)(G + j\omega C)I = 0$$

On differentiating eqn.(6.47) with respect to 'x' we have,

$$\frac{\partial^2 E_y}{\partial x^2} + (j\omega\mu)\frac{\partial}{\partial x} H_z = 0$$

$$\Rightarrow \frac{\partial^2 E_y}{\partial x^2} - (j\omega\mu)(\sigma + j\omega\varepsilon) E_y = 0 \qquad ...(6.49)$$

Similarly, $$\frac{\partial^2 H_z}{\partial x^2} - (j\omega\mu)(\sigma + j\omega\varepsilon) H_z = 0$$

The possible solution of these equations is of the form

$$V, I, E_y, H_z = Ae^{-\gamma x} + Be^{\gamma x} \qquad ...(6.50)$$

Here, $\gamma^2 = (R + j\omega L)(G + j\omega C)$ (from eqn.(6.48))

And, $\gamma^2 = (j\omega\mu)(\sigma + j\omega\varepsilon)$ (from eqn.(6.49))

An alternative solution to eqn.(6.48) and (6.49) is often used in transmission line theory. Here the exponentials combined differently and the solutions can be written as

$$V = A_1 \cosh \gamma x + B_1 \sinh \gamma x$$

$$I = A_2 \cosh \gamma x + B_2 \sinh \gamma x \qquad ...(6.51)$$

Let, at the receiving end, *i.e.*, at $x = 0$, $V = V_R, I = I_R$;

and, at the source end, *i.e.*, at $x = x_1$, $V = V_S, I = I_S$.

Using the boundary condition at the receiving end into eqn.(6.51), we have,

$$V_R = A_1, I_R = A_2$$

Using eqn.(6.46) and (6.51), we have

$$\frac{\partial V}{\partial x} + (R + j\omega L) I = 0$$

$$\Rightarrow \gamma [A_1 \sinh \gamma x + B_1 \cosh \gamma x] = -(R + j\omega L) I$$

Using again $V = V_R, I = I_R$ at $x = 0$, we get,

$$\gamma [0 + B_1] = -(R + j\omega L) I_R$$

$$\Rightarrow B_1 = -(R + j\omega L) I_R / \gamma$$

$$= -\frac{(R + j\omega L)}{\sqrt{(R + j\omega L)(G + j\omega C)}} I_R$$

$$\Rightarrow B_1 = -\sqrt{\frac{(R+j\omega L)}{(G+j\omega C)}}I_R$$

Similarly, $$B_2 = -\sqrt{\frac{(G+j\omega C)}{(R+j\omega L)}}V_R$$

For an e.m.wave the electric and magnetic fields become,

$$E = A_1\cosh\gamma x + B_1\sinh\gamma x$$
$$H = A_2\cosh\gamma x + B_2\sinh\gamma x$$

Let, at the receiving end, *i.e.*, at $x = 0$, $E = E_R, H = H_R$;

and, at the source end, *i.e.*, at $x = x_1$, $E = E_S, H = H_S$.

Using these boundary conditions and similarly as in the left half, we get,

$$B_1 = -\sqrt{\frac{(j\omega\mu)}{(\sigma+j\omega\varepsilon)}}H_R$$

And, $$B_2 = -\sqrt{\frac{(\sigma+j\omega\varepsilon)}{(j\omega\mu)}}E_R$$

In transmission line theory we know,

the impedance per unit length is $Z = (R+j\omega L)$,

the admittance per unit length is $Y = (G+j\omega C)$, ...(6.52)

and, $$Z_0 = \sqrt{\frac{Z}{Y}} = \sqrt{\frac{(R+j\omega L)}{(G+j\omega C)}}$$

Here, 'Z_0' is known as the Characteristic impedance or intrinsic impedance of the medium.

At the source end with $x = x_1 = -l$, $B_1 = -Z_0 I_R, B_2 = -\frac{V_R}{Z_0}$,

and eqn.(6.51) for transmission line becomes

$$V_S = V_R\cosh\gamma l + Z_0 I_R\sinh\gamma l$$

$$I_S = I_R\cosh\gamma l + \frac{V_R}{Z_0}\sinh\gamma l$$

At the source end with $x = x_1 = -l$, $B_1 = -\eta H_R, B_2 = -\frac{E_R}{\eta}$,

and eqn.(6.52) for e.m.wave becomes

$$E_S = E_R \cosh \gamma l + \eta H_R \sinh \gamma l$$

$$H_S = H_R \cosh \gamma l + \frac{E_R}{\eta} \sinh \gamma l$$

For long transmission line or very thick homogeneous medium, 'γl' is very large, and so,

$$\cosh \gamma l = \frac{e^{\gamma l} + e^{-\gamma l}}{2} \approx \frac{e^{\gamma l}}{2} \approx \frac{e^{\gamma l} - e^{-\gamma l}}{2} = \sinh \gamma l \qquad ...(6.53)$$

Using this into eqn.(6.53) for transmission line we have,

$$\frac{V_S}{I_S} = \frac{V_R \cosh \gamma l + Z_0 I_R \sinh \gamma l}{I_R \cosh \gamma l + \frac{V_R}{Z_0} \sinh \gamma l}$$

$$\approx \frac{V_R + Z_0 I_R}{I_R + \frac{V_R}{Z_0}}$$

$$= Z_0 \frac{V_R + Z_0 I_R}{V_R + Z_0 I_R} = Z_0 \qquad ...(6.54)$$

Using '$\cosh \gamma l = \sinh \gamma l$' into eqn.(6.54) for e.m.wave we have,

$$\frac{E_S}{H_S} = \frac{E_R \cosh \gamma l + \eta H_R \sinh \gamma l}{H_R \cosh \gamma l + \frac{E_R}{\eta} \sinh \gamma l} = \eta$$

Hence 'Z_0, η' are the characteristic impedances for the propagation of waves along uniform transmission lines or plane waves in homogeneous media respectively.

For lossless transmission line we have,

$$R = G = 0 \Rightarrow Z_0 = \sqrt{\frac{L}{C}}$$

$$\Rightarrow \gamma = \sqrt{(j\omega L)(j\omega C)} = j\omega\sqrt{LC}$$

But, $\gamma = \alpha + j\beta$

Hence, $\alpha = 0, \beta = \omega\sqrt{LC}$

Here, $\cos j\beta \approx \cos\beta$ and $\sin j\beta \approx j\sin\beta$,

The eqn.(6.53) becomes

$$V_S = V_R \cos\beta l + jZ_0 I_R \sin\beta l$$

$$I_S = I_R \cos\beta l + j\frac{V_R}{Z_0}\sin\beta l \quad ...(6.55)$$

For loss less medium, *i.e.*, free space we have for an e.m.wave,

$$\sigma = 0 \Rightarrow \eta = \sqrt{\frac{\mu}{\varepsilon}}$$

$$\Rightarrow \gamma = \sqrt{(j\omega\mu)(j\omega\varepsilon)} = j\omega\sqrt{\mu\varepsilon}$$

Hence, $\alpha = 0, \beta = \omega\sqrt{\mu\varepsilon}$

Here also, $\cos j\beta \approx \cos\beta$ and $\sin j\beta \approx j\sin\beta$,

The eqn.(6.54)) becomes

$$E_S = E_R \cos\beta l + j\eta H_R \sin\beta l$$

$$H_S = H_R \cos\beta l + j\frac{E_R}{\eta}\sin\beta l \quad ...(6.56)$$

The quantities ‘ $\frac{1}{\sqrt{LC}} = c \approx 3\times10^8$ mt/sec

and $\frac{1}{\sqrt{\mu_0\varepsilon_0}} = c \approx 3\times10^8$ mt/sec.

We expect that for a wave of arbitrary shape traveling through a conducting medium would decrease in amplitude exponentially, but its wave-shape remains the same as it progresses. However, by decomposing the wave into its fundamental and harmonic components by Fourier analysis we observe that the attenuation factor ‘α’ is different at different frequencies. Therefore such a wave-shape becomes distorted as it progresses.

6.14 Impedance Matching Techniques in Transmission Line

The impedance mismatches between the transmission line and load should be avoided to eliminate reflection losses (*i.e.*, $Z_R \neq Z_0$). There are techniques developed to avoid this mismatch loss and some of them are discussed as follows.

1. Quarter Wave Transformer: Impedance mismatch can be avoided by compensating it with a quarter wave transformer. Hence, a quarter wave, *i.e.*, ‘ $\lambda/4$ ’ length section of different transmission line (with characteristic impedance

'Z_0'' is inserted between the original transmission line and load as shown in Figs.6.11(a) and 11(b).

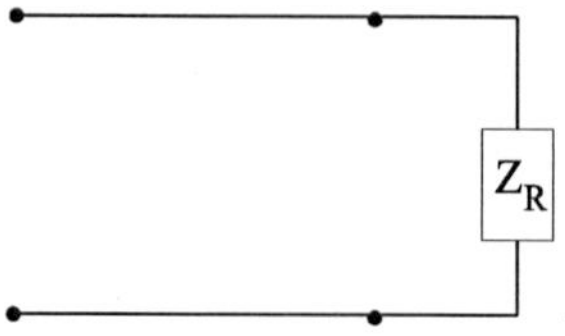

Fig. 6.11 (*a*) Transmission line with load.

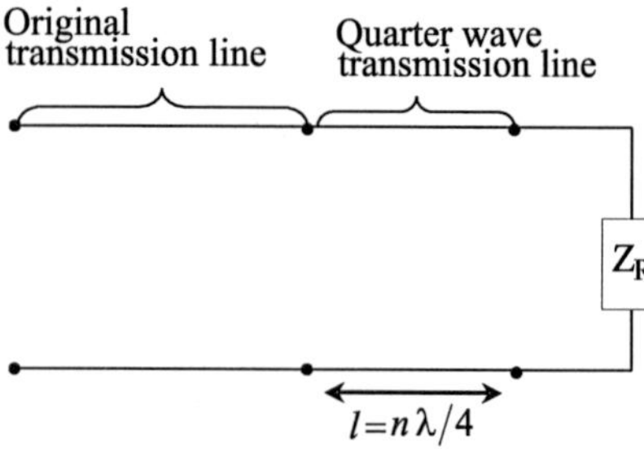

Fig. 6.11 (*b*) Quarter wavelength transmission line with load.

Input impedance is now given by

$$Z_{in} = Z_0'\frac{Z_R\cosh\gamma x + Z_0'\sinh\gamma x}{Z_R\sinh\gamma x + Z_0'\cosh\gamma x} \quad \text{(from eqn.(6.32))} \qquad ...(6.57)$$

For $x = l$ we have from eqn.(6.57),

$$Z_{in} = Z_0'\frac{Z_R\cosh\gamma l + Z_0'\sinh\gamma l}{Z_R\sinh\gamma l + Z_0'\cosh\gamma l} = Z_0'\frac{Z_R + Z_0'\tanh\gamma l}{Z_0' + Z_R\tanh\gamma l} \qquad ...(6.58)$$

For lossless lines we have $\alpha = 0$

Hence, $\gamma = 0 + j\beta = j\beta$ ...(6.59)

Using the value of 'γ' from eqn.(6.59) into eqn.(6.58) we have,

$$Z_{in} = Z_0'\frac{Z_R + jZ_0'\tan\beta l}{Z_0' + jZ_R\tan\beta l} \qquad ...(6.60)$$

For quarter wave transformer, $l = \frac{n\lambda}{4}$, hence,

$$\beta l = \frac{2\pi}{\lambda}\times\frac{n\lambda}{4} = \frac{n\pi}{2}$$

Using these values of 'βl' into eqn.(6.60) we have,

$$Z_{in} = Z_0'\frac{Z_R + jZ_0'\tan\beta l}{Z_0' + jZ_R\tan\beta l}$$

$$= Z_0'\frac{\dfrac{Z_R + jZ_0'\tan\beta l}{\tan\beta l}}{\dfrac{Z_0' + jZ_R\tan\beta l}{\tan\beta l}} = Z_0'\frac{\dfrac{Z_R}{\tan\beta l} + jZ_0'}{\dfrac{Z_0'}{\tan\beta l} + jZ_R}$$

$$= \frac{(Z_0')^2}{Z_R}$$

However, after impedance matching this impedance should equal the characteristic impedance of the original transmission line, hence,

$$\frac{(Z_0')^2}{Z_R} = Z_0$$

$$\Rightarrow Z_0' = \sqrt{Z_0 Z_R}$$

Hence if the above condition is fulfilled for an additional line added between the original line and the load, standing wave exists. However this transformer is a narrowband device.

2. Stub Matching: Quarter wave transformer is utilized for matching the resistive load 'R_L' with 'Z_0'. For complex load impedance, it can not be utilized. The 'stub' matching has been used for complex load impedance.

For any transmission line, where characteristic admittance equals the real part of input admittance, *i.e.*, $\frac{1}{Z_0} = Y_0$, the susceptance 'B' can be eliminated on inserting the proper reactive component in parallel at this point.

Here, $$Y_{in} = \frac{1}{Z_{in}} = Y_0 \pm jB$$

This is same as inserting inductance or capacitor in parallel with the transmission line. Due to high losses at used frequencies in these devices an open or short circuited segment of transmission line is used to obtain the required reactance. This is shown in Figs.6.12(a) and 6.12(b).

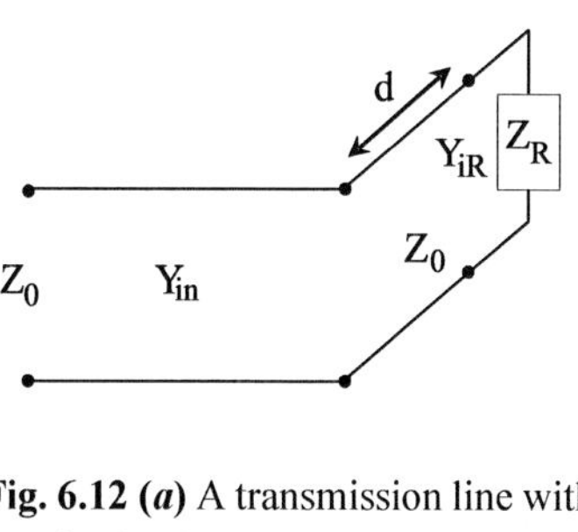

Fig. 6.12 (*a*) A transmission line with reactive load.

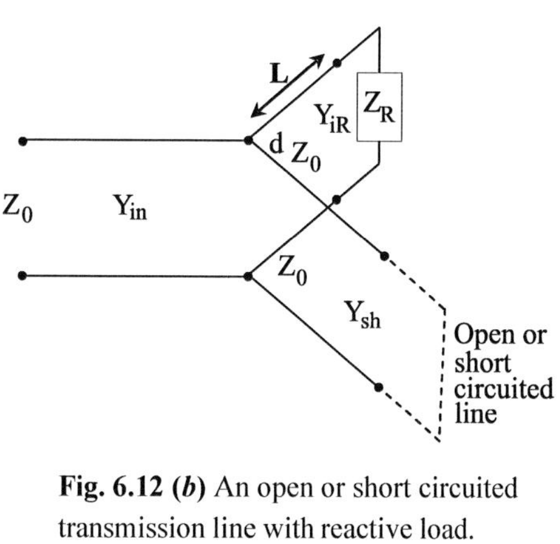

Fig. 6.12 (*b*) An open or short circuited transmission line with reactive load.

In Fig.6.12(b), Y_{sh}, Y_{iR}, Y_{in} are input admittances of the stub, terminated transmission line and original transmission line respectively.

Here, $Y_{sh} = -jB$, and,

$$Y_{iR} = Y_0 - Y_{sh} = Y_0 + jB$$

Hence, $Y_{in} = Y_{sh} + Y_{iR} = (-jB) + (Y_0 + jB) = Y_0$

This is the required admittance of the resultant transmission line with complex load.

❑❑❑

CHAPTER 7

INTRODUCTION TO SMITH CHART

7.1 Smith Chart

This is a graphical method of solving transmission line problems with graphical indication of the impedance of transmission line. It consists of group of circles (constant resistance and conductance circle). Comprising the values of impedance and admittance in the normalized form.

From mathematical point of view, the Smith chart is simply a representation of all possible complex impedances with respect to coordinates defined by the reflection coefficient. The domain of definition of the reflection coefficient is a circle of radius '1' in the complex plane. In Smith chart. The complex reflection coefficient circle is shown in Fig.7.1.

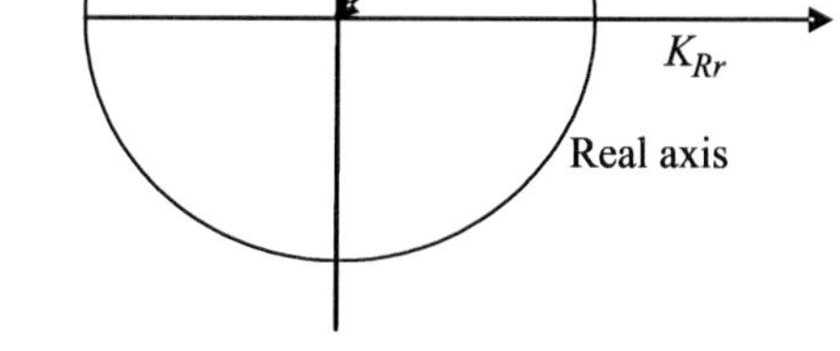

Fig. 7.1 Reflectivity Unit Circle

Here reflection coefficient is

$$K_R = K_{Rr} + jK_{Ri}$$

7.2 Theory

From the transmission line theory, the reflection coefficient is given by

$$K_R = \frac{Z_R - Z_0}{Z_R + Z_0}$$

So,
$$K_R = \frac{(Z_R - Z_0)/Z_0}{(Z_R + Z_0)/Z_0} = \frac{\frac{Z_R}{Z_0} - 1}{\frac{Z_R}{Z_0} + 1} = \frac{\exists_R - 1}{\exists_R + 1} \quad ...(7.1)$$

Here '$\exists_R$' is the impedance per unit load or the normalized impedance.

As both Z_R and Z_0 are complex quantities, so 'K_R' is also a complex one, hence, we can write

$$K_R = \frac{\exists_R - 1}{\exists_R + 1} = U + jV \quad ...(7.2)$$

Here 'U,V' are the real and imaginary parts of 'K_R' respectively.

However, for the impedance per unit load, we have,

$$\exists_R = r + jx \quad ...(7.3)$$

Here r is the resistive part of the impedance and represents the per unit resistive load. 'x' is the reactive part and represents the per unit reactive load; when 'x' is positive, the reactance is inductive and when 'x' is negative, the reactance is capacitative.

From eqn.(7.1),

$$K_R \exists_R + K_R = \exists_R - 1 \Rightarrow \exists_R = \frac{1 + K_R}{1 - K_R} \quad ...(7.4)$$

$$\Rightarrow \exists_R = \frac{1 + U + jV}{1 - U - jV} \qquad \text{(using eqn.(7.2))}$$

$$\Rightarrow r + jx = \frac{(1+U) + jV}{(1-U) - jV} \qquad \text{(using eqn.(7.3))}$$

$$\Rightarrow r + jx + 1 = \frac{(1+U) + jV}{(1-U) - jV} + 1$$

$$= \frac{2}{(1-U) - jV} = \frac{2\{(1-U) + jV\}}{(1-U)^2 + V^2} \quad ...(7.5)$$

So equating the real parts of eqn.(7.5),

$$\Rightarrow r + 1 = \frac{2(1-U)}{(1-U)^2 + V^2}$$

$$\Rightarrow (1-U)^2 + V^2 = \frac{2(1-U)}{r+1}$$

$$\Rightarrow U^2 - 2U + 1 + V^2 = \frac{2}{r+1} - \frac{2U}{r+1}$$

$$\Rightarrow U^2 + 2U\left[\frac{1}{r+1} - 1\right] + V^2 = \frac{2}{r+1} - 1$$

$$\Rightarrow U^2 + 2U\left(\frac{-r}{r+1}\right) + \left(\frac{-r}{r+1}\right)^2 + V^2 = \frac{2}{r+1} - 1 + \left(\frac{-r}{r+1}\right)^2$$

$$\Rightarrow \left[U - \frac{r}{r+1}\right]^2 + V^2 = \frac{2(1+r) - (1+r)^2 + r^2}{(1+r)^2} = \frac{2 + 2r - 1 - 2r - r^2 + r^2}{(1+r)^2}$$

$$\Rightarrow \left[U - \frac{r}{r+1}\right]^2 + V^2 = \left[\frac{1}{1+r}\right]^2 \quad ...(7.6)$$

This is the eqn. of a circle having center at $\left(\frac{r}{r+1}, 0\right)$ and radius $\left(\frac{1}{r+1}\right)$ along U-V axes.

Equating imaginary parts from eqn.(7.5) we have,

$$x = \frac{2V}{(1-U)^2 + V^2}$$

$$\Rightarrow (1-U)^2 + V^2 = \frac{2V}{x}$$

$$\Rightarrow (U-1)^2 + V^2 - \frac{2V}{x} = 0$$

$$\Rightarrow (U-1)^2 + \left[V^2 - 2V.\frac{1}{x} + \left(\frac{1}{x}\right)^2\right] = \left(\frac{1}{x}\right)^2$$

$$\Rightarrow (U-1)^2 + \left(V - \frac{1}{x}\right)^2 = \left(\frac{1}{x}\right)^2 \quad ...(7.7)$$

Eqn.(7.7) is also an equation of circle of radius $(1/x)$ with center at $\left(1, \frac{1}{x}\right)$.

We can now draw the curves in the rectangular coordinates U and V as below.

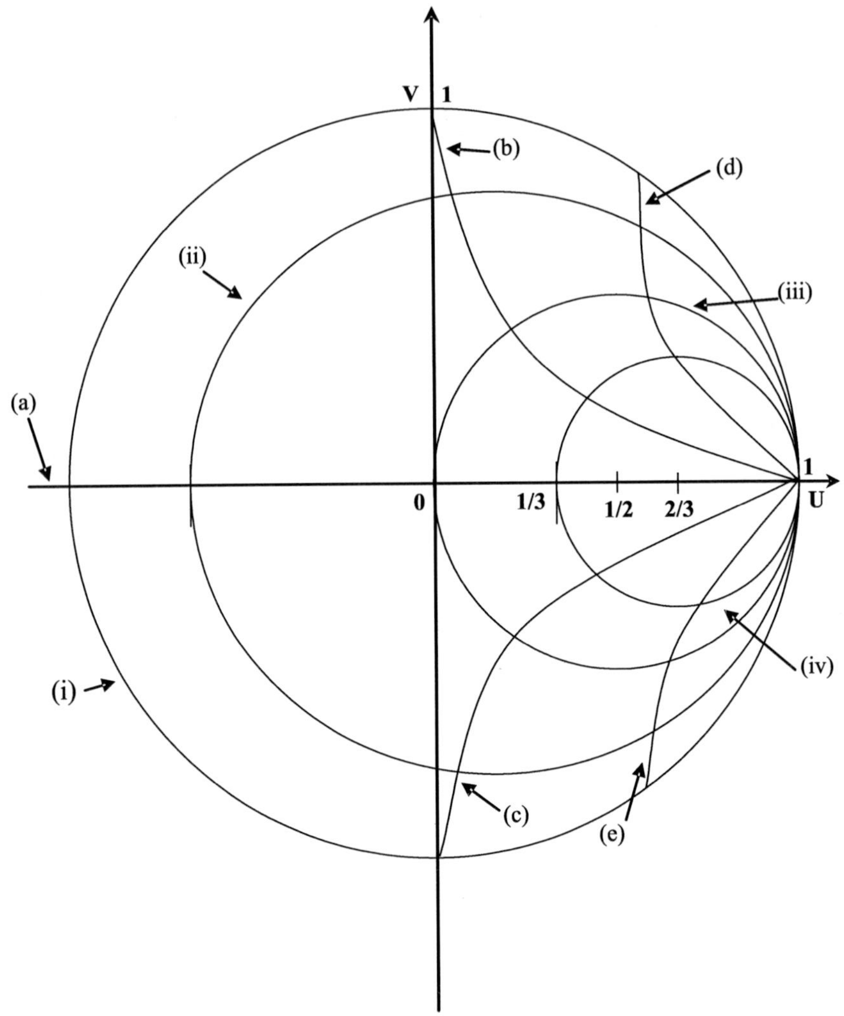

Fig. 7.2 U-V graphs for different 'r,x'.

For Circles-1

Using eqn.(7.6), Center is $\left(\dfrac{r}{r+1}, 0\right)$ and radius is $\left(\dfrac{1}{r+1}\right)$

Hence we have for the above chart in Fig.7.2,

Curve-(*i*)	For $r = 0$,	Center is at	$(0,0)$;	Radius is 1.
Curve-(*ii*)	For $r = 0.5$,	Center is at	(1/3, 0);	Radius is 2/3.
Curve-(*iii*)	For $r = 1$,	Center is at	(1/2, 0);	Radius is 1/2.
Curve-(*iv*)	For $r = 2$,	Center is at	(2/3, 0);	Radius is 1/3.

For Circles-2

Using eqn.(7.7), Center is $(1, 1/x)$ and radius is $(1/x)$.

Hence we have for the chart in Fig.7.2,

Curve-(a)	For $x=0$,	Center is at	$(0, \infty)$;	Radius is "∝".
Curve-(b)	For $x=1$,	Center is at	(1, 1);	Radius is 1.
Curve-(c)	For $x=-1$,	Center is at	(1, -1);	Radius is $\lvert -1 \rvert=1$.
Curve-(d)	For $x=2$,	Center is at	(1, 1/2);	Radius is 1/2.
Curve-(e)	For $x=-2$,	Center is at	(1, -1/2);	Radius is $\lvert -1/2 \rvert=1/2$.

7.3 Per Unit Impedance Chart

We have the per unit load impedance as $$\exists_R = \frac{Z_R}{Z_O}$$

and the reflection coefficient is given by $$K_R = \frac{\exists_R - 1}{\exists_R + 1}$$

$$\Rightarrow (K_R).e^{j\sigma} = \frac{r + jx - 1}{r + jx + 1} \qquad \text{(using eqn.(7.3))}$$

$$= \frac{(r-1) + jx}{(r+1) + jx} = \frac{[(r-1) + jx][(r+1) - jx]}{(r+1)^2 + x^2}$$

$$= \frac{[(r-1)(r+1) + x^2] + j[x(r+1) - x(r-1)]}{(r+1)^2 + x^2}$$

$$= \frac{(r^2-1) + x^2 + j.2x}{(r+1)^2 + x^2}$$

$$= a + j.b \qquad \text{...(7.8)}$$

Here, $$a = \frac{(r^2-1) + x^2}{(r+1)^2 + x^2} \quad \text{and} \quad b = \frac{2x}{(r+1)^2 + x^2}$$

Here from equation (7.8) we have,

$$(K_R)^2 = a^2 + b^2 = \frac{[(r^2-1) + x^2]^2 + 4x^2}{[(r+1)^2 + x^2]^2}$$

$$= \frac{r^4 + 1 + x^4 - 2r^2 - 2x^2 + 2x^2r^2 + 4x^2}{[(r+1)^2 + x^2]^2}$$

$$= \frac{r^4 + 1 + x^4 - 2r^2 + 2x^2 + 2x^2r^2}{[(r+1)^2 + x^2]^2}$$

$$= \frac{r^4 + 1 + x^4 + 2r^2 + 2x^2 + 2x^2r^2 - 4r^2}{[(r+1)^2 + x^2]^2}$$

$$= \frac{(r^2 + 1 + x^2)^2 - (2r)^2}{[(r+1)^2 + x^2]^2} = \frac{(r^2 + 1 + x^2 + 2r)(r^2 + 1 + x^2 - 2r)}{[(r+1)^2 + x^2]^2}$$

$$= \frac{(r^2 + 1 + x^2) - 2r}{(r+1)^2 + x^2} = \frac{(r-1)^2 + x^2}{(r+1)^2 + x^2} \quad ...(7.9)$$

Also,

$$\tan\sigma = \frac{b}{a}$$

$$\Rightarrow \sigma = \tan^{-1}\left[\frac{2x}{(r+1)^2 + x^2} \Big/ \frac{(r^2 - 1) + x^2}{(r+1)^2 + x^2}\right]$$

$$\Rightarrow \sigma = \tan^{-1}\left[\frac{2x}{(r^2 - 1) + x^2}\right] \quad ...(7.10)$$

So, $$\tan\sigma = \frac{2x}{(r^2 - 1) + x^2}$$

$$\Rightarrow (r^2 - 1 + x^2)\tan\sigma = 2x \quad ...(7.11)$$

In terms of voltage standing wave ratio (VSWR), S, we have $S = \frac{V_{max}}{V_{min}}$. This is shown in Fig.7.3)

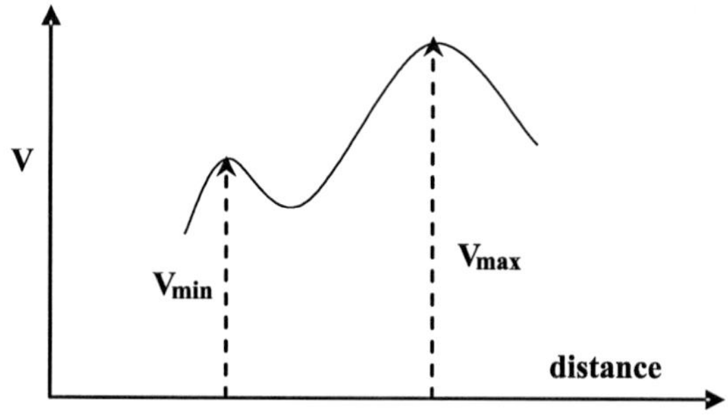

Fig. 7.3 Variation of voltage with distance.

Here 'd' is the distance between the two points in the line and

$$|K_R| = \frac{S-1}{S+1} \quad ...(7.12)$$

And $$\sigma = 2\beta d, \beta = 2\pi/\lambda$$

For eqns. (7.9) and (7.12),

$$\left(\frac{S-1}{S+1}\right)^2 = \frac{(r-1)^2+x^2}{(r+1)^2+x^2}$$

$$\Rightarrow (S-1)^2.(r+1)^2+(S-1)^2.x^2 = (S+1)^2(r-1)^2+x^2.(S+1)^2$$

$$\Rightarrow (S-1)2.r^2+2r.(S-1)^2+(S-1)^2-(S+1)^2.r^2+2r(S+1)^2$$
$$-(S+1)^2+x^2[(S-1)^2-(S+1)^2]=0$$

$$\Rightarrow [(S-1)^2-(S+1)^2]r^2+2r[(S-1)^2+(S+1)^2]+[(S-1)^2$$
$$-(S+1)^2]+x^2[(S-1)^2-(S+1)^2]=0$$

$$\Rightarrow -4S.r^2+4(S^2+1)r-4S+x^2(-4S)=0$$

$$\Rightarrow -4S[r^2+x^2]+4(S^2+1)r=4S$$

$$\Rightarrow r^2+x^2-\frac{S^2+1}{S}r=-1$$

$$\Rightarrow r^2-2r.\frac{S^2+1}{2S}+\left(\frac{S^2+1}{2S}\right)^2+x^2=\left(\frac{S^2+1}{2S}\right)^2-1$$

$$\Rightarrow \left[r-\frac{S^2+1}{2S}\right]^2+x^2=\frac{S^4+2S^2+1-4S^2}{4S^2}$$

$$\Rightarrow \left[r-\frac{S^2+1}{2S}\right]^2+x^2=\left(\frac{S^2-1}{2S}\right)^2 \qquad \text{...(7.13)}$$

This is a equation of a circle with center at $\left(\frac{S^2+1}{2S},0\right)$ and radius $\left(\frac{S^2-1}{2S}\right)$ along (r, x) coordinate system.

From, eqn.(7.11), we have

$$(r^2-1+x^2)\tan\sigma = 2x$$

$$\Rightarrow (r^2+x^2-1)\tan(2\beta d)=2x$$

$$\Rightarrow r^2+x^2-1=\frac{2x}{\tan 2\beta d}$$

$$\Rightarrow r^2+x^2-2x.\frac{1}{\tan 2\beta d}+\left(\frac{1}{\tan 2\beta d}\right)^2=1+\left(\frac{1}{\tan 2\beta d}\right)^2$$

$$\Rightarrow r^2+\left(x-\frac{1}{\tan 2\beta d}\right)^2=1+\left(\frac{\cos 2\beta d}{\sin 2\beta d}\right)^2=\frac{\sin^2 2\beta d+\cos^2 2\beta d}{\sin^2 2\beta d}=\left(\frac{1}{\sin 2\beta d}\right)^2$$

$$\Rightarrow r^2 + \left(x - \frac{1}{\tan 2\beta d}\right)^2 = \left(\frac{1}{\sin 2\beta d}\right)^2 \qquad ...(7.14)$$

This is also an equation of circle with at center at $\left(0, \frac{1}{\tan 2\beta d}\right)$ and radius '$\frac{1}{\sin 2\beta d}$' along (r, x) axes. So we can draw the graphs in Fig.7.4.

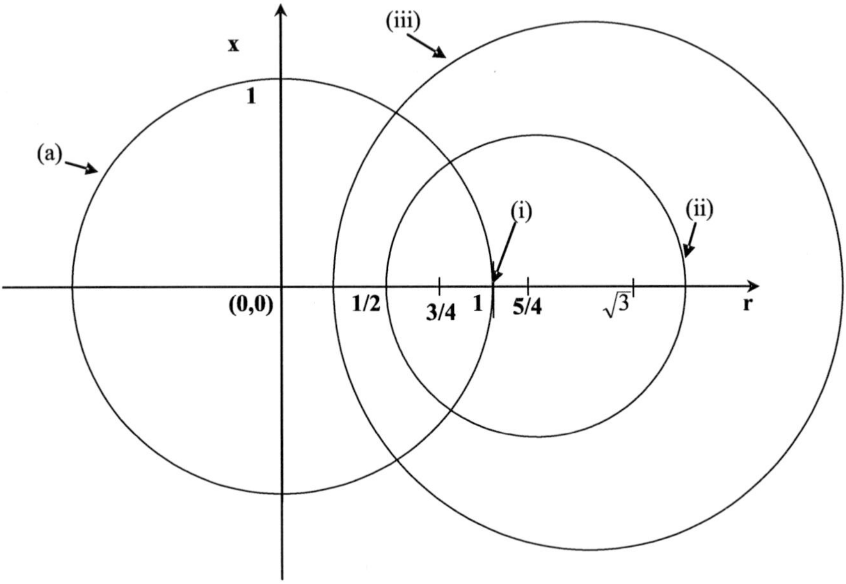

Fig. 7.4 Graphs for different values of ($s, \beta d$)

For Circles-1: Using eqn.(7.13), Center is $\left(\frac{S^2+1}{2S}, 0\right)$ and radius $\left(\frac{S^2-1}{2S}\right)$.

Hence we have for the above chart in Fig.7.4,

Curve-(*i*)	For $S=1$,	Center is at	(1,0);	Radius is 0.
Curve-(*ii*)	For $S=2$,	Center is at	(5/4, 0);	Radius is 3/4.
Curve-(*iii*)	For $S=3$,	Center is at	(10/6, 0);	Radius is 8/6=4/3.

For Circles-2: Using eqn.(7.14), Center is $\left(0, \frac{1}{\tan 2\beta d}\right)$ and radius '$\frac{1}{\sin 2\beta d}$'.

Hence we have for the above chart in Fig.7.4,

Curve-(a) For $\beta d = 45^\circ$, Center is at (0, 0); Radius is 1.

Curve-(b) (Not shown in Fig.7.4), For $\beta d = 15^\circ$, Center is at $(1, \sqrt{3})$;Radius is 2.

7.4 Complete Smith Chart

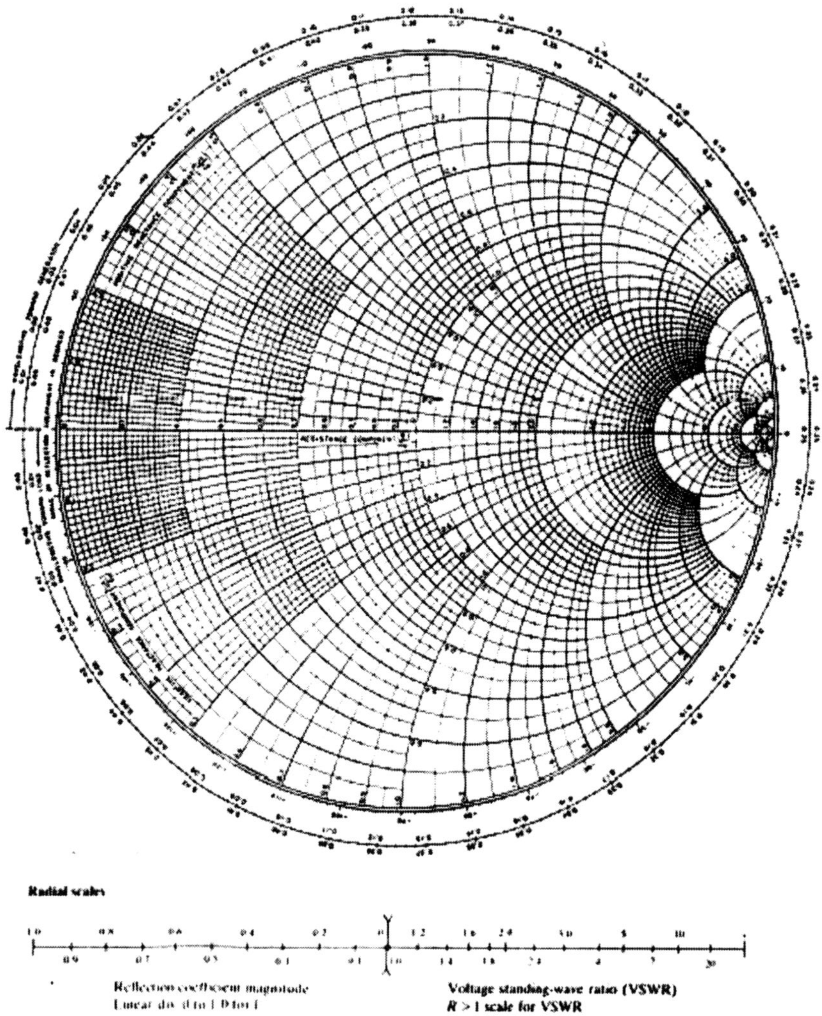

Fig. 7.5 A complete smith chart.

7.5 Pictorial Representation of Smith Chart

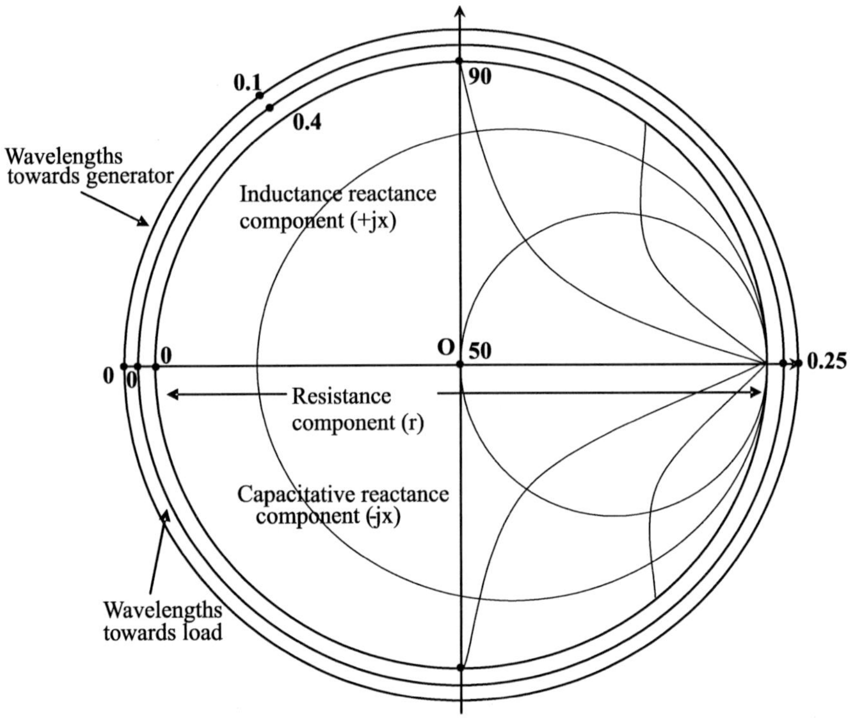

Fig. 7.6 Pictorial presentation of Smith Chart.

7.6 Characteristic of the Smith Chart

(*i*) The constant 'r' and 'x' form two families of orthogonal circles in the chart.

(*ii*) The constant 'r' and 'x' circles all pass through the point $K_{Rr} = 1; K_{Ri} = 0$.

(*iii*) The upper half of the diagram represents '$+jx$'.

(*iv*) The lower half of the diagram shows '$-jx$'.

(*v*) For admittance, the constant 'r' circles become constant 'g' circles, and constant 'x' circles become constant susceptible 'b' circles.

(*vi*) The distance around the Smith chart once is one half wavelength ($\lambda/2$).

(*vii*) At a point of $Z_{\min} = 1/K_R$, there is a $V_{\min}$ on the line.

(*viii*) At a point of $Z_{\max} = K_R$, there is a $V_{\max}$ on the line.

(*ix*) The horizontal radius to the right of the chart centre corresponds to $V_{\max}, I_{\min}, Z_{\max}, K_R (SWR)$.

(*x*) The horizontal radius to the left of the chart centre corresponds to

$V_{min}, I_{max}, Z_{min}, 1/K_R$.

(*xi*) Since the normalized admittance 'y' is a reciprocal of the normalized impedance 'Z', the corresponding quantities in the admittance chart are 180^0 out of phase with those in the impedance chart.

(*xii*) The normalized impedance or admittance is repeated for every half wavelength of distance.

(*xiii*) The distance are given in wavelengths towards the generator and also toward the load.

7.7 Some Important Definitions

(*i*) SWR Circle: This is the circle with centre as the centre of the chart and radius of circle is the distance between the centre of chart and the normalized impedance.

(*ii*) Load Line: The line passing through the centre of the chart and the given normalized impedance.

(*iii*) The point of intersection of the SWR circle and the axis of the chart (right hand to the centre of the chart) gives the SWR of the design.

7.8 Steps to Calculate the Reflection Coefficient

(*i*) Normalize the impedance as $\exists_R = \dfrac{Z_L}{Z_o} = r + jx$.

(*ii*) Find the circle of constant normalized resistance '*r*'.

(*iii*) Find the arc of constant normalized reactance '*x*'.

(*iv*) The intersection of the two curves indicates the reflection coefficient in the complex plane. The chart provides directly the magnitude and the phase angle of K_R.

7.9 Application of the Smith Chart

(*i*) To find SWR.

(*ii*) To find the location of voltage maxi mum and minimum from the load.

(*iii*) To find unknown load impedance from SWR or reflection coefficient.

(*iv*) To find the length and position of the stub used in the impedance matching for the perfect transmission (*i.e.*, $Z_l = 1$ *i.e.*, $Z_L = Z_o$).

7.10 Solution of Problems Using Smith Chart

Q 7.1. Find the input admittance of a 0.375λ line terminated in $100 + j150\Omega$ load. The characteristic impedance is 50 Ω.

Soln.: $\exists_R = \dfrac{Z_R}{Z_O} = \dfrac{100 + j150}{50} = 2 + j3$ per Ω.

So equating with $\exists_R = r + jx$, we have, $r = 2, x = 3$.

Procedure for Solution:

Steps:

1. In Fig.7.7 a point 'A_1' is located where resistive component is 100 and inductive reactive component is 150 (as).
2. The point 'A_1' to 'O' (center of the bigger circle) is joined. After joining 'OA_1' and we extend it to the outer circle with "toward the generator scale", *i.e.*, at A_2. The reading of the intersecting point in this outermost circle is 0.213λ.
3. The input admittance of 0.375λ is added to it to get 0.375λ +0.213λ = 0.588λ, which is equivalent to 0.088λ.
4. A point A_3 is now located on the outermost circle which have the value of 0.088λ as straight line OA_2 is drawn.
5. Now with 'O' as the center and OA_1 as radius, a circle is drawn which intersect OA_3 at A_4. The coordinate of A_4 is now (10, 30).

   So its (r, x) coordinate is $\left(\frac{10}{50}, \frac{30}{50}\right) \Rightarrow (0.2, 0.6)$.

   Hence, $\exists_i = 0.2 + j.(0.6)$ and, $z_i = 0.2 \times 50 + j0.6 \times 50 = 10 + j30\Omega$.

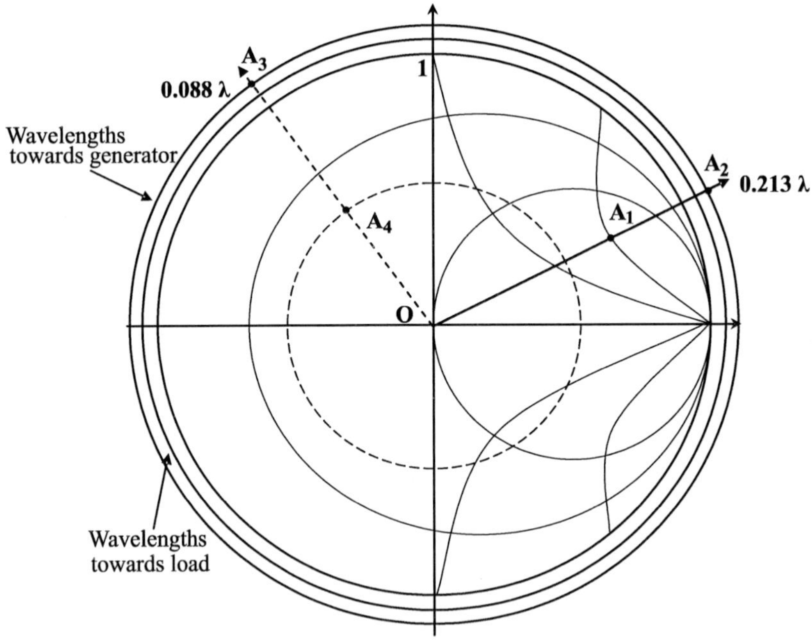

Fig. 7.7 Solution using pictorial Smith chart.

Q 7.2 Find the load impedance of 0.225λ line if the per unit load impedance is measured to be $1 - j.1$ per unit ohm.

Soln.: Here, we have to determine' $\exists_R$ '.

Steps:

1. A point 'A$_1$' is located with $r = 1, x = -1$ (*i.e.*, 50,-50) as in Fig.7.8.
2. 'OA$_1$' is joined and extended to the outer circle with 'toward load' scale up to A$_2$. The reading is 0.162λ.
3. Now 0.225λ is added to it. Now the load is $0.225\lambda + 0.162\lambda = 0.387\lambda$.
4. A point A$_3$ is now marked in the 'towards the load' scale having value 0.387λ.
5. With 'O' as a centre and OA$_1$ as radius, a circle is drawn and it intersects OA$_3$ at A$_4$.
6. At A$_4$, the coordinates are (30,33) $\Rightarrow r = \frac{30}{50} = 0.6$, $x = \frac{33}{50} = 0.66$.

   Hence, $\exists_R = 0.6 + j0.66$ per Ω.

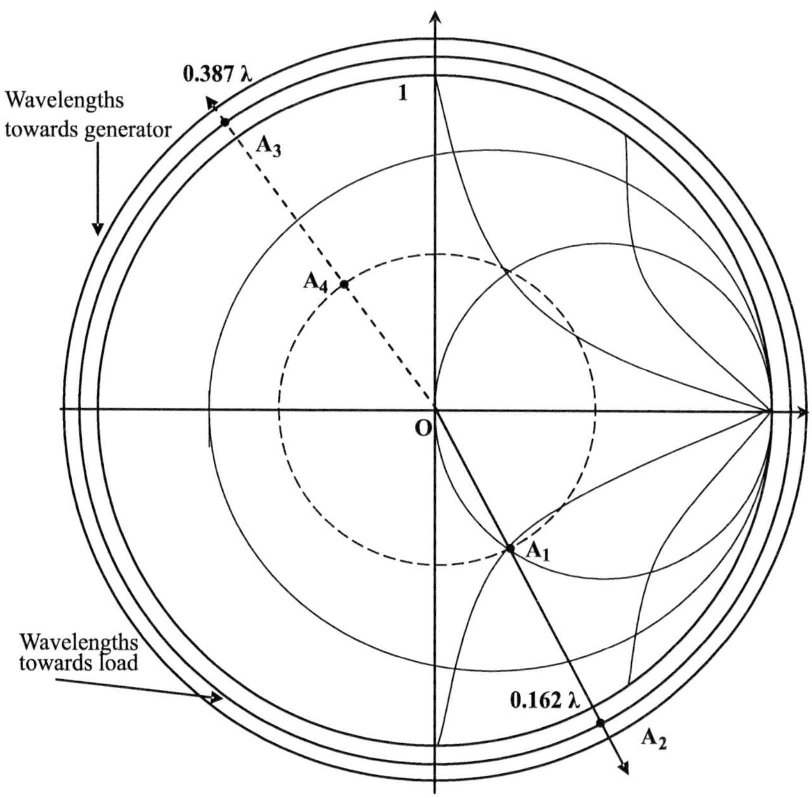

Fig. 7.8 Solution using pictorial Smith chart

Q 7.3. Find the length of the line when load impedance is $0.5 + j(0.7)$ per ohm and the input impedance is $1.4 - j(0.4)$ per ohm.

Solution: Steps:

1. The points A_1 and A_2 with co-ordinates $(0.5\times50, 0.7\times50)$ *i.e.*, (25,35) and, $(1.4\times50, -1.4\times50)$ *i.e.*, (70,-70) respectively are located as in Fig.7.9.
2. OA_1 and OA_2 are joined and extended to the outer circle with 'toward the generator' scale upto A_3 and A_4 respectively. The reading of A_3 is 0.113λ and of A_4 is 0.311λ. They are in opposite directions, so the differences between them is $0.311\lambda - 0.113\lambda = 0.198\lambda$.

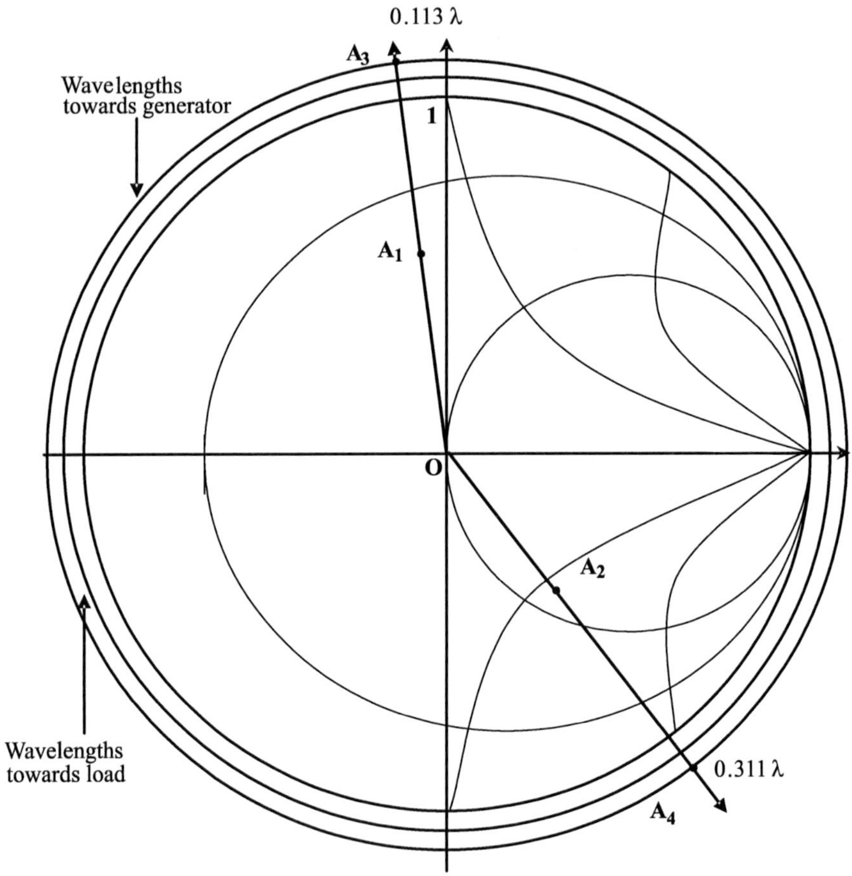

Fig. 7.9 Solution using pictorial Smith chart.

Q7.4. Determine the length of a 50Ω short circuited at one end and required to produce a reactance of (*i*) $j100\Omega$, (*ii*) $-j100\Omega$, (*iii*) 0Ω, (*iv*) infinite resistance.

Solution: Steps:

1. $\exists i = \frac{Z_i}{Z_0} = \frac{j100}{50} = j.2\ \Omega = 0 + j.2$ per Ω
2. A point A_1, where $r = 0, x = 0$, is located as shown in Fig.7.10.
3. Also point A_2 is located where $r = 0, x = 2 \times 50 = 100$.
4. OA_2 is joined and extended upto A_3 where the reading with "toward the generator scale" is 0.176λ, hence, the difference is $0.176\lambda - 0 = 0.176\lambda$.
5. (ii). Same process as in steps (1 to 4) for $x = -2 \times 50 = -100$.
6. (iii). Here, $\exists_i = 0$ and it is equivalent to the length of 0.5λ.
7. (iv). Here, $r = 0, x = \infty$ and so the reading is 0.25λ, *i.e.*, at the point of 'P'.

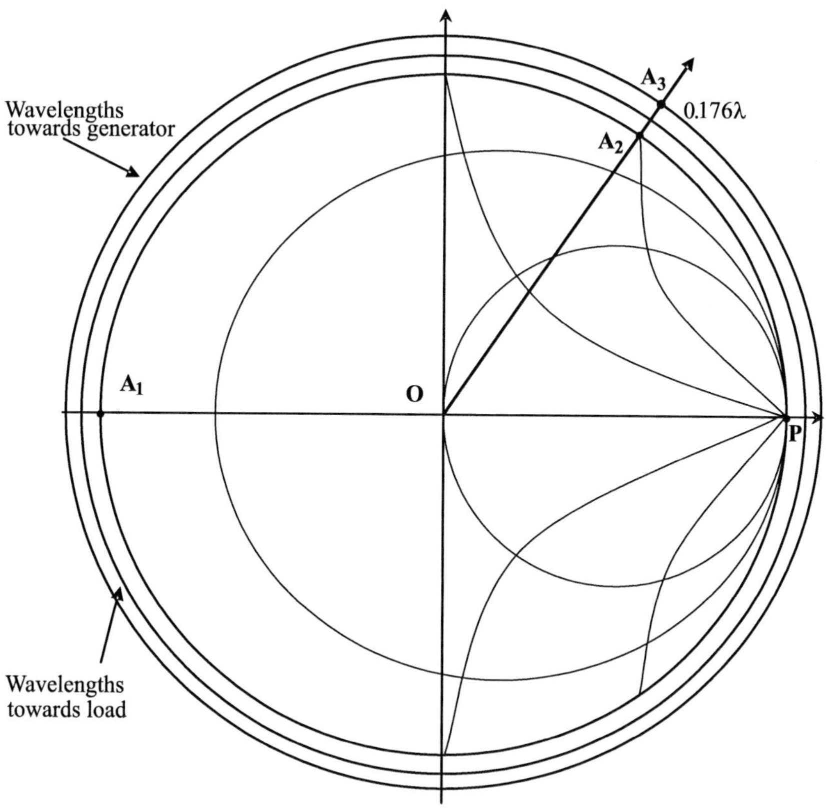

Fig. 7.10 Solution using pictorial Smith chart.

Q 7.5. The characteristic admittance of a line is 0.02 mho and short circuited at one end. Determine the length of a line to produce an admittance of

(*i*) $j(0.032)$ mho

(*ii*) $-j(0.032)$ mho

(*iii*) $-j(0.07)$ mho

(*iv*) $j(0.07)$ mho

Solution: Here, let the admittance is given by $Y = g + jb$. 'g' and 'b' are conductance and susceptance respectively. For inductive susceptance, 'b' is positive and for capacitative susceptance, 'b' is negative.

Steps:

1. (i). Here, $y_i = \frac{Y_i}{Y_0} = \frac{(0.032)}{(0.02)} = (1.6)$

2. A point is located with $g = \infty, b = \infty$ at 'P' shown in Fig.7.11.

3. At 'P' the reading in 'generator scale' is 0.25λ.

4. We now locate a point 'P_1' with $g = 0, b = 1.6 \times 50 = 80$.

5. Extending OP_1 to the 'generator scale' it intersects at P_2. The reading is 0.162λ, which is equivalent to $0.162\lambda + 0.5\lambda = 0.662\lambda$.

6. Hence the difference is $0.662\lambda - 0.25\lambda = 0.412\lambda$. This is the required length.

7. We have to follow the same for (ii), (iii) and (iv).

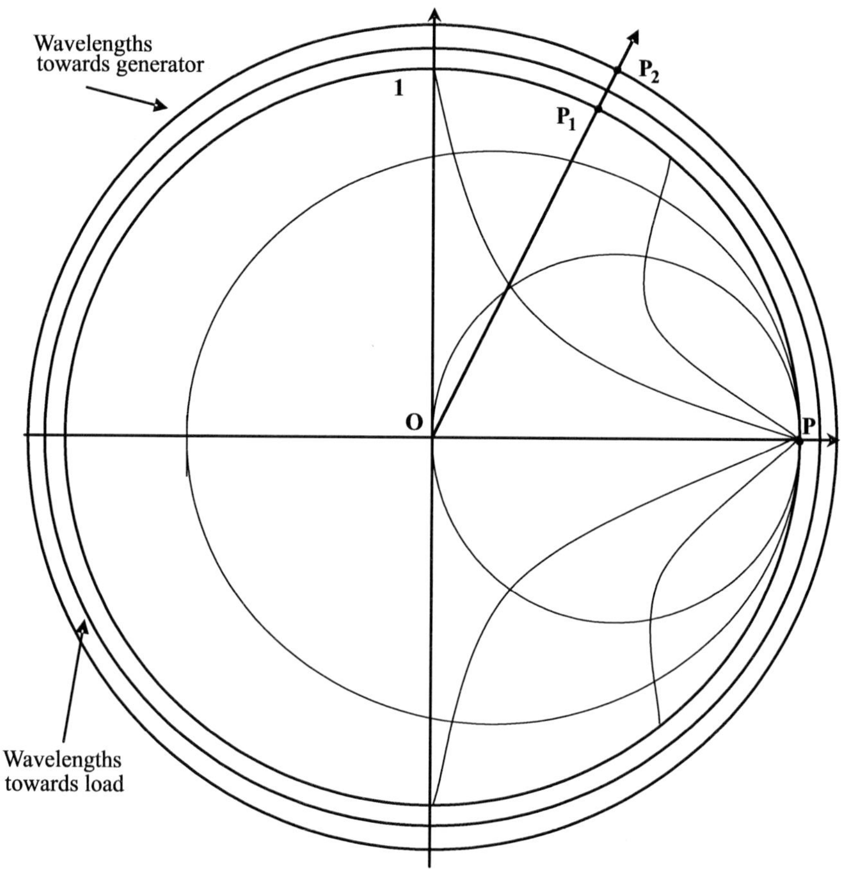

Fig. 7.11 Solution using pictorial Smith chart.

❑❑❑

NUMERICAL PROBLEMS

Q.1. Calculate the electrostatic force between two protons in a nucleus of iron with which they repel each other assuming a separation of $4\times10^{-15}m$ between them.

Soln.:

$$F=\frac{1}{4\pi\varepsilon_o}.\frac{q_1q_2}{r^2}$$

$$=\frac{1}{4\pi\times\frac{1}{36\pi\times10^9}}\times\frac{(1.6\times10^{-19})\times(1.6\times10^{-19})}{(4\times10^{-15})^2}=14.4N$$

Q.2. In Rutherford scattering experiment gold nuclei were bombarded with α particles which were energetic enough to reach within $2\times10^{-14}m$ of the nucleus. Calculate the force of electrostatic repulsion experienced by the α -particles. (Z=79 for Au).

Soln.:

$$F=\frac{1}{4\pi\varepsilon_o}.\frac{79q\times2q}{r^2}$$

$$=\frac{1}{4\pi\times\frac{1}{36\pi\times10^9}}\times\frac{(79\times1.6\times10^{-19})\times(2\times1.6\times10^{-19})}{(2\times10^{-14})^2}=91.008N$$

Q3. The concentrated charges of $0.25\,\mu C$ are placed at the vertices of an equilateral triangle while side is $100mm$. Determine the magnitude and direction of the resultant force on one charge due to the other charges.

Soln.:

Following Fig.1, force along BA arm is given by

$$F_{BA} = 9\times10^{9}\times\frac{(0.25\mu C\times0.25\mu C)}{(100mm)^{2}} = 56.25\times10^{-3}\text{ N (Directed from B to A)}$$

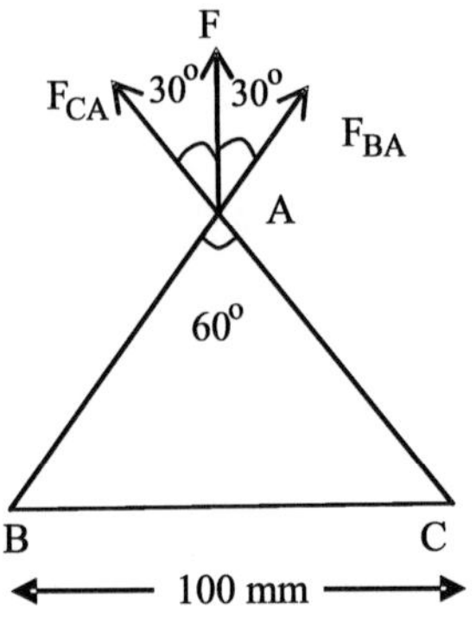

Fig. 1

Similarly, force along CA arm is

$$F_{CA} = 9\times10^{9}\times\frac{(0.25\mu C\times0.25\mu C)}{(100mm)^{2}} = 56.25\times10^{-3}\text{ N (Directed from C to A)}$$

Hence the resultant force on A is

$$\vec{F} = \vec{F}_{BA} + \vec{F}_{CA} = F_{BA}\cos 30^{o} + F_{CA}\cos 30^{o}$$

$$= 2\times(56.25\times10^{-3})\times\sqrt{3}/2 = 97.425\times10^{-3}\text{ N}$$

And this is perpendicular to BC.

Q4. What is the electric field due to a positive charge and a negative charge of equal magnitude 'Q' separated by a distance '2a' at a distance 'r' along the perpendicular bisector of the line joining the charges. This configuration is called electric dipole. Here $r \rangle\rangle a$.

Soln.:

Here as shown in Fig.2, net electric field is

$$\vec{E} = \vec{E}_1 + \vec{E}_2$$

Now,

$$E_1 = E_2 = \frac{1}{4\pi\varepsilon_o}\cdot\frac{Q}{\left(\sqrt{a^2+r^2}\right)^2}$$

And, $E = E_1\cos\theta + E_2\cos\theta$

$$= 2E_1\cos\theta = 2E_1\cdot\frac{a}{\sqrt{a^2+r^2}}$$

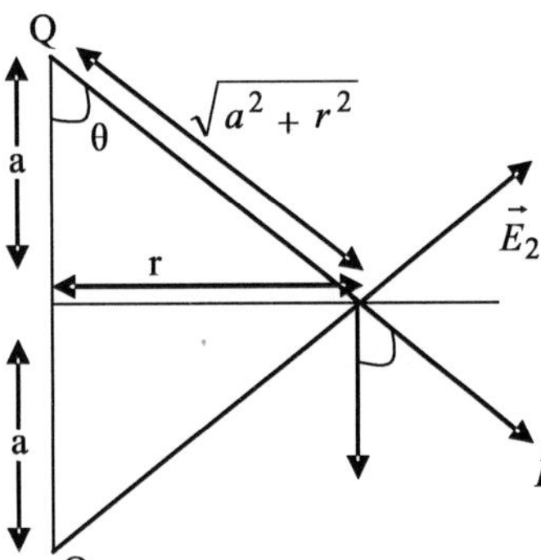

Fig. 2

Hence, $E = \frac{1}{4\pi\varepsilon_o} \cdot \frac{2aQ}{r^3} = \frac{1}{4\pi\varepsilon_o} \times \frac{p}{(r)^3}$ (as $r \rangle\rangle a$)

Here $p = 2aQ$ is the dipole moment.

Q.5. Two charges of similar sign and magnitude 1×10^{-12} coulomb are located 1m apart. What is the potential at point that is midway between two charges and 50cm from the line connecting the charges? What is the potential if the charges are of opposite sign?

Soln.:

From Fig.3 the potential is given by

$$V = \frac{1}{4\pi\varepsilon_o}\left[\frac{Q}{AO} + \frac{Q}{BO}\right]$$

$$= 9\times10^9 \left[\frac{1\times10^{-12}}{\sqrt{(0.5)^2 + (0.5)^2}} \times 2\right] = 25.45\times10^{-3}\,V$$

For opposite charges the potential becomes

$$V = \frac{1}{4\pi\varepsilon_o}\left[\frac{1\times10^{-12}}{\sqrt{(0.5)^2 + (0.5)^2}} + \frac{-1\times10^{-12}}{\sqrt{(0.5)^2 + (0.5)^2}}\right] = 0V$$

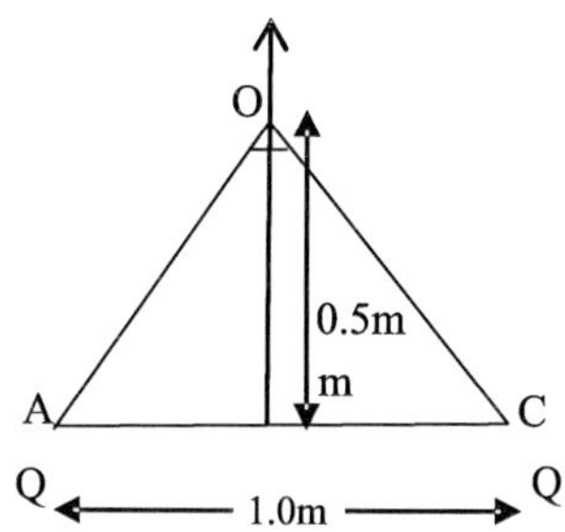

Fig. 3

Q.6 **(*a*)** Determine the electric potential at a point on the axis of a uniformly charged disc.

(*b*) The potential at any point about a long pair of wires having equal and opposite charges distributed along their length is given by

$$\frac{\rho_l}{2\pi\varepsilon_o}\log\left(\frac{r_b}{r_a}\right)$$

Here 'ρ_l' is the linear charge density distributed along with the wires and the point is at distance 'r_a' and 'r_b' for the wires respectively. Show that the equipotential surfaces are non-concentric cylinders.

Soln.:

Let the radius of disc is 'a' and $Z = OP = h$.

Hence as shown in Fig.4, $R = \sqrt{r^2 + h^2}$

Potential at point P can be evaluated by considering of a large number of elemental rings. We also consider the disc along XY plane have charge density 'ρ_s' coulomb/m^2. For an elemental annular ring of radius 'r' and of radial thickness 'dr', the annular area '$2\pi r dr$' and this surface element carries a charge 'dQ' is $dQ = \rho_S \times 2\pi r dr$

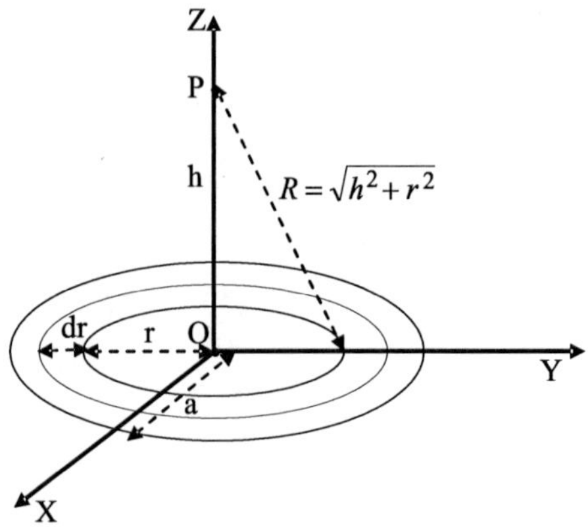

Fig. 4

So elementary potential dV at P due to Q is

$$dV = \frac{1}{4\pi\varepsilon_o} \times \frac{\rho_S \times 2\pi r dr}{\sqrt{r^2+h^2}}$$

Hence, net potential for the whole plate is

$$V = \frac{\rho_S}{4\pi\varepsilon_o} \times \int_0^a \frac{2\pi r dr}{\sqrt{r^2+h^2}}$$

$$= \frac{\rho_S}{2\varepsilon_o} \times \left[\sqrt{r^2+h^2}\right]_0^a = \frac{\rho_S}{2\varepsilon_o}\left[\sqrt{r^2+h^2} - h\right] \text{ V}$$

(*b*) Here, as shown in Fig.5, we have

$$V_{AB} = V_A - V_B = -\int_{r_a}^{r_b} E dr$$

$$= -\int_{r_a}^{r_b} \frac{\rho_l}{2\pi\varepsilon_o}\frac{dr}{r} = \frac{\rho_l}{2\pi\varepsilon_o}\log\left(\frac{r_a}{r_b}\right)$$

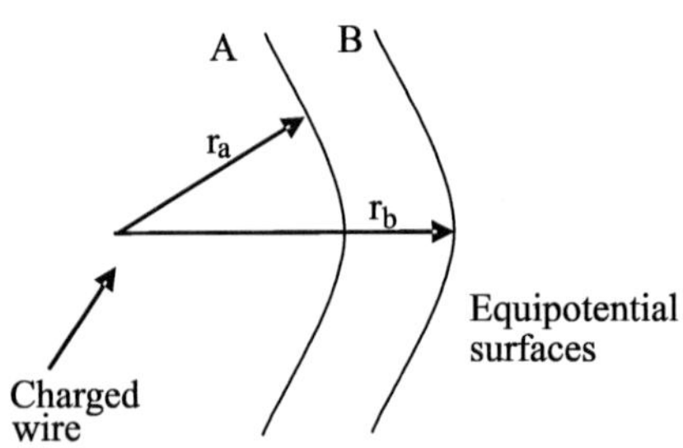

Fig. 5

From Gauss's Law we have,

$$\oint_S Dds = q = \int \rho_l dl$$

$$\Rightarrow \varepsilon_o E \times 2\pi r \int dl = \rho_l \int dl$$

$$\Rightarrow \vec{E} = \frac{\rho_l}{2\pi\varepsilon_o r}$$

Q.7. Find the field outside a uniformly charged sphere of radius 'a'.

Soln.:

Net electric flux is given by

$$\oint \vec{E}_o.\hat{n}dS = \oint E_o dS = E_o 4\pi r^2$$

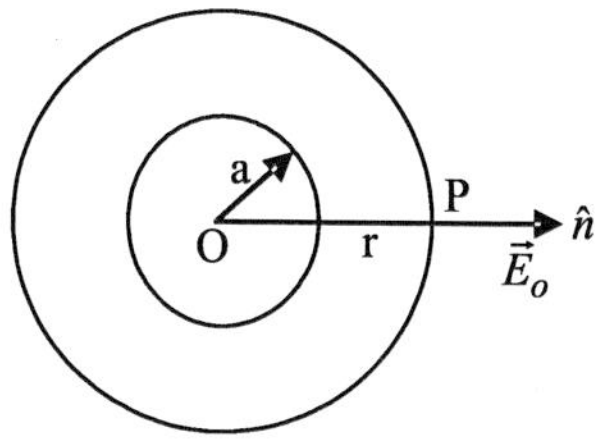

Fig. 6

However from Gauss's law we have,

$$\int \vec{D}.d\vec{S} = q \Rightarrow \int \vec{E}.d\vec{S} = \frac{q}{\varepsilon_o}$$

$$\Rightarrow E_o \times 4\pi r^2 = \frac{q}{\varepsilon_o}$$

$$\Rightarrow E_o = \frac{1}{4\pi\varepsilon_o}.\frac{q}{r^2}$$

Q.8. A spherical volume of radius 'R' has a volume charge density of $\rho = kr$, here 'r' is radial distance and 'k' is constant. Find the expression for electric field in the region of $0 \le r \le \infty$.

Soln.:

Given, $\rho = kr$

But, $Q = \int_V \rho dV$

$$= \int_o^R (kr).(4\pi r^2 dr) = 4\pi k \int_0^R r^3 dr$$

$$= 4\pi k \times \frac{R^4}{4} = \pi k R^4$$

From Gauss's Law we have,

$$\int Dds = Q \Rightarrow EdS = Q / \varepsilon$$

$$\Rightarrow E \times 4\pi r^2 = \pi k R^4 / \varepsilon$$

$$\Rightarrow E = \frac{kR^4}{4\varepsilon r^2}$$

Vectorically, as this is outward electric flux, we have $\vec{E} = \vec{E}_{out}$

$$\therefore \vec{E}_{out} = \frac{kR^4}{4\varepsilon r^2}\hat{r}$$

This is true for $r \rangle R$, *i.e.*, outside the charged sphere.

At $r = R$, $$\vec{E}_{out} = \frac{kR^4}{4\varepsilon R^2}\hat{r} = \frac{k}{4\varepsilon}R^2\hat{r}$$

At $r \langle R$, $$q_{inside} = \int_0^r \rho dV = \int_o^r (kr).(4\pi r^2 dr) = \frac{4k\pi r^4}{4} = k\pi r^4$$

So,

$$E_{in}\left(=\frac{Q}{\varepsilon d\vec{S}}\right) = \frac{k\pi r^4}{\varepsilon \times 4\pi r^2}\hat{r} = \frac{k}{4\varepsilon}r^2\hat{r}$$

Q9. In a spherical coordinate system, volume charge density is $\rho = \rho_o (r/a)^{3/2}$

(*i*) How much charge lies in sphere of radius 'a'?

(*ii*) Find electric flux density at $r = a$.

Soln.:

We have here, $$\rho = \rho_o (r/a)^{3/2}$$

(*i*) $$Q = \int_0^a \rho dV = \int_0^a \left(\rho_o \left(\frac{r}{a}\right)^{3/2}\right)\left(4\pi r^2 dr\right) = \frac{4\pi\rho_o}{a^{3/2}}\int_0^a r^{7/2} dr$$

$$\therefore Q = \frac{4\pi \ell_o}{a^{3/2}}\left[\frac{2}{9}a^{9/2}\right] = \frac{8\pi}{9}\ell_o a^3 \text{ coulomb}$$

(*ii*) Using Gauss's law, $$E \times 4\pi r^2 = \frac{Q}{\varepsilon}$$

$$\Rightarrow D = \frac{Q}{4\pi a^2} = \frac{8\pi\rho_o a^3/9}{4\pi a^2} = \frac{2}{9}\rho_o a^3$$

$$\therefore \vec{D} = \frac{2}{9}\rho_o a^3 \hat{r} \text{ C/m}^2$$

Q.10. Three coaxial cylindrical sheets are present in free space with

$\rho_S = 5$ C/m² at r=2 m

$\rho_S = -2$ C/m² at r=4 m

$\rho_S = -3$ C/m² at r=5 m

Find 'D' at R=1,3,4,5 and 6m

Soln.:

For R=1m:

(*i*) We now determine the effect of $\rho_S = 5coul/m^2$ on $r = 2$ m from Gauss's law:

$$D_1 \times dS = q \Rightarrow D_1 \times 2\pi R \times z = \int \rho_s dS = \int_0^z \int_0^{2\pi} \rho_S r d\phi dz$$

$$\Rightarrow D_1 \times 2\pi R \times z = z \times \int_q^{2\pi} 5 \times 2 \times d\phi$$

$$\Rightarrow D_1 \times 2\pi \times 1 \times z = z \times 10 \times 2\pi$$

$$\Rightarrow D_1 = 10C/m^2$$

(*ii*) We now determine the effect of $\rho_S = -2C/m^2$ on $r = 4$ m from Gauss's law:

$$D_2 \times 2\pi \times 1 \times z = z \times \int_0^{2\pi} (-2) \times 4 \times d\phi = z \times -8 \times 2\pi$$

$$\Rightarrow D_2 = -8C/m^2$$

(*iii*) We now determine the effect of $\rho_S = -3coul/m^2$ on $r = 5$ m from Gauss's law:

$$D_3 \times 2\pi \times 1 \times z = z \times \int_0^{2\pi} (-3) \times 5 \times d\phi = z \times -15 \times 2\pi$$

$$\Rightarrow D_3 = -15C/m^2$$

Finally net value of 'D' is $= D_1 + D_2 + D_3 = 10 - 8 - 15 = -13C/m^2$

Similar steps will follow for solution with $R = 3, 4, 5, 6$ m.

Q.11. Determine the electric field due to spherical cloud of electrons giving the volume charge density of

$$\rho = -\rho_o \text{ at } a \le r \le R$$
$$= 0 \text{ at } r \rangle R$$

Soln.: Total enclosed charges are

$$Q_{enclosed} = \int \rho dV = \int_0^R (-\rho_o).(4\pi r^2 dr) = -\rho_0 . \frac{4}{3}\pi R^3$$

Using Gauss's Law we have the electric field as,

$$E_1 \times 4\pi r^2 = \frac{Q}{\varepsilon} = -\frac{\rho_0}{\varepsilon}\frac{4\pi}{3}R^3$$

$$\Rightarrow E_1 = -\frac{\rho_0}{3\varepsilon r^2}R^3$$

So for $r \rangle\rangle R$: $\overrightarrow{E_{out}} = -\frac{\rho_0 R^3}{3\varepsilon r^2}\hat{r}$

For charges inside,

$$Q_{in} = \int \rho dV = \int_0^r (-\rho_o) 4\pi r^2 dr = -\frac{4\pi}{3}\rho_o r^3$$

Hence, $E_{in} = \frac{1}{4\pi r^2}\frac{Q}{\varepsilon} = -\frac{\frac{4\pi}{3}\rho_o r^3}{4\pi\varepsilon r^2}$

$$\Rightarrow \overrightarrow{E_{in}} = -\frac{\rho_o r}{3\varepsilon}\hat{r}$$

Q.12. Using Gauss's Law in integral form obtain electric field at all points due to the following volume charge distribution in cylindrical coordinates as

$$\rho(r,\phi,z) = \rho_o(r/a) \quad \text{for} \quad 0\langle r \langle a$$
$$= 0 \quad \text{for} \quad a \langle r \langle \infty$$

Soln.:

Using cylindrical symmetry the amount of enclosed charges is given by

$$Q_{enclosed} = \int \rho dV = \int_0^{2\pi}\int_0^a\int_0^z \rho(r d\phi) dr dz$$

$$= \int_0^{2\pi} d\phi \int_0^z dz \int_0^a \rho_o \frac{r}{a} r dr = \frac{2\pi z \rho_o}{a}\int_0^a r^2 dr$$

$$= \frac{2\pi\rho_o z}{a} \times \frac{a^3}{3} = \frac{2\pi\rho_o a^2 z}{3}$$

Using Gauss's Law for the electric field 'E' we have,

$$E\int dS = Q/\varepsilon$$

$$\Rightarrow E \times 2\pi r z = Q/\varepsilon \Rightarrow E = \frac{Q}{2\pi\varepsilon r z}$$

At $r = a$: $E = \frac{2\pi\rho_o a^2 z/3}{2\pi\varepsilon z a} = \frac{\rho_o a}{3\varepsilon}$

$$\Rightarrow \vec{E} = \frac{\rho_o a}{3\varepsilon}\hat{r}$$

At $r < a$:

$$Q_{inside} = \int \rho dV = \int_0^{2\pi}\int_0^{z}\int_0^{r} \rho_o \frac{r}{a} r dr d\phi dz$$

$$= \frac{2\pi\rho_o z r^3}{3a}$$

Hence the electric field becomes

$$E_{in} = \frac{2\pi\rho_o z r^3 / 3a}{\varepsilon \times 2\pi r z} = \frac{\rho_o r^2}{3\varepsilon a}$$

Q.13. A parallel plate capacitor has internal separation 'd' between the plates. A dielectric slab with 'ε_r' of thickness 'a' is placed on the lower plate of the capacitor as in Fig.7. Show that

(*a*) Electric intensity in the dielectric is $E_1 = \dfrac{V}{\varepsilon_r d - a(\varepsilon_r - 1)}$ 'V' is the potential difference between the plates.

(*b*) Electric field intensity in the air space is $E_o = \varepsilon_r E_1$

(*c*) Capacitance of the capacitor is

$$C_T = \frac{\varepsilon_o A}{d}\left[\frac{\varepsilon_r}{\left(1 - \frac{a}{d}\right)\varepsilon_r + (a/d)}\right] \text{F.}$$

Soln.:

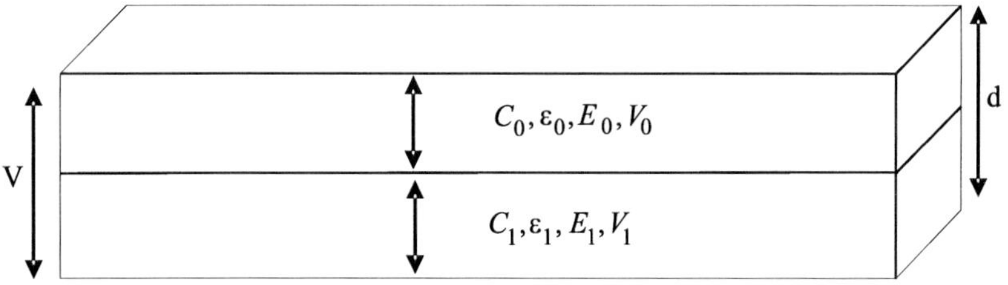

Fig. 7

(*a*) As the normal component of D is continuous, we have

$$\varepsilon_o E_o = \varepsilon_1 E_1$$

$$\Rightarrow E_o = \frac{\varepsilon_1}{\varepsilon_o} E_1 = \varepsilon_r E_1 \qquad \text{(here } \varepsilon_r = \frac{\varepsilon_1}{\varepsilon_o}\text{)}$$

Also $\quad V_1 = E_1 \times a$ and $V_o = E_o(d - a)$

However, $V = V_o + V_1$

$$= E_1 a + E_o(d-a) = E_1 a + (\varepsilon_r E_1)(d-a)$$

$$= E_1(a + \varepsilon_r(d-a))$$

$$= \frac{V}{a+\varepsilon_r(d-a)}$$

$$\Rightarrow E_1 = \frac{V}{\varepsilon_r d - a(\varepsilon_r - 1)}$$

(*b*) Electric field intensity in the air space is given by

$$E_0 = \frac{V}{\varepsilon_r d} = \frac{E}{\varepsilon_r} = \varepsilon_r E \qquad \text{(as } \varepsilon_r = 1 \text{ for free space)}$$

(*c*) Total capacitance 'C_T' is given by

$$\frac{1}{C_T} = \frac{1}{C_o} + \frac{1}{C_1} \Rightarrow C_T = \frac{C_o \times C_1}{C_o + C_1}$$

Here, $C_o = \varepsilon_o \times \frac{A}{d-a}$ and $C_1 = \varepsilon_1 \frac{A}{a}$

Hence, $$C_T = \frac{\frac{\varepsilon_o A}{d-a} \times \frac{\varepsilon_1 A}{d}}{\frac{\varepsilon_o A}{d-a} + \frac{\varepsilon_1 A}{a}} = \frac{\varepsilon_o \varepsilon_1 A^2}{a(d-a)} \times \frac{a(d-a)}{\varepsilon_o A(a) + \varepsilon_1 A(d-a)}$$

$$= \frac{\varepsilon_o \varepsilon_1 A^2}{a\varepsilon_o A + A\varepsilon_1(d-a)}$$

$$= \frac{\varepsilon_o A}{d} \cdot \frac{\varepsilon_1}{\varepsilon_o \frac{a}{d} + \varepsilon_1\left(\frac{d-a}{d}\right)} = \frac{\varepsilon_o A}{d}\left[\frac{\varepsilon_r \varepsilon_o}{\varepsilon_o \frac{a}{d} + \varepsilon_o \varepsilon_r \times (1 - a/d)}\right]$$

$$\Rightarrow C_T = \frac{\varepsilon_o A}{d} \times \frac{\varepsilon_r}{(1-\frac{a}{d})\varepsilon_r + a/d}$$

Q.14. (*a*) Find the capacitance per unit area of the condenser whose parallel plates are separated by 'h'.

(*b*) An infinite uncharged sheet of metal of thickness 'a' is introduced between the plate as in Fig.8. Show that the change in capacitance per unit area is $\frac{\varepsilon_o a}{h(h-a)}$.

Soln:

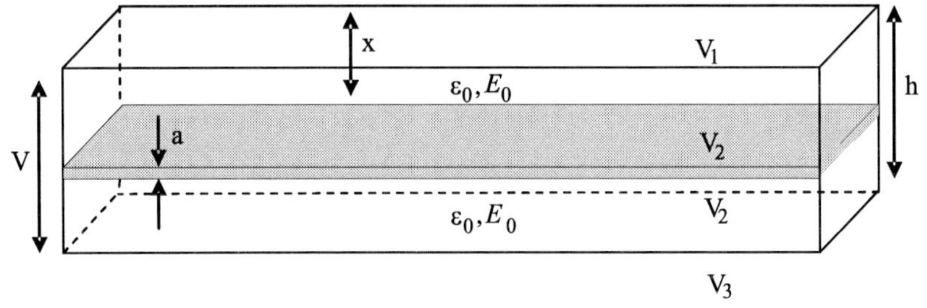

Fig. 8

(a) When no metal sheet is inserted inside the capacitor, the capacitance of it is given by

$$C = \frac{Q}{V}$$

$$\Rightarrow \frac{C}{A} = \frac{Q}{AV} = \frac{\rho_S}{V}$$

Potential difference between the two plates now is given by

$$V = V_1 - V_3$$

Also the potential is $V = E_o h$

$$= \frac{D}{\varepsilon_o} h = \frac{\rho_S}{\varepsilon_o} h \quad \text{(using Gauss's law)}$$

So capacitance per unit area is

$$\frac{C}{A} = \frac{\rho_s}{V} = \frac{\rho_S}{\rho_S \cdot \frac{h}{\varepsilon_o}} = \frac{\varepsilon_o}{h} \qquad (1)$$

(b) Now a metal sheet is inserted inside the capacitor.

Then the potential difference between the upper capacitor plate and top face of the inserted sheet is

$$V_1 - V_2 = E_o x = \frac{D_o}{\varepsilon_o} x = \frac{\rho_S}{\varepsilon_o} x$$

Similarly, the potential difference between the lower capacitor plate and bottom face of the inserted sheet is

$$V_2 - V_3 = \frac{\rho_S}{\varepsilon_o}\left(h - (x + a)\right)$$

'V_2' is same across the metal sheet. Hence the net potential difference across the capacitor plates now is

$$V_1 - V_3 = (V_1 - V_2) + (V_2 - V_3)$$

$$= \frac{\rho_S}{\varepsilon_o} x + \frac{\rho_S}{\varepsilon_o}\left(h - (x+a)\right)$$

$$= \frac{\rho_S}{\varepsilon_o}(h - x)$$

So capacitance per unit area is

$$\frac{C}{A} = \frac{Q}{AV} = \frac{\rho_S}{V} = \frac{\rho_S}{\frac{\rho_S}{\varepsilon_o}(h-a)} = \frac{\varepsilon_o}{h-a} \qquad (2)$$

Hence using eqns.(1) and (2), change in capacitance per unit area is

$$\frac{\varepsilon_o}{h-a} - \frac{\varepsilon_o}{h} = \frac{a\varepsilon_o}{h(h-a)}$$

Q.15. Maximum potential difference between inner and outer conductor sheath of coaxial cable is $200KV$ as in Fig.9 with $E = 25 \times 10^6 V/m$

(*a*) Find R_1 and R_2 if $R_1 = \frac{R_2}{2}$.

(*b*) Find capacitance of 10 Km length cable.

(*c*) What is the energy stored in 10 Km cable?

Soln.:

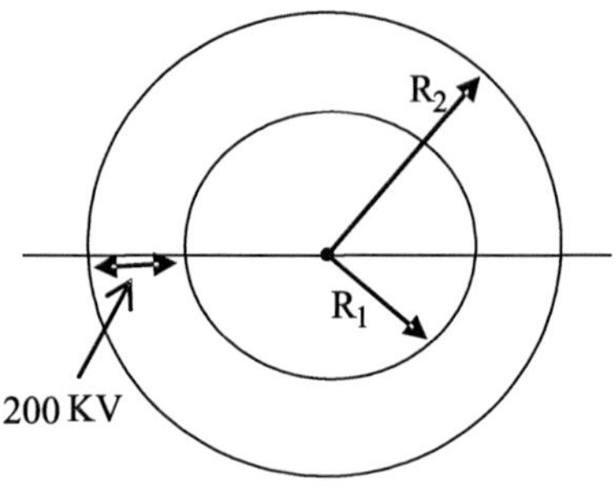

Fig. 9

Here, $V = 200KV, l = 10Km$ and $E = 25 \times 10^6 V/m$

For cylindrical cable the electric field is

$$E = \frac{D}{\varepsilon} = \frac{Q}{A\varepsilon} = \frac{\rho_L \times L}{\varepsilon \times 2\pi r L} = \frac{\rho_L}{2\pi r\varepsilon} \text{ (using Gauss's law)} \qquad (3)$$

Hence the potential is given by

$$V = -\int_{R_{11}}^{R_2} E dr = -\frac{\rho_L}{2\pi\varepsilon}\int_{R_2}^{R_1}\frac{dr}{r}$$

$$= \frac{\rho_L}{2\pi\varepsilon}\ln\left(\frac{R_2}{R_1}\right)$$

$$\Rightarrow \rho_L = \frac{2\pi\varepsilon V}{\ln(R_2/R_1)} \qquad (4)$$

(a) Given $E = 25\times10^6 V/m$

Hence using eqn.(3) at $R = R_1$, we have,

$$\frac{\rho_L}{2\pi R_1\varepsilon} = 25\times10^6$$

$$\Rightarrow \frac{2\pi\varepsilon V}{\ln(R_2/R_1)}\times\frac{1}{2\pi R_1\varepsilon} = 25\times10^6 \quad \text{(from eqn.(4))}$$

$$\Rightarrow R_1 = \frac{V}{25\times10^6\times\ln\left[\frac{R_2}{R_1}\right]}$$

$$= \frac{200\times10^3}{25\times10^6\times\ln(2)} = \frac{2}{250\times\ln 2} = 0.0115 \text{ m}$$

And $R_2 = 2R_1 = 0.023\,\text{m}$

(b) Capacitance of 10 Km length cable is

$$C = \frac{Q}{V} = \frac{\rho_L\times l}{\frac{\rho_L}{2\pi\varepsilon}\ln\left(\frac{R_2}{R_1}\right)}$$

$$= \frac{2\pi\times8.85\times10^{-12}\times10\times10^3}{\ln(2)} = 0.802\mu F$$

(c) The energy stored in 10 Km length cable is

$$W = \frac{1}{2}CV^2 = \frac{1}{2}\times0.802\times10^{-6}\times200\times10^3 = 16KJ$$

Q.16. A plane sheet containing charges with density $\rho_s = 40\ \mu C/m^2$ is located at $z = -0.5m$. A uniform line charge of $\rho_l = -6\mu C/m$ lies along the Y-axis. What is the net flux crosses the surface of a cube 2 m on an edge, centered at the origin, as shown in Fig.10?

Soln.:

The net electric flux is equal to the net charge enclosed and so $\Psi = q_{encl}$

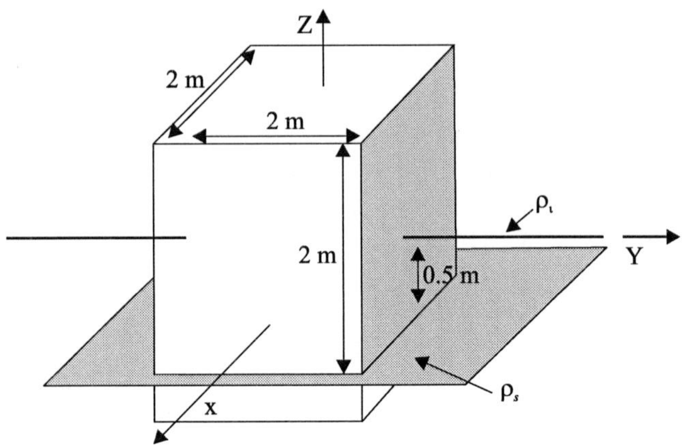

Fig. 10

The charge in the plane sheet is

$$Q_1 = (2m \times 2m)(40C/m^2) = (4m^2)(40C/m^2) = 160\mu C$$

Net charge along the line is

$$Q_2 = (2m)(-6\mu C/m) = -12\mu C$$

Thus, the amount of charge enclosed is

$$q_{enc} = \Psi = Q_1 + Q_2 = 160 - 12 = 148\mu C$$

Q.17. A uniform line charge of density $\rho_\ell = 3\mu C/m$ lies along Z-axis. A concentric circular cylinder of radius 2 m has surface charge density $\rho_\ell = (-1.5/4\pi)\ \mu C/m^2$. Both distributions are infinite in extent along Z-direction as shown in Fig.11. Using Gauss's law find $\vec{D}$ in all regions.

Soln:

From Gauss's law, $q = \oint_S \vec{D}.\vec{dS}$

Since line charge is distributed along the Z-axis, therefore, $\vec{D}$ with respect to line charge is at 90 with cylindrical surface and is shown in Fig.2. Thus if 'L' is the length of the cylinder, then, we have,

$$q = \rho_l L = D \times 2\pi r \times L \Rightarrow D = \frac{\rho_l}{2\pi r}$$

Vectorially, $\vec{D} = \frac{\rho_\ell}{2\pi r}\hat{r}$ for $0 < r < 2$ m (5)

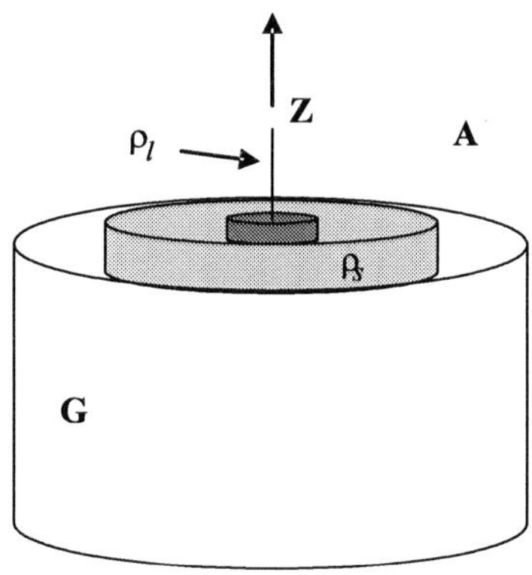

Fig. 11

For Gaussian surface 'G' we have from Gauss's law the enclosed charge is

$$q_{enc} = \oint \vec{D}.\vec{dS}$$

$$\Rightarrow (\rho_\ell + 4\pi\rho_s)L = D(2\pi rL) \Rightarrow D = \frac{(\rho_\ell + 4\pi\rho_s)}{2\pi r}$$

Vectorically, $\vec{D} = \dfrac{\rho_\ell + 4\pi\rho_s}{2\pi r}\hat{r}$ for $r > 2\,\text{m}$ (6)

Substituting given data into eqn.(5) and (6) we have,

$$\vec{D} = \frac{0.477}{r}\hat{r}\ \ \mu C/m^2 \qquad \text{for } 0 < r < 2\ \text{m}$$

And, $$\vec{D} = \frac{0.239}{r}\hat{r} \qquad \text{for } r > 2\,\text{m}$$

Q18. Given that $\vec{A} = 30e^{-r}\hat{r} - 2z\hat{z}$ in cylindrical coordinates, evaluate both sides of the divergence theorem for the volume enclosed by $r = 2$, $z = 0$, and $z = 5$ as shown in Fig.12.

Soln.:

From Gauss's divergence theorem for any vector $\vec{A}$ is

$$\oint \vec{A}.\vec{dS} = \int (\vec{\nabla}.\vec{A})dV$$

Divergence of a vector field is also shown in Fig.12.

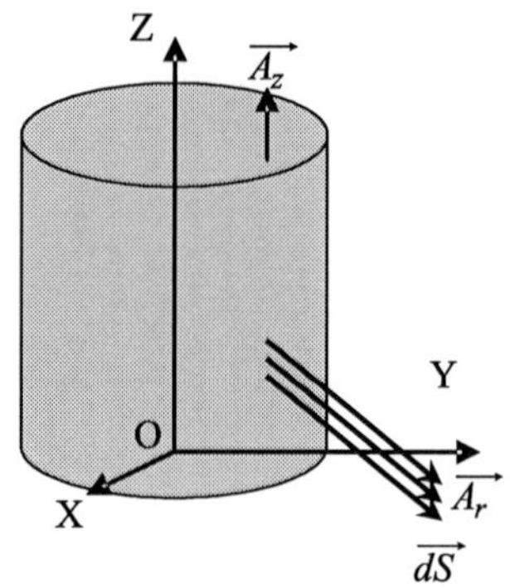

Fig. 12

Here, $A_z = 0$ for $z = 0$ and hence $\vec{A}.\vec{dS}$ is zero over this part of the surface. Therefore surface integral of vector field $\vec{A}$ under the given boundary condition for cylindrical co-ordinates is given by

$$\oint_S \vec{A}.\vec{dS} = \int_0^{2\pi}\int_0^{5} 30e^{-2}\hat{r}.2d\phi dz\hat{r} + \int_0^{2\pi}\int_0^{2} (-2)5\hat{z}.rdrd\phi\hat{z}$$

$$= 60e^{-2}(2\pi)(5) - 10(2\pi)(2) = 129.4$$

Now, $$\vec{\nabla}.\vec{A} = \frac{1}{r}\frac{\partial}{\partial r}(30re^{-r}) + \frac{\partial}{\partial z}(-2z) = \frac{30e^{-r}}{r} - 30e^{-r} - 2$$

Hence, right side of the divergence theorem for cylindrical surface is given by

$$\int\left(\vec{\nabla}.\vec{A}\right)dV = \int_0^{5}\int_0^{2\pi}\int_0^{2}\left(\frac{30re^{-r}}{r} - 30e^{-r} - 2\right)rd\phi drdz = 129.4$$

Hence, $$\oint_S \vec{A}.\vec{dS} = \int\left(\vec{\nabla}.\vec{A}\right)dV$$

Q.19. For an electric field of $\vec{E} = 2x\hat{i} - 4y\hat{j}$ (V/m), calculate the work done in moving a point charge of '+2' Coulomb

(a) From a point of $(2,0,0)$ m to $(0,0,0)$ and then from $(0,0,0)$ to $(0,2,0)$;

(b) From $(2,0,0)$ to $(0,2,0)$ along the straight-line path joining the two points.

As shown in Fig.13.

Soln.:

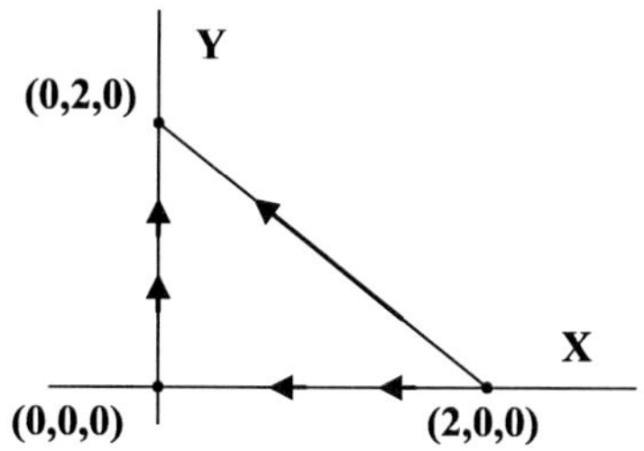

Fig. 13

(*a*) Movement of charge along the X-axis is

$$y = dy = dz = 0$$

And so the work done is

$$dW_1 = -2(2x\hat{i}).(dx\hat{i}) = -4xdx$$

Movement of charge along the Y-axis is

$$x = dx = dz = 0$$

And so the work done is

$$dW_2 = -2(-4y\hat{j}).(dy\hat{j}) = 8ydy$$

Thus total work done for the given displacement of the point charge is

$$W = \int_2^0 (dW_1)dx + \int_0^2 (dW_2)dy = -4\int_2^0 xdx + 8\int_0^2 ydy = 24 \text{ J}$$

(*b*) From Fig.13 the equation of the straight line XY is given by

$$\frac{x-2}{0-2} = \frac{y-0}{2-0} = \frac{z-0}{0-0} = t, \text{ say and } 0 \le t \le 1.$$

Hence, $x = 2-2t\,;\, y = 2t\,;\, z = 0$

For the elementary displacement along the path XY the amount of work done is

$$dW = -2[2(2-2t)\hat{i} - 4(2t)\hat{j}].[(-2dt)\hat{i} + (2dt)\hat{j}] = 16(1+t)dt$$

And the net displacement along XY the amount of work done is

$$W = 16\int_0^1 (1+t)dt = 24J$$

Q. 20. Find the work done in moving a point charge $q = 5\mu C$ from the origin to the point with $(2m, \pi/4, \pi/2)$ in spherical coordinates, in the electric field of

$$\vec{E} = 5e^{-r/4}\hat{r} + \frac{10}{r\sin\theta}\hat{\phi} \text{ (V/m).}$$

Soln.:

The path in spherical coordinates is given by

$$\overrightarrow{dl} = \hat{r}dr + \hat{\theta}rd\theta + \hat{\phi}r\sin\theta d\phi$$

For any arbitrary path chosen along segment-I of Fig.14 is

$$d\theta = d\phi = 0\,.$$

So work done from the origin 'O' is

$$dW = -q\vec{E}.\overrightarrow{dl} = (-5\times10^{-6})(5e^{-r/4}dr)$$

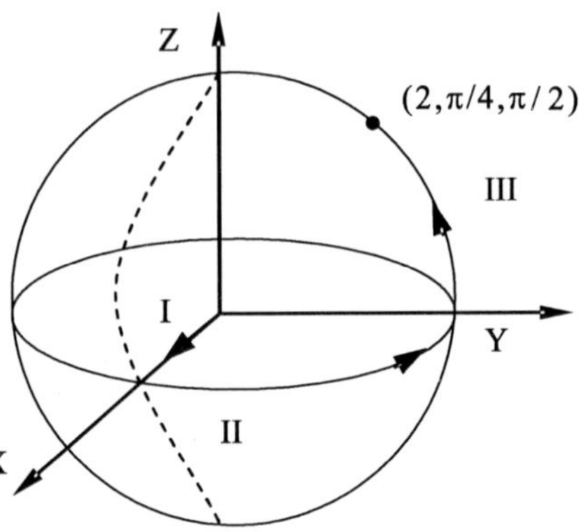

Fig. 14

Along segment-II we have

$$dr = d\theta = 0$$

And work done from the origin 'O' is

$$dW = -q\vec{E}.\overrightarrow{dl} = (-5\times10^{-6})(10d\phi)$$

Along segment-III we have

$$dr = d\phi = 0$$

And work done from the origin 'O' is

$$dW = -q\vec{E}.\overrightarrow{dl} = 0$$

Therefore the total work done on the moving charge is given by

$$W = \int[dW_1 + dW_2 + dW_3] = (-25\times10^{-6})\int_0^2 e^{-r/4}dr + (-50\times10^{-6})\int_0^{\pi/2} d\phi = 117.9\text{ J}$$

Q.21. 40 nano-coulombs of charge is uniformly distributed around a circular ring of a radius 2 m. Find the potential at a point on the axis 5 m from the plane of the ring. Compare with the result when all the charge is at the origin in the form of a point charge.

Soln.:

A circular ring containing charges 'dQ' is shown in Fig.15. Here, as the given charges are distributed around a closed ring, we have

$$q = \int \rho_l dl$$

With the charges along a line the potential at distance 'R' is given by

$$V = \int \frac{\rho_\ell d\ell}{4\pi\varepsilon_0 R}$$

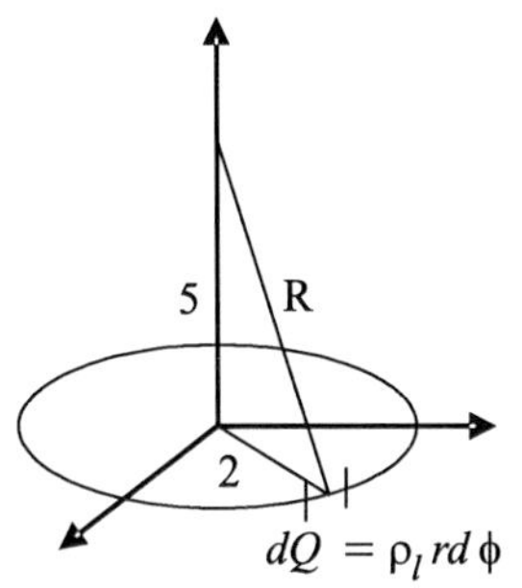

Fig. 15

From the given data, $\rho_l = \frac{40\times10^{-9}}{2\pi(2)} = \frac{10^{-8}}{\pi} C/m$

From Fig.15, we have $R = \sqrt{29} m$, $d\ell = (2)d\phi$.

Hence, $$V = \int_0^{2\pi} \frac{(10^{-8}/\pi)(2)d\phi}{4\pi(10^{-9}/36\pi)\sqrt{29}} = 66.9V$$

If the charges are concentrated at the origin, then,

$$V = \frac{q}{4\pi\varepsilon_0 r} = \frac{40\times10^{-9}}{4\pi\varepsilon_0(5)} = 72 \text{ V}$$

Q.22. Find the stored energy in a system of 4 identical point charges with $q = 4$ nC placed at the corners of a square 1 m on a side as shown in Fig.16. What is the stored energy in this system when only two charges at opposite corners are in place?

Soln.:

Total work done in assembling four charges along the vertices of the square is

$$2W_E = q_1V_1 + q_2V_2 + q_3V_3 + q_4V_4 = 4q_1V_1 \quad \text{(as all are equal charges)}$$

Here 'V_1, V_2, V_3, V_4' are work done per unit charge for the respective charges, however they are equal for equal charges.

Now the potential V_1 for the other three charges is given by

$$V_1 = \frac{q_2}{4\pi\varepsilon_0 R_{12}} + \frac{q_3}{4\pi\varepsilon_0 R_{13}} + \frac{q_4}{4\pi\varepsilon_0 R_{14}} = \frac{4\times10^{-9}}{4\pi\varepsilon_0}\left(\frac{1}{1}+\frac{1}{1}+\frac{1}{\sqrt{2}}\right) = 97.5 \text{ V}$$

Hence total energy is

$$W_E = 2q_1V_1 = 2(4\times10^{-9})(97.5) = 780 \text{ nJ}$$

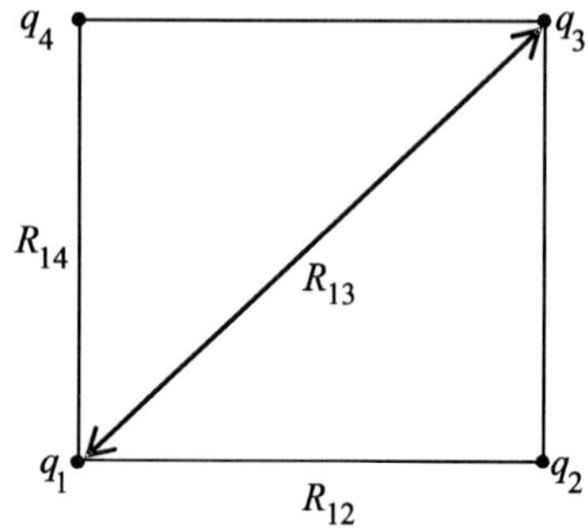

Fig. 16

For only two charges in place the total energy becomes,

$$2W_E = q_1V_1 = (4\times10^{-9})\left(\frac{4\times10^{-9}}{4\pi\varepsilon_0\sqrt{2}}\right) = 102 \text{ nJ}$$

Q.23. A thin conducting sheet lies in the $z = 0$ plane for $0 < x < 0.05m$. A current of 25 A directing along Y-axis is sinusoidally distributed across the sheet, with linear density zero for $x = 0$ and $x = 0.05m$ and maximum at $x = 0.025m$ (as in Fig.17). Obtain an expression for $\overrightarrow{\rho_{sh}}$.

Soln.:

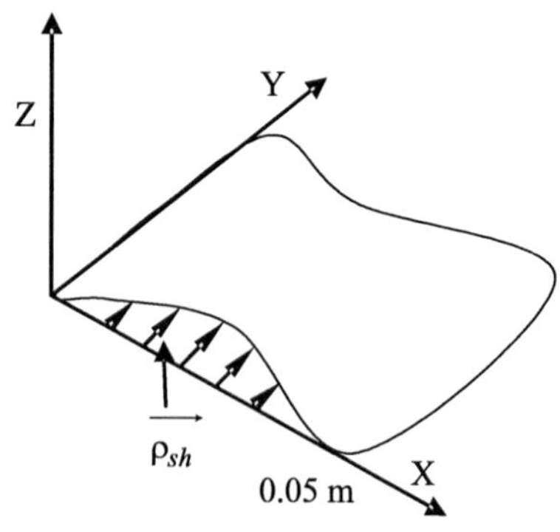

Fig. 17

With reference to Fig.17, is expressed as

$$\overrightarrow{\rho_{sh}} = \hat{j}k\sin(20\pi x)\ A/m,$$

Here 'k' is an unknown constant and represents amplitude of current sheet density for sinusoidal variations.

Hence current is given by

$$I = 25 = \int \rho_{sh}dx = k\int_{0}^{0.05} \sin(20\pi x)dx$$

$$\Rightarrow 25 = k/10\pi \Rightarrow k = 250\pi \text{ A/m}.$$

So the expression of $\overrightarrow{\rho_{sh}}$ becomes

$$\overrightarrow{\rho_{sh}} = \hat{j}250\pi\sin(20\pi x)\ A/m$$

Q.24. Two concentric cylindrical conductors with radii $r_a = 0.01$ m and $r_b = 0.08$ m as shown in Fig.18, have charge densities $\rho_{sa} = 40pC/m^2$ and ρ_{sb}. Here $\vec{D}$ and $\vec{E}$ fields exist only between the two cylinders and are zero elsewhere. Find ρ_{sb} and write the expressions for $\vec{D}$ and $\vec{E}$ between the cylinders.

Soln.:

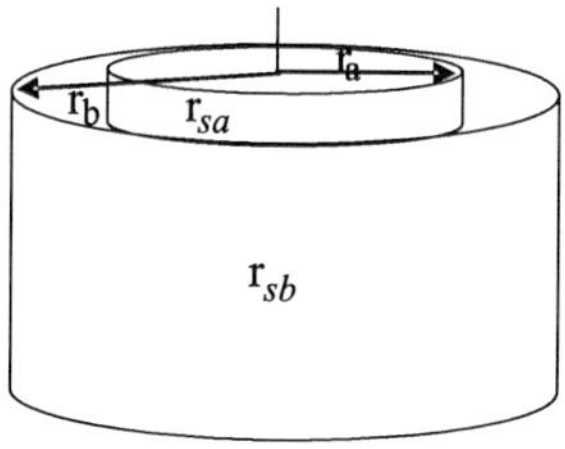

Fig. 18

By symmetry, field between the cylinders must be radial and a function of 'r' only. Then, for $r_a < r < r_b$ in cylindrical co-ordinates, the outward flow of $\vec{D}$ is expressed as

$$\vec{\nabla}.\vec{D} = \frac{1}{r}\frac{d}{dr}(rD_r) = 0 \Rightarrow rD_r = c$$

To evaluate the constant 'c', we have

at $r = r_a = 0.01$ m, $\qquad D_n = D_r = \rho_{sa}$, then,

$$c = (0.01)(40\times10^{-12}) = 4\times10^{-13} \text{ C/m}$$

and so

$$\vec{D} = \frac{4\times10^{-13}}{r}\hat{r} \quad \text{C/m}^2$$

and $$\vec{E} = \frac{D}{\varepsilon_0} = \frac{4.52\times10^{-2}}{r}\hat{r} \quad \text{V/m}$$

The charge density ρ_{sb} is given as

$$\rho_{sb} = D_n\Big|_{r=rb-0} = -D_r\Big|_{r=rb-0} = -\frac{4\times10^{-13}}{0.08} = -5\,pC.m^2$$

Q.25. Find the capacitance of a parallel plate capacitor containing two dielectrics with $\varepsilon_{r1} = 1.5$ and $\varepsilon_{r2} = 3.5$ with each one comprising one-half the total volume as shown in Fig. 19. (Given $A = 2$ m ^{2} and $d = 10^{-3}\,m$).

Soln.:

The capacitance for dielectric ε_{r1} is given by

$$C_1 = \frac{\varepsilon_0\varepsilon_{r1}A_1}{d} = \frac{(8.854\times10^{-12})(1.5)1}{10^{-3}} = 13.3 \text{ nF}$$

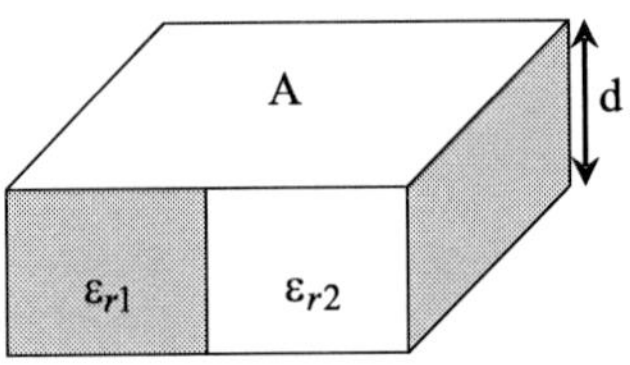

Fig. 19

Similarly we have, $C_2 = 31.0$ nF.

Hence the total capacitance of the constituted system is

$$C = C_1 + C_2 = 44.3 \text{ nF}$$

Q.26. Find the voltage drop across each dielectric in Fig.20 where $\varepsilon_{r1} = 2.0$ and $\varepsilon_{r2} = 5.0$. The inner conductor is at $r_1 = 2$ cm and the outer at $r_2 = 2.5$ cm with the dielectric interface halfway between.

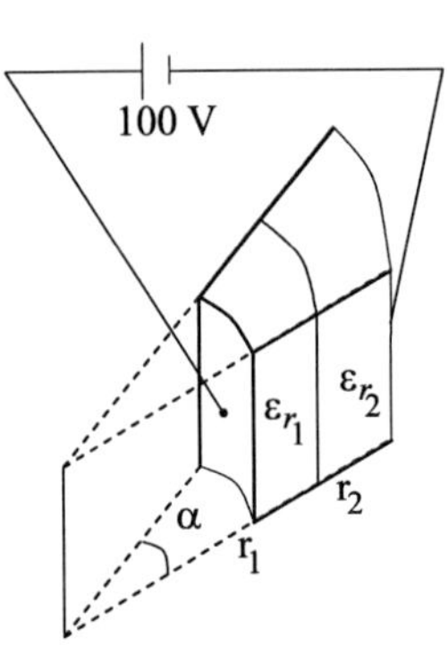

Fig. 20

Soln.:

For concentric cylinders of inner radius 'a' and outer radius 'b' the change on the inner conducting cylinder is given as

$$V = \frac{2\pi\varepsilon_0\varepsilon_{r1}L}{\log_e(b/a)}$$

Here, 'L' is the length of cylinder.

The voltage division is the same as it would be for

complete right circular cylinders. The shown segment with angle α will have a capacitance $\alpha/2\pi$ times of that of the complete coaxial capacitor. Hence,

$$C_1 = \left(\frac{\alpha}{2\pi}\right)\frac{2\pi\varepsilon_0\varepsilon_{r1}L}{\log_e(2.25/2.0)} = \alpha L(1.5\times 10^{-10})\text{ F}$$

Similarly, $C_2 = \alpha L(4.2\times 10^{-10})$ F (as $\varepsilon_{r2} = 5.0$)

Since $Q = C_1V_1 = C_2V_2$

and $V_1 + V_2 = V,$

so we have,

$$V_1 = \frac{C_2}{C_1+C_2}V = \frac{4.2}{1.5+4.2}(100) = 74V$$

$$V_2 = \frac{C}{C_1+C_2}V = \frac{1.5}{1.5+4.2}(100) = 26V$$

Q.27. Find the potential function and the electric field intensity for the region between the two concentric right circular cylinders as shown in Fig.21. Here $V = 0$ at $r = 1$ mm and $V = 150$ V at $r = 20$ mm. Neglect fringing.

Soln.:

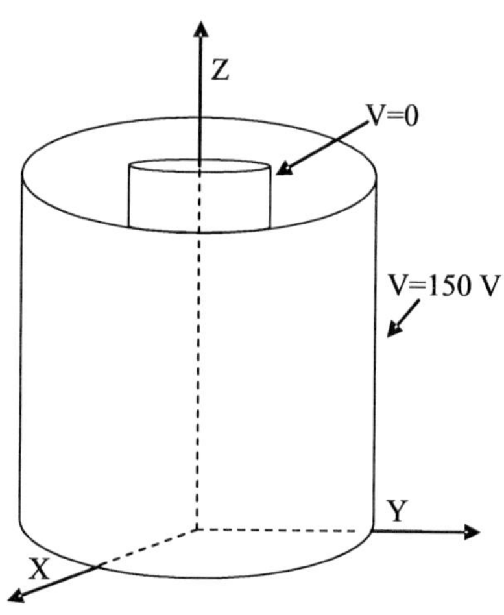

Fig. 21

Two concentric circular cylinders with given potentials at different values of 'r' is shown in Fig.21. If the potential is constant with ϕ and z, then Laplace's equation reduces to

$$\frac{1}{r}\frac{d}{dr}\left(r\frac{dV}{dr}\right) = 0$$

Integrating once we have

$$r\frac{dV}{dr} = A$$

And again we have,

$$V = A\log_e r + B\,.$$

Here 'A, B' are integration constants.

Applying the boundary conditions at $r = 1$ mm, $V = 0$ we have

$$0 = A\log_e(0.001) + B$$

Applying the boundary conditions at $r = 20$ mm, $V = 150$ V we have

$$150 = A\log_e(0.02) + B$$

On solving, we get $A = 50.1,\ B = 345.9.$

Using the values of A, B into the expression of V we have,

$$V = 50.1\log_e(r) + 345.9 \quad \text{V}$$

And the electric field is

$$\vec{E} = \frac{50.1}{r}(-\hat{r})\ \text{V/m}$$

Q.28. In spherical coordinates, $V = 0$ for $r = 0.10$ m and $V = 100V$ for $r = 2.0$ m. Assuming free space between these concentric spherical shells, find $\vec{E}$ and $\vec{D}$.

Soln.:

Here V is not function of θ or ϕ, so Laplace's equation reduces to

$$\frac{1}{r^2}\frac{d}{dr}\left(r^2\frac{dV}{dr}\right) = 0$$

On integrating we have $r^2\dfrac{dV}{dr} = A$

On second integration we get

$$V = \frac{-A}{r} + B$$

The given boundary conditions give

$$0 = \frac{-A}{0.10} + B \text{ and } 100 = \frac{-A}{2.00} + B$$

On solving $A = 10.53$ V m $B = 105.3$ V

Then the potential expression is

$$V = \frac{-10.53}{r} + 105.3\ \text{V}$$

Hence

$$\vec{E} = -\vec{\nabla} V = -\frac{dV}{dr}\hat{r} = -\frac{10.53}{r^2}\hat{r} \text{ V/m}$$

And $$\vec{D} = \varepsilon_0 \vec{E} = \frac{-9.32\times 10^{-11}}{r^2}\hat{r} \text{ C/m}^2$$

Q.29. Determine the magnetic flux density for a current carrying wire at a point P as shown in Fig.22.

Soln.:

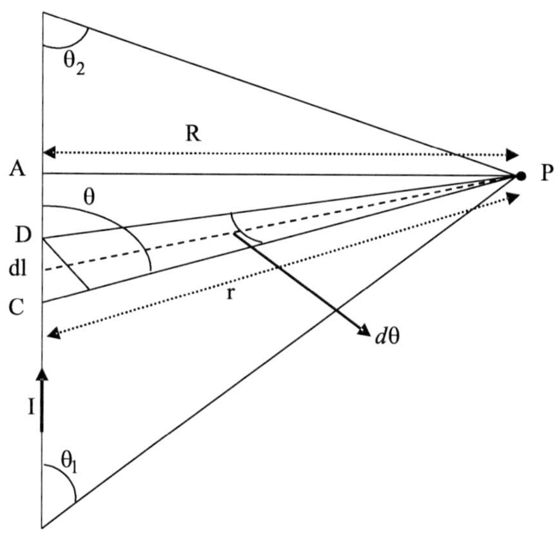

Fig. 22

From Fig.22, in ΔAPC, we have $\sin\theta = R/r$ (7)

Also, $$\frac{DE}{dl} = \sin\theta \Rightarrow DE = dl\sin\theta \quad (8)$$

And, $DE \approx rd\theta$ (9)

Hence, $dl\sin\theta = rd\theta$ (using eqns.(8) and (9))

$$\Rightarrow dl = \frac{rd\theta}{\sin\theta} = \frac{rd\theta}{R/r} = \frac{r^2 d\theta}{R} \quad \text{(using eqn.(7))} \quad (10)$$

Using Biot-savart's law for an current element we have,

$$dB = \frac{\mu}{4\pi}\frac{Idl\sin\theta}{r^2} = \frac{\mu}{4\pi}\times\frac{r^2 d\theta}{R}\times\frac{I\sin\theta}{r^2} \quad \text{(using eqn.(10))}$$

$$= \frac{\mu I}{4\pi R}\sin\theta d\theta$$

Hence net magnetization is

$$B = \int dB = \frac{\mu I}{4\pi R}\int_0^{\pi}\sin\theta d\theta = -\frac{\mu I}{4\pi R}\left[\cos\theta\right]_0^{\pi} = \frac{\mu I}{2\pi R}$$

Q.30. Determine the magnetic flux density for a circular current carrying loop at a point P as shown in Fig.23.

Soln.:

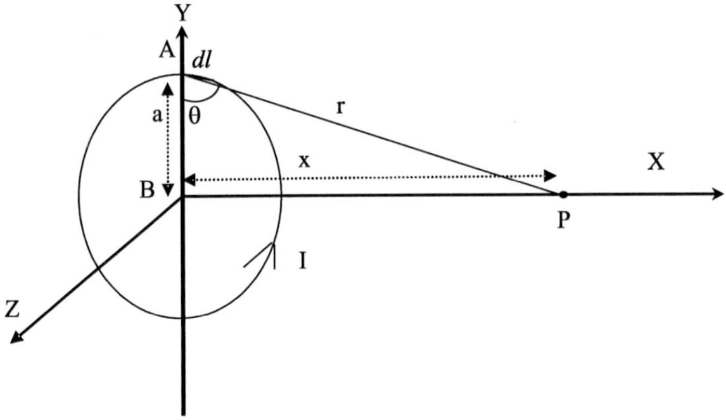

Fig. 23

The coil of radius 'a' is in XY-plane with center is at the origin and is carrying a current 'I'. 'P' is the observation point. 'r' is the distance between 'P' and current element 'dl'. '$\overrightarrow{dB}$' is in a direction perpendicular to both '$\overrightarrow{dl}$' and '$\vec{r}$'.

So using Biot-savart's law we have,

$$dB_x = \frac{\mu}{4\pi}\cdot\frac{Idl\sin(90-\theta)}{r^2} = \frac{\mu}{4\pi}\times\frac{Idl\cos\theta}{r^2} \quad (11)$$

From ΔABP we have,

$$\cos\theta = \frac{AB}{AP} = \frac{a}{r}$$

and $$r^2 = x^2 + a^2$$

Thus using these into eqn.(11) we have,

$$dB_x = \frac{\mu}{4\pi}\times\frac{Idl}{r^2}\times\frac{a}{r}$$

Hence the net magnetic flux density is

$$B_x = \int dB_x = \frac{\mu a I}{4\pi r^3}\int_0^L dl$$

$$\Rightarrow B_x = \frac{\mu a I}{4\pi r^3} \times 2\pi a \qquad [L = 2\pi a]$$

$$\Rightarrow B_x = \frac{\mu a^2 I}{2r^3} = \frac{\mu a^2 I}{2\left[x^2 + a^2\right]^{3/2}} \tag{12}$$

For 'N' nos. of turns in the coil, we have,

$$B_x = \frac{\mu a^2 I}{2\left[x^2 + a^2\right]^{3/2}} \times N$$

Hence from eqn.(12) we observe that 'B_x' decreases with 'x'.

(*i*) At the center of the coil:
Here $x = 0$, hence from eqn.(12),

$$B_x = \frac{\mu a^2 I}{2\left[0 + a^2\right]^{3/2}} = \frac{\mu I}{2a}$$

(*ii*) For $x >> a$:
Using eqn.(12), we have,

$$B_x \approx \frac{\mu a^2 I}{2\left[x^2 + 0\right]^{3/2}} = \frac{\mu a^2 I}{2x^3} = \frac{\mu a^2 I}{2r^3} \quad \left[r^2 = x^2 + a^2 \Rightarrow x \approx r\right]$$

$$= \frac{\mu I}{2\pi r^3} \times \pi a^2 = \frac{\mu I}{2\pi r^3} A$$ ('A' is the area of the loop, so, $A = \pi a^2$)

However, dipole moment of the loop is given by $p = IA$, hence,

$$B_x = \frac{\mu p}{2\pi r^3}$$

Q.31. Determine the magnetic flux density for a solenoid at a point 'P' on it as shown in Fig.24.

Soln.:

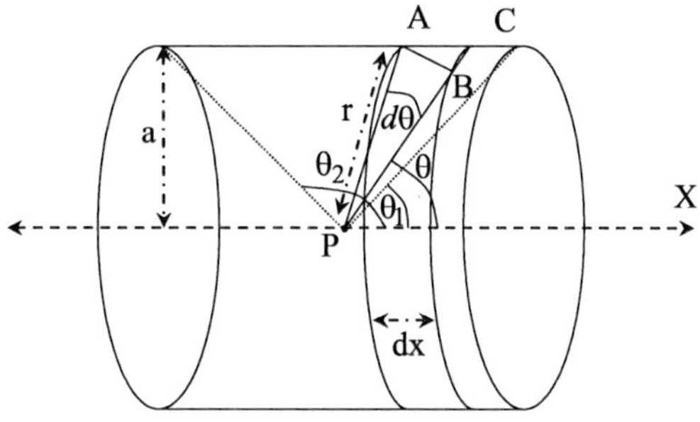

Fig. 24

A solenoid is a helical coil. Let 'N' is the number of terms per unit length in the solenoid.

From ΔABC, we have, $AC = dx, AB = rd\theta$

And $\angle ACB = \theta$,

Hence, $\frac{AB}{AC} = \sin\theta \Rightarrow \frac{rd\theta}{dx} = \sin\theta$

$$\Rightarrow dx = \frac{rd\theta}{\sin\theta} \tag{13}$$

So the total no. of turns in length 'dx' of the solenoid is 'Ndx' and net current flowing through it is '$INdx$'. Hence magnetic flux density is given by

$$B_x = \int dB_x = \int \frac{\mu I a^2}{2r^3} \times INdx$$

$$= \frac{\mu IN}{2} \int_\theta \left(\frac{rd\theta}{\sin\theta}\right) \cdot \frac{a^2}{r^3} = \frac{\mu IN}{2} \int_\theta \left(\frac{a^2 d\theta}{r^2 \sin\theta}\right)$$

$$= \frac{\mu IN}{2} \int_\theta \left(\frac{(r\sin\theta)^2 d\theta}{r^2 \sin\theta}\right) \quad \left[\because \frac{a}{r} = \sin\theta\right]$$

$$= \frac{\mu IN}{2} \int_{\theta_1}^{\theta_2} \sin\theta d\theta = \frac{\mu IN}{2}[\cos\theta_1 - \cos\theta_2] \tag{14}$$

***(i)* Long Solenoid:** Here, $\theta_1 = 0, \theta_2 = \pi$, so using eqn.(14) we have,

$$B = \frac{\mu IN}{2}[\cos 0 - \cos\pi] = \mu IN$$

***(ii)* Point 'P' is at one end of the Solenoid:** Here, $\theta_1 = 0, \theta_2 = \pi/2$, so using eqn.(14) we have,

$$B = \frac{\mu IN}{2}[\cos 0 - \cos\pi/2] = \mu IN/2$$

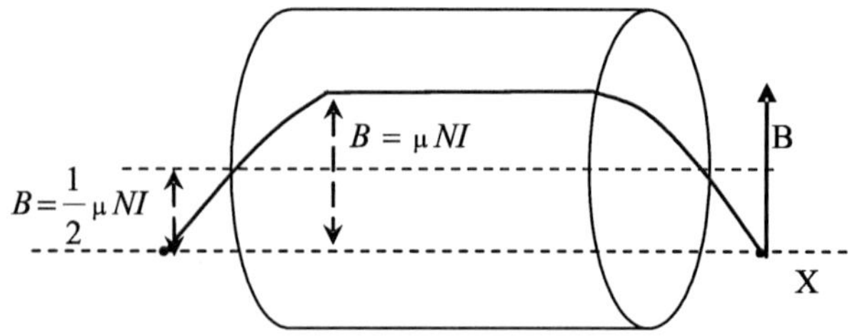

Fig. 25

The variation of 'B' along the length of the solenoid is shown in Fig.25.

Q.32. A square has a size of length 'a' carries a current 'I' as shown in Fig.26. Show that the value of '$\vec{B}$' at its center is $B = 2\sqrt{2}\frac{\mu I}{\pi a}$.

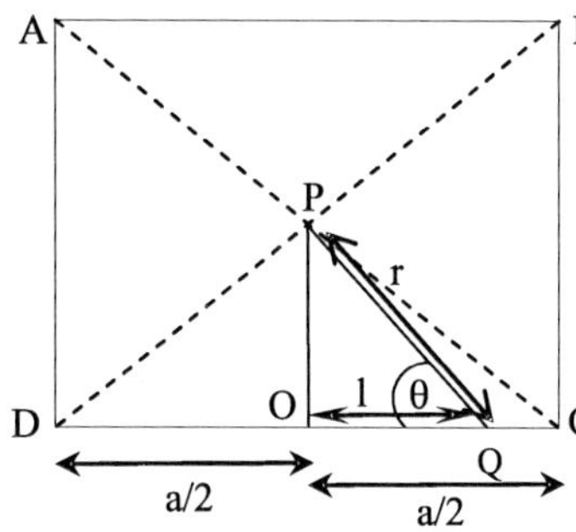

Fig. 26

Soln.:

From Biot-savart's law we have,

$$dB = \frac{\mu}{4\pi}\times\frac{Idl\sin\theta}{r^2}$$

Considering 'O' as the origin with only one side of the square DC as in Fig.26 we have,

$$\sin\theta = \frac{OP}{PQ} = \frac{a/2}{r};$$

Also, $$r^2 = (a/2)^2 + l^2 = \frac{a^2}{4} + l^2$$

Net magnetization over the whole side DC becomes

$$B = \int_{-a/2}^{a/2} dB = \frac{\mu I}{4\pi}\int_{-a/2}^{a/2}\frac{dl}{r^2}\cdot\left[\frac{a/2}{r}\right] \quad \text{(putting the value of } \sin\theta\text{)}$$

$$= \frac{\mu Ia}{8\pi}\int_{-a/2}^{a/2}\frac{dl}{r^3}$$

$$= 2\times\frac{\mu Ia}{8\pi}\int_0^{a/2}\frac{dl}{\left(\frac{a^2}{4}+l^2\right)^{3/2}} \quad \text{(putting the value of 'r')}$$

Let, $$l = \frac{a}{2}\tan\theta \Rightarrow dl = \frac{a}{2}\sec^2\theta d\theta .$$

But, at $l = 0, \theta = 0$ and $l = a/2, \theta = \pi/4$.

Using these we have,

$$B = \frac{\mu I a}{4\pi}\int_{0}^{\pi/4}\left[\frac{\frac{a}{2}\sec^2\theta d\theta}{\left(\frac{a^2}{4}+\frac{a^2}{4}\tan^2\theta\right)^{3/2}}\right]$$

$$= \frac{\mu I a}{4\pi\left(\frac{a^2}{4}\right)}\int_{0}^{\pi/4}\left[\frac{d\theta}{(\sec\theta)}\right] = \frac{\mu I}{\pi a}\int_{0}^{\pi/4}\cos\theta d\theta$$

$$= \frac{\mu I}{\pi a}[\sin\theta]_0^{\pi/4} = \frac{\mu I}{\pi a}\times\frac{1}{\sqrt{2}} = \frac{\mu I}{\pi\sqrt{2}a}$$

Now for all the four sides of the square, the resultant magnetic field at 'P' is given by

$$= 4\times\frac{\mu I}{\pi a\sqrt{2}} = \frac{\mu I}{a}\times\frac{2\sqrt{2}}{\pi}\text{ Tesla}$$

Q.33. Find the current in a circular wire of radius 2 mm when the current density in the conductor is $\vec{J} = 30\left[1-e^{-1000r}\right]\hat{a}_z$ A/m².

Soln.:

$$I = \int_S \vec{J}.\vec{dS} = \int_{\phi=0}^{2\pi}\int_{r=0}^{0.002} 30\left[1-e^{-1000r}\right]\hat{a}_z.(rdrd\phi) \qquad (\text{as } dS = rdrd\phi)$$

$$= 30\times 2\pi\left[\int_0^{0.002} rdr - \int_0^{0.002} re^{-1000r}dr\right]$$

$$= 60\pi\left[\frac{r^2}{2}\Bigg|_0^{0.002} - \left\{\frac{re^{-1000r}}{-1000}\Bigg|_0^{0.002} - \int_0^{0.002}\frac{e^{-1000r}}{-1000}dr\right\}\right]$$

$$= 60\pi\left[4\times10^{-6} + \left(\frac{2\times10^{-3}}{1000}e^{-1000\times2\times10^{-3}} - 0\right) + \frac{e^{-1000r^{-3}}}{1000\times-1000}\Bigg|_0^{0.002}\right]$$

$$= 60\pi\left[4\times10^{-6} + \left(2\times10^{-6}\times e^{-2}\right) - \left(10^{-6}\times e^{-2} - 10^{-6}\right)\right] \approx 0.2649\text{ mA}$$

Q.34. Compute the total magnetic flux 'ϕ' crossing the $z = 0$ plane in cylindrical co-ordinates for $0 < r < 5\times10^{-2}$ mt if $\vec{B} = \frac{0.2}{r}\sin^2\phi\hat{a}_z$ tesla.

Soln.:

$$\phi = \int \vec{B}.\overrightarrow{dS} = \int_{\phi}\int_{r}\left(\frac{0.2}{r}\sin^2\phi\right).(rdrd\phi)$$

$$= 0.2\int_0^{2\pi}\sin^2\phi.\int_0^{5\times10^{-2}} dr$$

$$= 0.2\int_0^{2\pi}\left(\frac{1-\cos 2\phi}{2}\right)d\phi.[r]_0^{5\times10^{-2}} = 3.1\times10^{-2}\ \text{Wb/mt}^2.$$

Q.35. A stationary 10 turn square coil of 1 m side is situated with its lower left corner coincident with the origin and with sides x_1, y_1 along X and Y-axes as shown in Fig.27. If the field '$\vec{B}$' is normal to the plane of the coil and has the amplitude

$$B_0 = \sin\left(\frac{\pi x}{x_1}\right)\sin\left(\frac{\pi y}{y_1}\right)\text{Tesla}$$

Find the rms value of the emf introduced in the coil if 'B' varies harmonically at a frequency of 1 kHz.

Soln.:

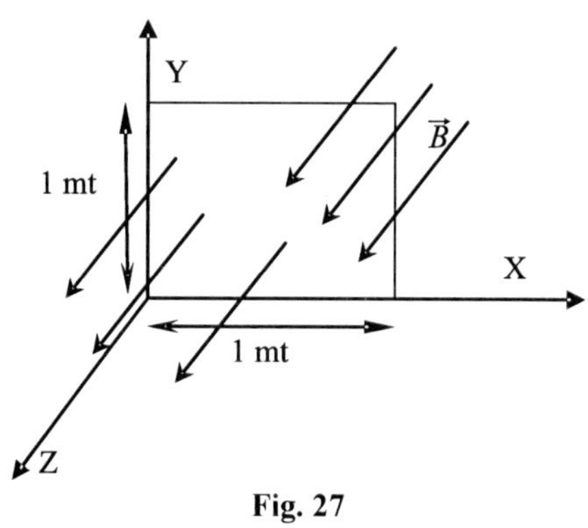

Fig. 27

Magnetic field is given by

$$B = B_0 \sin\omega t \qquad \text{where,} \quad B_0 = \sin\left(\frac{\pi x}{x_1}\right)\sin\left(\frac{\pi y}{y_1}\right).$$

Here, $x_1 = 1\,\text{m}$ and $y_1 = 1\,\text{m}$.

Using Faraday's law, we have,

$$emf = e = \int_S\left(\vec{\nabla}\times\vec{E}\right).\hat{n}dS = -\int_S\left(\frac{\partial\vec{B}}{\partial t}\right).\overrightarrow{dS} \qquad \left(\text{as } e = -\left(\frac{\partial\phi}{\partial t}\right)\right)$$

$$= -\int_S (\omega B_0 \cos\omega t) dS = \int_x \int_y \omega \left[\sin\left(\frac{\pi x}{x_1}\right) \sin\left(\frac{\pi y}{y_1}\right) dxdy \right] \cos\omega t$$

So the rms value of emf (*i.e.*, at $\sin\omega t = 1$) is given by

$$emf = \omega \int_0^{x_1} \sin\left(\frac{\pi x}{x_1}\right) dx \int_0^{y_1} \sin\left(\frac{\pi y}{y_1}\right) dy$$

$$= 2\pi v \int_0^1 \sin\left(\frac{\pi x}{1}\right) dx \int_0^1 \sin\left(\frac{\pi y}{1}\right) dy$$

$$= 2\pi \times 1000 \times \left.\frac{-\cos\pi x}{\pi}\right|_0^1 \times \left.\frac{-\cos\pi y}{\pi}\right|_0^1$$

$$= \frac{2\pi \times 1000 \times 2 \times 2}{\pi^2} \text{ V/turn}$$

Hence the net emf is

$$N \times emf = \frac{10 \times 2\pi \times 1000 \times 2 \times 2}{\pi^2} = 18.015 \text{ KV}$$

Q.36. Find the flux crossing the portion of the plane $\phi = \pi/4$ defined by $0.01 < r < 0.05$ m and $0 < z < 2$ m (see Fig.28). A current filament of 2.5 A is flowing along the Z-axis.

Soln.:

The intensity of magnetization for a given current 'I' is

$$\vec{B} = \mu_0 \vec{H} = \frac{\mu_0 I}{\pi r} \hat{\phi}$$

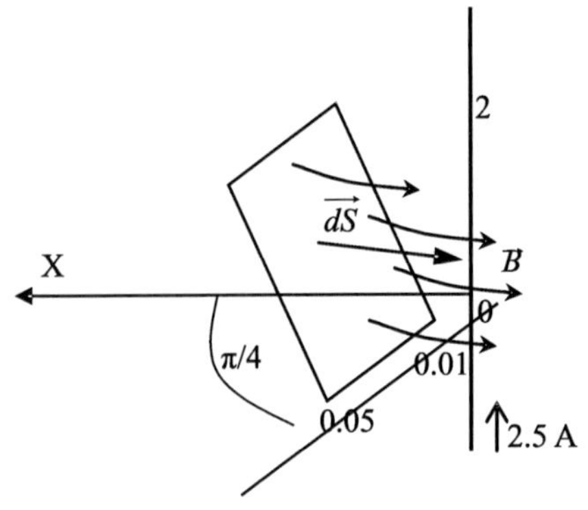

Fig. 28

As shown in Fig.28, the current element is

$$d\vec{S} = drdz\hat{\phi}$$

Hence the magnetic flux is given by

$$\Phi = \oint_S \vec{B}.\overrightarrow{dS} = \int_0^2 \int_{0.01}^{0.05} \frac{\mu_0 I}{2\pi r}\hat{\phi}.(drdz\hat{\phi})$$

$$= \frac{2\mu_0 I}{2\pi}\log_e \frac{0.05}{0.01} = 1.61\times10^{-6}\text{ Wb}$$

Q.37. In a certain region $\vec{B} = 5.0\times10^{-4}\hat{k}$ T and $\vec{E} = 5.0\hat{k}$ V/m. A proton ($q_p = 1.602\times10^{-19}C,\ m_p = 1.673\times10^{-27}kg$ enters the fields at the origin with an initial velocity $\vec{u}_0 = 2.5\times10^5\hat{i}$ m/s. Describe the proton's motion and give its position after three complete revolutions.

Soln.:

Initially Lorentz force acting on the particle is

$$\vec{F}_0 = q(\vec{E} + \vec{u}_0 \times \vec{B}) = q_p(E\hat{k} - u_0 B\hat{j})$$

The Z-component (electric component) of the force is constant and produces a constant acceleration in the Z-direction. We know the force equation as

$$m_p a = q_p E \Rightarrow a = \frac{q_p E}{m_p}$$

Thus the equation of motion along the Z-direction is

$$z = 0 + \frac{1}{2}at^2 = \frac{1}{2}\left(\frac{q_p E}{m_p}\right)t^2$$

For the magnetic component we have the force equation as

$$\frac{m_p u^2}{r} = Bq_p u \Rightarrow u = \frac{2rBq_p}{m_p}$$

The magnetic component produces circular motion perpendicular to the Z-axis, with period

$$T = \frac{2\pi r}{u} = \frac{2\pi r}{\frac{2rBq_p}{m_p}} = \frac{2\pi m_p}{Q_p B}$$

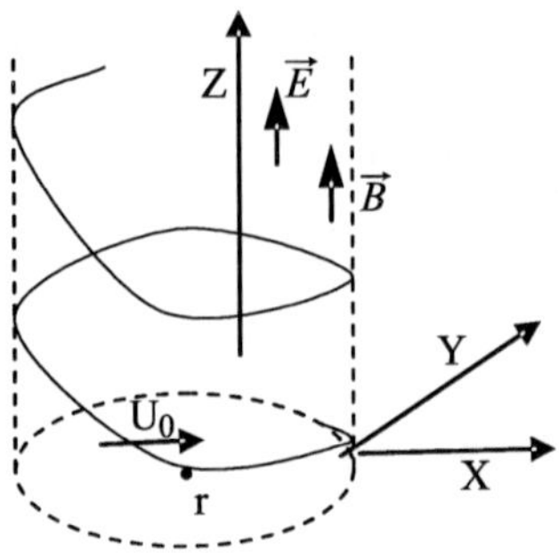

Fig. 29

The resultant motion is helical, as shown in Fig.29.

After three revolutions, $x = y = 0$ and $t = 3T$, hence the displacement along Z-axis is

$$z = \frac{1}{2}\left(\frac{q_p E}{m_p}\right)(3T)^2 = \frac{18\pi^2 E m_p}{q_p B^2} = 37.0 \text{ m}$$

Q.38. In region-1of Fig.30, $\vec{B} = 1.2\hat{i} + 0.8\hat{j} + 0.4\hat{k}$ T. Find magnetic field at region-2, *i.e.*, $\overrightarrow{H_2}$ (*i.e.*, $\vec{H}$ at $z = +0$) and the angles between the field vectors and a tangent to the interface.

Soln.:

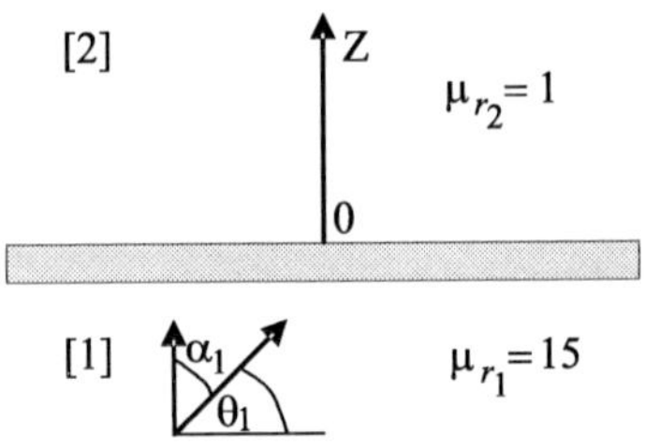

Fig. 30

From the boundary conditions across the interface between two dielectrics we know that $\vec{B}$ normal is continuous and $\vec{H}$ tangential is continuous across a current-free interface.

We have,

$$\vec{B}_1 = 1.2\hat{i} + 0.8\hat{j} + 0.4\hat{k} \qquad \text{T}$$

So,
$$\vec{H}_1 = \frac{1}{\mu_0 \mu_{r1}}\vec{B}_1 = \frac{1}{15\mu_0}\left(1.2\hat{i} + 0.8\hat{j} + 0.4\hat{k}\right)$$

$$= \frac{1}{\mu_0}(8.0\hat{i} + 5.33\hat{j} + 2.67\hat{k})10^{-2} \text{ A/m}$$

As 'H' is continuous across X-Y plane, X and Y-components of 'H' are same in both the mediums. With new Z-component of 'H' in medium-2 we have

$$\vec{H}_2 = \frac{1}{\mu_0}(8.0\hat{i} + 5.33\hat{j} + H_{z2}\hat{k})10^{-2} \text{ A/m} \quad (15)$$

As 'B' is continuous across Z-axis, X and Y-components of 'B' are not same in both the mediums. With same Z-component of 'B' in medium-2 we have the magnetic flux density as

$$\vec{B}_2 = B_{x2}\hat{i} + B_{y2}\hat{j} + 0.4 \quad \text{T} \quad (16)$$

On comparing eqns.(15) and (16) we have

$$B_{x2} = \mu_0\mu_{r2}H_{x2} = \mu_0 \times 1 \times \frac{\left(8.0\times10^{-2}\right)}{\mu_0} = 8.0\times10^{-2} \quad \text{T}$$

Similarly, $B_{y2} = 5.33\times10^{-2}$ T

$$H_{z2} = \frac{B_{z2}}{\mu_0\mu_{r2}} = \frac{0.4}{\mu_0} \quad \text{A/m}$$

Also as shown in Fig.30, the angle θ_1 is '$90° - \alpha_1$'. Here' α_1 ' is the angle between '$\vec{B_1}$' and the normal $\hat{z}$. Hence,

$$\cos\alpha_1 = \frac{\vec{B_1}.\hat{k}}{\left|\vec{B_1}\right|} = \frac{0.4}{\sqrt{(1.2)^2 + (0.8)^2 + (0.4)^2}} = 0.27$$

$$\Rightarrow \alpha_1 = 74.5° \text{ and } \theta_1 = 15.5°.$$

Now using $\frac{\tan\theta_1}{\tan\theta_2} = \frac{\mu_{r2}}{\mu_{r1}}$

We have $\theta_2 = 76.5°$.

Q.39. Find the magnetic field of a transverse electromagnetic (TEM) wave with $E = 1\ \mu V/mt$ in air.

Soln.:

In free space the characteristic impedance in using the properties of e.m.wave is given by

$$\eta = \frac{E}{H} = 377\Omega .$$

Also, the characteristic impedance in using the properties of medium is given by

$$\eta = \sqrt{\frac{\mu_0}{\varepsilon_0}}$$

Hence, in air,

$$\sqrt{\frac{\mu_0}{\varepsilon_0}} = \frac{E}{H} = 377\Omega$$

$$\Rightarrow H = \frac{E}{377} = \frac{1\times10^{-6}}{377} = 2.65\times10^{-9} \text{ A/m}^2$$

Q.40. Show that $E_y = E_0 \sin(\omega t - \beta z)$ and $H_x = -\beta \frac{E_0}{\omega\mu_0} \sin(\omega t - \beta z)$ travels with velocity of light in free space and determine the value of '$\frac{E}{H}$'.

Soln.:

We have from Maxwell's third equation,

$$\vec{\nabla}\times\vec{E} = -\mu\frac{\partial\vec{H}}{\partial t}$$

Now, as $E_x = 0 = E_z$, then,

$$\vec{\nabla}\times\vec{E} = \begin{vmatrix} \hat{i} & \hat{j} & \hat{k} \\ \frac{\partial}{\partial x} & \frac{\partial}{\partial y} & \frac{\partial}{\partial z} \\ 0 & E_y & 0 \end{vmatrix} = \hat{i}\left[-\frac{\partial}{\partial z}E_y\right] + \hat{k}\left[\frac{\partial}{\partial x}E_y\right]$$

$$= \hat{i}\left[-\frac{\partial}{\partial z}E_0\sin(\omega t - \beta z)\right] + \hat{k}\left[\frac{\partial}{\partial x}E_0\sin(\omega t - \beta z)\right]$$

$$= \hat{i}\left[\beta E_0\cos(\omega t - \beta z)\right] + 0$$

$$= \hat{i}\left[\beta E_0\cos\left\{\omega(t - \frac{z}{\omega/\beta})\right\}\right]$$

$$= \hat{i}\left[\beta E_0\cos\left\{\omega(t - \frac{z}{v_\omega})\right\}\right]$$

Similarly the magnetic field vector exists in X-direction only. So both the electric and magnetic vector components generates an e.m.wave propagating along Z-direction with a velocity 'v_ω'.

So the velocity of the wave is given by

$$v_\omega = \frac{\omega}{\beta} = \frac{2\pi\nu}{2\pi/\lambda} = \nu\lambda = c = 3\times10^8 \text{ m/sec.}$$

Hence,

$$\frac{E}{H} = \frac{E_y}{H_x} = \frac{E_0 \sin(\omega t - \beta z)}{\beta \frac{E_0}{\omega\mu_0} \sin(\omega t - \beta z)}$$

$$= \frac{\omega\mu_0}{\beta} = v_\omega \mu_0 = c\mu_0$$

$$= \frac{1}{\sqrt{\mu_0\varepsilon_0}} \times \mu_0 = \sqrt{\frac{\mu_0}{\varepsilon_0}} = 377\Omega$$

Q.41. Verify that $E_y = f_1(x - v_0 t)$ is a solution of the equation $\frac{\partial^2 E_y}{\partial x^2} = \mu\varepsilon \frac{\partial^2 E_y}{\partial t^2}$.

Soln.:

Given $E_y = f_1(x - v_0 t)$

Hence, $$\frac{\partial E_y}{\partial x} = \frac{\partial f_1(x - v_0 t)}{\partial x} = \frac{\partial f_1(x - v_0 t)}{\partial (x - v_0 t)} \times \frac{\partial (x - v_0 t)}{\partial x}$$

$$= f_1'(x - v_0 t) \times 1 = f_1'(x - v_0 t)$$

Similarly, $$\frac{\partial^2 E_y}{\partial x^2} = f_1''(x - v_0 t)$$

Now, $$\frac{\partial E_y}{\partial t} = \frac{\partial f_1(x - v_0 t)}{\partial t} = \frac{\partial f_1(x - v_0 t)}{\partial (x - v_0 t)} \times \frac{\partial (x - v_0 t)}{\partial t}$$

$$= f_1'(x - v_0 t) \times (-v_0) = -v_0 f_1'(x - v_0 t)$$

So, $$\frac{\partial^2 E_y}{\partial t^2} = v_0^2 f_1''(x - v_0 t)$$

$$= \left(\frac{1}{\sqrt{\mu\varepsilon}}\right)^2 f_1''(x - v_0 t) = \left(\frac{1}{\mu\varepsilon}\right) f_1''(x - v_0 t)$$

Hence, $$\mu\varepsilon \frac{\partial^2 E_y}{\partial t^2} = \mu\varepsilon \times \left(\frac{1}{\mu\varepsilon}\right) f_1''(x - v_0 t)$$

$$= f_1''(x - v_0 t) = \frac{\partial^2 E_y}{\partial x^2}$$

Q.42. Show that any function $F = e^{-\alpha z}\sin\left\{\frac{\omega}{v}(x - vt)\right\}$ satisfies the wave equation $\nabla^2 F = \frac{1}{c^2}\frac{\partial^2 F}{\partial t^2}$ provided that the wave velocity is given by

$$v = \frac{c}{\sqrt{1 + \frac{\alpha^2 c^2}{\omega^2}}}.$$

Soln.:

Here, $$F(x, z, t) = e^{-\alpha z}\sin\left\{\frac{\omega}{v}(x - vt)\right\}$$

Now, $$\frac{\partial F}{\partial x} = e^{-\alpha z}.\left(\frac{\omega}{v}\right)\cos\left\{\frac{\omega}{v}(x - vt)\right\}$$

$$\frac{\partial^2 F}{\partial x^2} = -e^{-\alpha z}.\left(\frac{\omega}{v}\right)^2 \sin\left\{\frac{\omega}{v}(x - vt)\right\}$$

$$= -\left(\frac{\omega}{v}\right)^2 F(x, z, t)$$

Similarly, $$\frac{\partial^2 F}{\partial z^2} = (\alpha)^2 F(x, z, t) \text{ and } \frac{\partial^2 F}{\partial y^2} = 0$$

$$\frac{\partial F}{\partial t} = e^{-\alpha z}.(-\omega)\cos\left\{\frac{\omega}{v}(x - vt)\right\}$$

$$\frac{\partial^2 F}{\partial t^2} = -e^{-\alpha z}.(\omega^2)\sin\left\{\frac{\omega}{v}(x - vt)\right\} = -\omega^2 F(x, z, t)$$

So, $$\nabla^2 F = \frac{\partial^2 F}{\partial x^2} + \frac{\partial^2 F}{\partial z^2} + \frac{\partial^2 F}{\partial y^2}$$

$$= \left[-\left(\frac{\omega}{v}\right)^2 + \alpha^2\right] F(x, z, t)$$

$$= \left[\alpha^2 - \left(\frac{\frac{\omega}{c}}{\sqrt{1+\frac{\alpha^2 c^2}{\omega^2}}} \right)^2 \right] F(x,z,t) = \left[\alpha^2 - \frac{\omega^2}{c^2}\left\{1+\frac{\alpha^2 c^2}{\omega^2}\right\} \right] F(x,z,t)$$

$$= \left[\alpha^2 - \frac{\omega^2}{c^2} - \frac{\omega^2}{c^2} \times \frac{\alpha^2 c^2}{\omega^2} \right] F(x,z,t) = \left[\alpha^2 - \frac{\omega^2}{c^2} - \alpha^2 \right] F(x,z,t)$$

$$= \left[-\frac{\omega^2}{c^2} \right] F(x,z,t) = \frac{1}{c^2}\frac{\partial^2 F}{\partial t^2}$$

Q.43. Using $\vec{\nabla}.\vec{D} = \rho$, Ohm's law and the equation of continuity show that if at any instant a charge density 'ρ' existed within a conductor, it would decrease to '$1/e$' times this value in a time of 'ε/σ' sec.

Soln.:

We have, $\vec{\nabla}.\vec{D} = \rho \Rightarrow \vec{\nabla}.\vec{E} = \rho/\varepsilon$.

From the equation of continuity,

$$\vec{\nabla}.\vec{J} + \frac{\partial \rho}{\partial t} = 0$$

$$\Rightarrow \vec{\nabla}.\vec{J} = -\frac{\partial \rho}{\partial t} \Rightarrow \vec{\nabla}.\sigma\vec{E} = -\frac{\partial \rho}{\partial t}$$

$$\Rightarrow \sigma\vec{\nabla}.\vec{E} = -\frac{\partial \rho}{\partial t} \Rightarrow \sigma\left(\frac{\rho}{\varepsilon}\right) = -\frac{\partial \rho}{\partial t}$$

$$\Rightarrow \frac{\partial \rho}{\partial t} + \left(\frac{\sigma}{\varepsilon}\right)\rho = 0$$

$$\Rightarrow \frac{\partial \rho}{\rho} = -\left(\frac{\sigma}{\varepsilon}\right)dt$$

Integrating,

$$\ln(\rho) = -\left(\frac{\sigma}{\varepsilon}\right)t + K \qquad (1)$$

K is integration constant.

At $t = 0, \rho = \rho_0$; hence,

$$\Rightarrow K = \ln(\rho_0),$$

Substituting the value of 'K', we get from eqn.(1),

$$\ln(\rho) = -\left(\frac{\sigma}{\varepsilon}\right)t + \ln(\rho_0)$$

$$\Rightarrow \rho = \rho_0 e^{-\left(\frac{\sigma}{\varepsilon}\right)t} \qquad (2)$$

Now at $t = \left(\frac{\varepsilon}{\sigma}\right)$, then from eqn.(2) we get,

$$\rho = \rho_0 e^{-\left(\frac{\sigma}{\varepsilon}\right)t} = \rho_0 e^{-\left(\frac{\sigma}{\varepsilon}\right)\left(\frac{\varepsilon}{\sigma}\right)} = \frac{\rho_0}{e}.$$

Q.44. An electric field $\vec{E} = 1.0e^{-az}e^{j(\omega t - \beta z)}\hat{i}$ V/m and frequency $f = \omega/2\pi = 100MHz$, is assumed at the surface of a copper conductor of conductivity $\sigma = 58$ MS/m, located at $z > 0$, as shown in Fig.31. Examine the attenuation as the wave propagates into the conductor.

Soln.:

From the definition of the skin depth 'δ' we have the amplitude of the field is attenuated to '1/e' times of its initial value and so as $\left|\vec{E}\right| = 1.0e^{-az}$

we have $\delta = \dfrac{1}{\sqrt{\pi f \mu \alpha}} = 6.61\ \mu m$

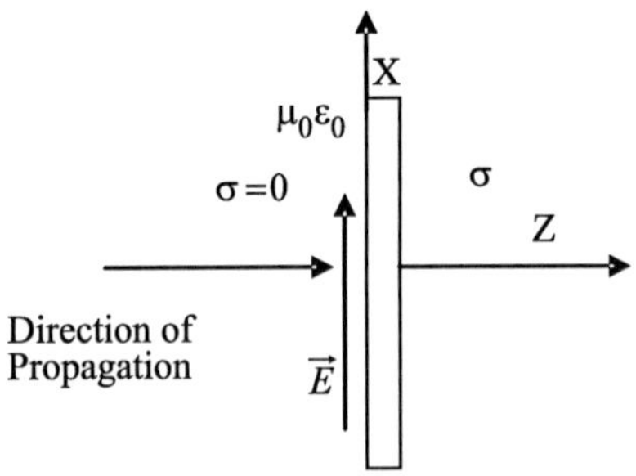

Fig. 31

Thus after just 6.61 microns, the field is attenuated to $e^{-1}(=36.8\%)$ of its initial value.

❑❑❑

SAMPLE QUESTIONS

1. Give the mathematical expressions and uses of Poisson's and Laplace' equations.
2. State and prove Gauss's Law. Also give its salient features, limitations and applications.
3. State and prove Electrostatic Uniqueness Theorem and discuss the boundary condition types.
4. With suitable diagrams discuss the conditions at a boundary between dielectrics.
5. Discuss and derive:
   (*a*) Gauss's Theorem
   (*b*) Electric field due to surface charge.
6. Derive an expression for field due to a sheet of charges.
7. Determine the electric field due to spherical cloud of electrons, giving the volume charge density.
8. Discuss in detail the concept and meaning of equipotential surfaces and method of electrical images along with their applications.
9. For the case of steady magnetic field derive the far field of a current distribution.
10. Give the alternative derivation of magnetic vector potential.
11. With suitable diagrams derive Ampere's Force Law and Ampere's Law for a Current Element.
12. With suitable diagram discuss the derivation of the magnetic field due to volume distribution of current and the Dirac-Delta.
13. Briefly discuss the energy stored in magnetic field.
14. With suitable diagrams and mathematical expressions define and discuss:
    (*a*) Linear polarization
    (b) Circular polarization and
    (c) Elliptical polarization.
15. Derive the wave propagation characteristics in:
    (*a*) Good conductors and
    (*b*) Good dielectrics.

16. Derive the proof of Maxwell's equations.
17. In case of electromagnetic waves derive the solution for free space condition.
18. Give the word statement of Maxwell's field equations.
19. Give the interpretation of Maxwell's field equations.
20. Derive the wave equations for a conducting medium.
21. State derive and explain continuity equation.
22. Why Ampere's Law is inconsistent? Explain the reasons and remedies related to above fallacy.
23. Explain Maxwell equations along with the derivations in Phasor notations both in electrostatics as well as magnetostatics.
24. Explain the physical interpretation of displacement current.
25. Write a note on depth of penetration.
26. State and prove Poynting's theorem.
27. What is Brewster's angle?
28. With diagram derive for surface impedance in case of electric field.
29. With diagram discuss the concepts of reflection and transmission coefficients in case of electromagnetic wave.
30. Briefly discuss:
    (*a*) Travelling wave
    (*b*) Standing wave
    (*c*) Characteristic Impedance
    (*d*) Input Impedance
    (*0e*) Reflection Coefficient.
31. Using Poynting Theorem, derive the expression for power loss in a Plane conductor.
32. Give at least five applications of Smith Chart.
33. What is meant by VSWR? Derive the relation between Reflection coefficient and VSWR.
34. Give at least five applications of transmission lines.
35. With suitable diagrams derive for surface impedance.
36. Assuming transmission line is a distributed circuit with suitable diagrams, derive the expressions for transmission line theory.
37. Discuss the solution of Transmission Line equations.
38. Derive an expression for input impedance of the transmission line. Discuss line acts as impedance transformer.
39. Derive an expression for 'γ, Z_0' for lossless, distortion less and low loss lines.

❑❑❑